10/03

RAISI
THE
HUNLEY

RAISING THE HUNLEY

*The Remarkable History and Recovery
of the Lost Confederate Submarine*

BRIAN HICKS
and
SCHUYLER KROPF

BALLANTINE BOOKS • NEW YORK

For the pioneers

A Presidio Press Book
Published by The Ballantine Publishing Group

www.ballantinebooks.com

Library of Congress Cataloging-in-Publication Data
is available from the publisher upon request.

ISBN 0-345-44772-7

Manufactured in the United States of America

Text design by Holly Johnson

First Hardcover Edition: April 2002
First Tradepaper Edition: April 2003

2 4 6 8 10 9 7 5 3 1

After the chassepots came the torpedoes, after the torpedoes came the submarine rams, then—the reaction.

—JULES VERNE, *TWENTY THOUSAND LEAGUES UNDER THE SEA*

No news of the torpedo boat.

—TELEGRAM FROM CHARLESTON

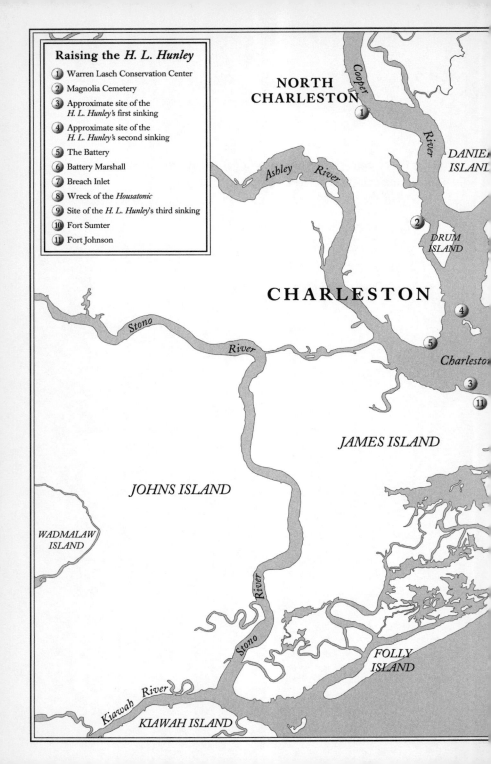

Raising the *H. L. Hunley*

1. Warren Lasch Conservation Center
2. Magnolia Cemetery
3. Approximate site of the *H. L. Hunley*'s first sinking
4. Approximate site of the *H. L. Hunley*'s second sinking
5. The Battery
6. Battery Marshall
7. Breach Inlet
8. Wreck of the *Housatonic*
9. Site of the *H. L. Hunley*'s third sinking
10. Fort Sumter
11. Fort Johnson

NORTH CHARLESTON

Cooper

River

Ashley *River*

DANIEL ISLAND

DRUM ISLAND

CHARLESTON

Stono

River

Charleston

JAMES ISLAND

JOHNS ISLAND

WADMALAW ISLAND

Stono River

FOLLY ISLAND

Kiawah River

KIAWAH ISLAND

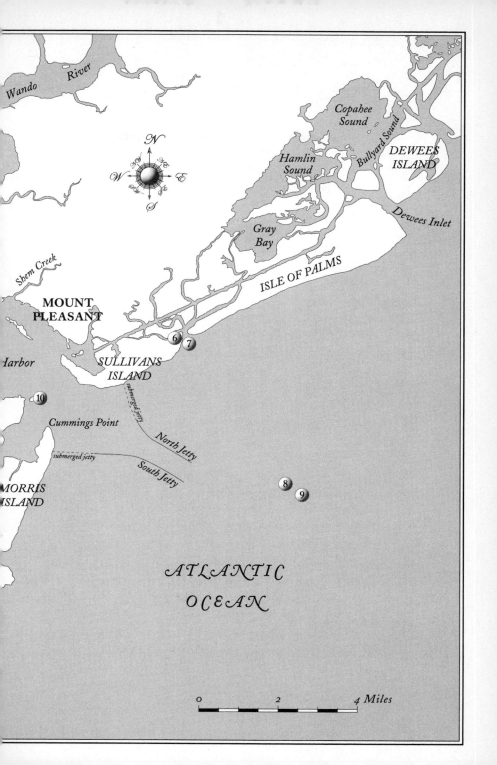

CONTENTS

CONTENTS

ACKNOWLEDGMENTS

No book that spans this many years and touches this many lives can be done alone. We were fortunate to follow this story in our role as journalists and to have the help of dozens of people, many of whom spent hours re-creating important scenes from their lives, explaining the intricacies of engineering and archaeology, or finding some document that we just knew was out there somewhere.

First, we would like to thank Sen. Glenn McConnell and Warren Lasch, chairmen, respectively, of the *Hunley* Commission and Friends of the *Hunley*, for giving us unparalleled assistance and access during the recovery and excavation of the *H. L. Hunley*. McConnell opened the files of the *Hunley* Commission to us and took the time to point out all of the most intriguing tidbits in that vast repository. The senator has an unquenchable dedication to and enthusiasm for the *Hunley*.

Lasch is the man who made things happen, who delivered on every promise, and who said yes when all others said no. Thanks for important views inside the submarine, of Lt. George E. Dixon's gold coin and everything else. Warren, it's always a pleasure.

We would also like to thank the folks at the lab, including Dr. Robert Neyland, Paul Mardikian, Maria Jacobsen, Harry Pecorelli III, Shea McLean, and Darlene Russo. Cramer Gallimore, who shot many of the Friends of the *Hunley* photographs in this book, was exceptionally helpful. All of these people were gracious with time they didn't really have. Thanks especially to "Dr. Bob" for the daily chats. At Friends of the *Hunley*, we also are indebted to Cindy Elenberger, Kellen Butler, and Mark Regalbuto. John P. Hazzard V of the *Hunley* Commission was of great help, as was Ms. Beckie Gunter, our heroine in Columbia.

Clive Cussler and the rest of the sea hunters were fabulous—including the NUMA (National Underwater and Marine Agency) team that was ultimately credited with discovering the *Hunley*: Ralph Wilbanks, Wes Hall, and the aforementioned, ever-humble, all-around great guy Harry Pecorelli III. His Authorship was kind enough to read the manuscript of this book twice, while Wilbanks, Hall, and Pecorelli all sat for hours-long interviews. *Veni, vidi, vici,* dudes.

Lee Spence and Mark Newell were kind enough to share their recollections and observations with us, even as they fought uphill battles to prove their claims. We were happy to tell their sides of the story. Steve Wright and Leonard Whitlock were extremely patient and helpful in explaining the engineering behind the lift. We also owe much to Randy Burbage and the dedicated men and women who reenact Civil War battles, ensuring that no one ever forgets. Also, the staff archaeologists at the National Park Service Submerged Cultural Resources Unit, Rick Hatcher at Fort Sumter, Chris Amer and Jonathan Leader of the South Carolina Institute of Archaeology and Anthropology, and their staff members were most kind. The U.S. Coast Guard Group Charleston, the U.S. Navy, the Naval Historical Center, the National Archives, and the Submarine Force Museum in Groton, Connecticut, also provided technical assistance. Jamie Downs, John Downs, John Hunley, Charlie Peery, Carole Bartholomeaux, Colleen Nelson, Bill Albergotti, Richard Cleeve, Jr., Andrew Nash, R. Theodor Kusiolek, and

Darren Milford also paved our way. Jenkins Montgomery of Titan Maritime Industries shared his story along with venison hamburgers. And for financial assistance during the writing of this book, we'd like to thank the guys at the weekly chapel meeting—Fred, Tom, Bryce, Mic, Robert, Tony, and especially Arlie.

It was an honor and a privilege to come to know the few surviving family members of the people involved in this story. Mary Elizabeth McMahon—the great-great-granddaughter of *Hunley* crewman James Wicks—and her sister-in-law, Hope Barker, were great sources of information and inspiration, and good friends. For the use of the Queenie Bennett photo, thanks to Sally Necessary, the great-granddaughter of Bennett, from whose hand passed the gold coin.

The librarians helped us sleuth out all these facts, especially Suzanne Henderson of *The Post and Courier*'s library, Charlotte Chamberlain of the Mobile Public Library, and the staffs at the Charleston and New Orleans public libraries. At the Museum of Mobile, Joan Layne and Chuck Torrey were especially kind, as was Dr. Bill Meneray in the Howard-Tilton Memorial Library of Tulane University in New Orleans. We made great discoveries at the Louisiana Historical Society and the South Carolina Historical Society—both of which are staffed by knowledgeable, courteous people.

For reading this manuscript in its earliest forms, we are forever indebted to the great novelist and editor Steve Knickmeyer, who does not suffer substandard prose. Jan Snouck-Hurgronje, president of the Nautical & Aviation Publishing Company of America, did many things to shepherd this book along, not the least of which was to offer valuable editing tips. Tracy Brown at Ballantine Books has been a great and patient editor, diplomatically making wise suggestions and answering all 861 E-mails with which we bombarded him—weekly. Thanks also to Nancy Delia for making this book come together seamlessly and to Susan Cohan for knowing what we really meant to say.

We are extremely grateful to the editors of *The Post and Courier*, who allowed us to cover the amazing story of the *Hunley*, in particular Barbara Williams, John Huff, Steve Mullins, and the late Grace Kutkus, who was a very special person. An extra nod goes to *The*

P&C's publisher, Larry Tarleton, for giving us the blue light to write this book. Thanks, LT.

We are grateful to our families for their encouragement, including Tish and Charles Kropf and the entire extended Kropf network. You are valued—Mom, especially, for keeping Grandfather's submarine service dolphins framed and ever present in our household, and Tracey O'Brien for just being there always. We are thankful for the moral support and kind words of Larry Hicks, Judy Spangler, Alan and Donna Spears, as well as Bill and Mary Ellen Spears, who provided shelter, great food, and better conversation for a traveling researcher. Beth Hicks deserves her name on this book as much as anyone, for reading countless early (and bad) versions of the manuscript, repairing the computer, watching the energetic Cole Hicks, taking photographs, and making sure the rest of the world continued to spin as this book was being written. You are simply the best.

And finally, we owe our greatest appreciation to Dan Conover, for the nudge.

Brian Hicks and Schuyler Kropf
Charleston
August 8, 2001

THE THREE CREWS
OF THE CONFEDERATE
SUBMARINE H. L. HUNLEY

FIRST CREW
Lost August 29, 1863, during training mission in Charleston Harbor

Lt. John Payne*	Absolum Williams
Lt. Charles Hasker*	Nicholas Davis
Frank Doyle	Michael Cane
John Kelly	Unknown*

SECOND CREW
Lost October 15, 1863, during training mission in Charleston Harbor

Horace Lawson Hunley	Charles Sprague
Thomas W. Park	Henry Beard
Robert Brockbank	John Marshall
Joseph Patterson	Charles McHugh

*Survived

THIRD CREW
Disappeared the night of February 17, 1864

Lt. George E. Dixon	C. Simpkins
James Wicks	Joseph Ridgeway
Arnold Becker	C. F. Carlson
Fred Collins	Unknown

Union losses aboard the USS *Housatonic*, February 17, 1864

John Williams	Edward C. Hazeltine
Charles O. Muzzey	John Walsh
Theodore Parker	

AUGUST 8, 2000

THE SEA WAS RESTLESS.

Aboard the crane barge *Karlissa B*, Jenkins Montgomery rehearsed the lift one more time, mentally playing out his role in one of the most significant maritime recovery efforts in history. Suspended high over the Atlantic in the chilly, predawn ocean breeze, Montgomery sat alone stuffed inside the glass control booth of one of the world's mightiest seagoing cranes. In a few hours he would pluck the lost Civil War submarine from the muddy grave where it had lain hidden for more than a century. Nervous or just killing time—or both—he went over the process again. In this weather he had to be perfect.

On paper anyway the lift was textbook-simple. A diver would give "Jinx," as his friends called him, the thumbs-up sign for him to begin reeling in his spool of industrial cable–like fishing line. Three hundred tons of reverse power would whine into action, and 28 feet below the surface, the deceptively small submarine, secure in a metal lift cage, would rise off the ocean floor at one-third the speed of an apartment building elevator. In a matter of seconds—if everything went correctly—Montgomery would be the first man to see the Confederate submarine *H. L. Hunley* break water since the moonlit night of February 17, 1864, when Union sailors on board the USS *Housatonic* thought a crazed porpoise was charging their ship. Lifting the sub, Montgomery had said earlier, would be "like picking a piece of pie off the plate."

On board *Karlissa* Montgomery had traveled the world recovering the things other men lost. In Scotland it was radioactive pipes, in Puerto Rico a Russian freighter blown by Hurricane Lenny into the Spanish fort guarding San Juan. Now, in the oddest twist of fate, he had been called home to Charleston to recover something in his own backyard. Yet for all his experience, all his confidence, the aggressive pitch of the sea had him worried. Ever since the final lift crew had come aboard at 4:00 A.M., the ocean had churned in the same unseasonable rolling pattern it had followed the entire month. As it smacked the base of the crane, lightning swatted a moonless southern sky. If this was going to be the day, Mother Nature was letting Montgomery know she would not cooperate.

In his perch Montgomery, still youthful at thirty-nine, had plenty of time to reflect on his role as he waited for the ocean to settle and the sun to rise. He was in a daunting position: at the end of his line hung the Holy Grail of the Civil War. For the moment, anyway, he controlled its fate—something men had been trying to do for years. Across the South the *Hunley* had become an obsession for countless people. Ordinary men acted as if they had a stake in its safe recovery, two states had battled over its ownership, and the reputations of several underwater explorers were tarnished in the conflicting stories of its discovery. The submarine was pure history, and history at the end of the twentieth century had become big business. It was a mystery that had puzzled men for more than 130 years, and now the answers were almost within reach. Because on this day—finally—the *Hunley* was coming home.

The *Hunley* was the first successful ship in the silent service. Built in an Alabama machine shop, the 40-foot, hand-cranked iron submarine made history the night it sank the *Housatonic*, then, less than an hour after the attack, abruptly disappeared. For 131 years men had searched for the tiny warship, which had vanished in relatively shallow water within sight of the South Carolina coast. Its crew—particularly its captain, George E. Dixon—had earned a notable place among maritime pioneers. In 1971 the U.S. Navy had named a submarine tender after the daring young Confederate lieutenant. Yet the submarine and its crew remained largely an enigma. The *Hunley* was a Confederate state secret. It was built to be a privateer vessel but eventually operated in a limbo between private hands and active government control. It left no paper trail in its wake. There were no diagrams, schematics, or detailed records known to prove that it even existed in the last days of the Civil War. But in the years following its disappearance, finding the *Hunley* became an endless quest for both the men who fought in the war and those who dreamed of traveling under the sea. P. T. Barnum offered a $100,000 reward for recovery of the submarine, French writer Jules Verne wove it into his science fiction, and scores of divers would swear that they had touched it. But no proof would come until May 1995, when another fiction writer said that he had found it.

As he waited for the seas to flatten, Montgomery's thoughts drifted back to his own family's role in the Civil War. It was December 1860, and the Secession Convention was meeting in Charleston after an alleged outbreak of smallpox had forced the delegates out of the capital in Columbia. There actually may have been a single case of fever, but the anti-Union fervor was weakening as Christmas approached, and the delegates used the threat of disease as a cover story for a move to Charleston and its friendlier atmosphere for revolt. In the Holy City—a nickname that referred to both Charleston's role in religious freedom and its dozens of stalagmite church steeples— cotton baron Joseph Evans Jenkins of nearby Edisto Island stood out among the delegates. Jenkins was a fiery coastal aristocrat, quick of temper and eager to break away from the Union. He was also Montgomery's great-great-great-grandfather, the forebear from whom he took his name. Jenkins was so determined to lead the march of secession that he daringly announced, "If South Carolina refuses to secede,

Edisto Island will!" Jenkins was a persuasive speaker; the delegates chose secession 169–0.

While Montgomery watched the skies and nervously fingered his controls, he wondered—for the first time, oddly enough—whether his secessionist grandfather had ever seen the tiny submarine now tethered at the end of his cable.

FOR MORE THAN 130 YEARS, THE *HUNLEY* HAD BEEN ON what veteran submariners call "eternal patrol"—lost at sea with little explanation of its fate for the mothers and widows back home. Every ship that sets sail in time of war—or even in time of peace—runs the risk of not coming back. But the stakes were higher for the *Hunley* than for almost any other ship of war ever built in North America. It was the first in its class, and to any rational-thinking military mind, its mission bordered on insanity. Eight volunteers sealed themselves up inside its iron belly, submerged, and navigated almost blindly toward an enemy ship miles away. They attacked with a ramming torpedo stuffed with 90 pounds of highly volatile black powder explosives at the end of a 20-foot iron pole. Because the submarine's two snorkel tubes never quite worked, fresh air was hard to come by. Since arm strength was its only source of power, the crew was always exhausted. And as a result of its being the first one, there were no sister ships to prowl underwater looking for it. Rescue, if necessary, was impossible. The risks were so great that Confederate general P.G.T. Beauregard eventually declared the *Hunley* more dangerous to those who operated it than to the enemy.

At the time the *Hunley* was launched, the Confederacy was dying. The submarine arrived in Charleston only weeks after the calamity at Gettysburg, an untested vessel that its benefactors hoped would break the Union naval blockade, part of U.S. president Abraham Lincoln's greatly effective "Anaconda Plan" to strangle the South by closing ports from Virginia to Texas. The *Hunley* was a response to that blockade, built out of necessity and desperation by men motivated by patriotism, money, and a lust for fame. At a time when most great minds were exploring improvements in medicine or agriculture, these men studied the physical properties of water and resistance, propulsion and pressure, weight and balance, iron and gunpowder. They built their creation in secrecy, yet it was only one of several submarines being developed during the Civil War in an underground—or underwater—arms race with the North. For the South the *Hunley* was simply the best response of a nation that was outgunned, outmanned, and outmaneuvered. But ultimately the *Hunley* represented much more than that. It was stealth technology in embryo. At the time, however, most military leaders and the brave sailors who piloted it never recognized it as a submarine; they simply dubbed it the "fish-boat."

The *Hunley* was by no means the world's first submersible vessel. By the time it was christened, history had recorded nearly twenty-five other manned boats in North America and Europe with the ability to dive and surface. Most of them sailed for peaceful reasons. Alexander the Great was reported to have used a glass diving bell; Dutchman Cornelis Drebbel built a leather-covered rowing boat in 1620 that he claimed could stay under for hours; Yale graduate David Bushnell's bubble-shaped *Turtle* of 1776 had one hand-cranked propeller for forward movement and another for vertical. During the Revolutionary War, the *Turtle* made one unsuccessful try at sinking a British ship in New York harbor by stabbing it with a screwlike spar, trying to affix a mine. The submarine's pilot grew frustrated and gave up when he couldn't get through the vessel's copper siding. In the years after Bushnell, dozens of men tried to make submarines work, but with limited success. In 1864, when the *Hunley* attacked and sank a ship, it became the first operational submarine, the first ever to accomplish the goal for which it was built. It was a marvel of nineteenth-century engineering. As has often been the case, war—and not necessity—was the mother of the invention.

NORMALLY MONTGOMERY KNEW THE CAROLINA COAST IN AUGUST to be a sauna, when pockets of steamy air suppress the waves, but since mid-May the weather offshore had been contrary, continually delaying the recovery. A rogue trough had planted itself over the Outer Banks of North Carolina, foiling coastal air as far south as Jacksonville, Florida, and bringing gusts that normally didn't arrive until fall. Those gusts had turned the seas around the *Hunley* wreck into a choppy, unpredictable mess. Already an earlier attempt at raising the submarine had been scrapped because the first crane barge had bobbed up and down so violently it resembled a channel buoy in a hurricane. Had the *Hunley* even made it off the ocean floor, recovery team leaders were afraid that it might crack open in the violent rise and fall of the swells. Without a steady deck from which to work, prospects for lifting the sub were decreasing. And the team was running out of time. Off the coast of Africa, the Atlantic hurricane season was beginning to percolate.

When Montgomery's bosses at Titan Maritime Industries of Fort Lauderdale got the call about the *Hunley*, they immediately thought of him and the *Karlissa B*. The *KB* was portable, could be towed anywhere in the world. In the industry it was known as a jack-up crane. At first glance it resembled nothing more than a work barge cluttered with trailers and generators, pipes and cables, shops and tools—all the makings of a tender ship. But once moved into place, the *Karlissa* became a steel island. It would release six 100-foot-long metal legs into the sea, raise itself high above the churning waves, and—in a move resembling a child's toy—morph over the course of several hours into something akin to an offshore oil rig. It would provide the *Hunley* recovery team with a dry, steady platform measuring half the size of a football field. When the *Karlissa B* sailed into Charleston, the stability problem, it seemed, had been overcome. But not even the mighty *KB* could protect against the weather.

IT MIGHT AS WELL HAVE BEEN A NATIONAL HOLIDAY. A ragtag armada had assembled in a semicircle around the *Karlissa B* by the time the sun rose over the Atlantic—an auditorium at sea waiting for a glimpse of the lost submarine of the Lost Cause. The fleet numbered in the hundreds, everything from sea kayaks to 100-foot yachts. Under the wet clouds, the only stain of color on the gray morning was the red, white, and deep blue of a Confederate flag the size of a tennis court whipping in the breeze over an anchored sailboat. By six A.M. the waves had calmed to 3-foot swells, but Montgomery still considered it too dangerous to lift the submarine and set it on the recovery barge. "I can lift it," he told the project's managers, "but you won't like what you get."

The *Hunley* was just about the lightest thing Montgomery had ever lifted, even though no one knew for sure how much it weighed. Engineers calculated that the iron-hulled submarine filled with silt and seawater might weigh 30 tons, a fraction of the *Karlissa B*'s load limit. But it wasn't the lift that was the problem; it was what to do with the *Hunley* after it broke buoyancy. Below the surface the seas were relatively calm; the water around the submarine was like fluid in the womb, partially protecting it. Once it broke the surface, however, there would be an urgent race to get the submarine and its truss set down gently on the transport barge before it started swinging like a pendulum and before its innards were exposed to the almost instant process of oxidation and decay. It would take nature only seconds to begin eating away at the most complete nineteenth-century time capsule ever found.

As the fleet of onlookers waited, National Park Service divers cruised the length of the hull to make sure no stray wiring or debris hung over the *Hunley*'s steel-framed lift cage that could snag the submarine when it was lifted. For several days the *Hunley* had been hanging in a state of suspended animation just inches off the ocean floor, cradled in a sling of thirty-three 1-foot-wide plastic pillows filled with foam. Through the miracles of chemical engineering, the pillows had turned rock-hard, like a cast for a broken bone, conforming to the elliptical shape of the *Hunley*.

By seven a.m. the lift had fallen behind schedule, even though the seas had calmed somewhat. Montgomery had tried to ease the tension aboard the crane barge earlier by dropping a full cup of coffee in front of the recovery team leaders. "Dang, I seem to be dropping things today," he said. Most of them were far too nervous to appreciate the joke.

By eight a.m. it was time. Montgomery, who alone held the controlling authority to make the lift, had to choose: "Either we can or we can't." He decided to bring it up. To wait any longer risked choppier seas. The ocean had calmed as much as it would for the morning; it would only grow more agitated again as the day wore on. Gingerly Montgomery pulled back on the levers controlling his cable spool to reel in his catch.

At the end of the line, the *Hunley* reacted slowly. The submarine was encrusted with coral-like marine growth, which had sealed the 40-foot hull in a concrete-hard sarcophagus. It weighed a little more than Montgomery had figured, and it had to be handled carefully. Scientists knew that the submarine had suffered some damage, three patched holes that had to be nursed: a 3-foot tear in the starboard side near the stern; a dish-shaped puncture in the forward starboard, low on the waterline; and a gaping hole as big as a grapefruit in the forward conning tower. Montgomery reminded himself to be gentle as he gunned the gears a little more, and slowly the *Hunley*'s 30-foot trip to the surface began. When the cable started moving, breathing on board the crane barge stopped. After a century buried beneath the Atlantic, the *Hunley* was about to surface once again.

With ten feet to go, Montgomery paused the *Hunley*'s ascent for a full minute, stomping his feet on the brake pedals, waiting for a signal from divers making last-second checks beneath the surface. It was the longest minute of the *Hunley*'s 136 years of missing time. Finally Montgomery got the thumbs-up and radio okay to reel her in.

On board the *Karlissa* the people who had waited five years for this moment peered over the rail at a patch of water where the steel cables tethered to the crane reached into the swells. As the crane's winch retracted its line, the light gray form of the lifting truss began to show just beneath the waves, followed by the optic yellow foam bags that collectively made up the lift hammock. Cradled in that rescue sling, only a few feet below the surface now, something else was coming into view.

It was glorious.

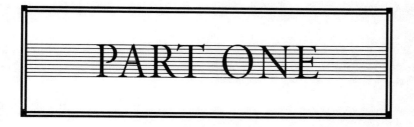

PART ONE

Chapter 1

PIONEERS

SHE WAS SLEEK, CIGAR-SHAPED, AND BLACK. WHEN SHE broke the choppy surface of Lake Pontchartrain, water rippled over her pectoral fins, and her flank glistened in the warm sunlight of early Louisiana spring. She was 34 feet long and dove underwater and resurfaced gracefully, slowly, like a porpoise. She was, her builders thought, beautiful.

It was such a shame to sink her.

Pioneer had only just begun to live up to its potential. In trial runs on the lake, the little submarine had performed well, had even blown up an old wreck once in mock combat. There were a few minor annoyances: it had buoyancy problems, was slow to turn, and couldn't be trusted to keep an even keel. But those things could be improved. Most important, it had accomplished something few boats that came before it had: it could travel underwater and surface at will.

Still, there wasn't any choice—it had to be scuttled. It was April 25, 1862, and Farragut was closing in on New Orleans. Since

Easter weekend the Union fleet had fought its way through Rebel fire-rafts and a barrage of cannon fire from the banks of the lower Mississippi. The Confederate Army had stood its ground for a week, but it couldn't hold forever. For the South in 1862, Good Friday did not live up to its name.

New Orleans was in a panic. Rear Adm. David Glasgow Farragut was not a man to be trifled with. The feisty, sixty-year-old naval genius credited with the phrases "full steam ahead" and "damn the torpedoes" was nothing short of an American legend. He had been a sailor since he was nine, when he served aboard the USS *Essex* during the War of 1812. Now Farragut was leading the Union's fleet in the Gulf of Mexico, and when he moved on New Orleans, it would only be a matter of time before it was his. A day earlier word had reached the city that the admiral's ships had just finished off Fort Jackson and Fort St. Philip 75 miles downriver. Those forts had been the city's only defense from the open sea, and now they were gone, destroyed. If the largest and most important city in the South couldn't be guarded against invasion, what chance did the Confederacy stand? People burned belongings they couldn't carry and couldn't bear to see fall into Yankee hands. Soon the wrought-iron balconies of the French Quarter would resemble bones, the skeleton of the old city. Very few would stand their ground to fight. New Orleans was a lost cause.

Pioneer could not be allowed to fall into Union hands. It was the South's newest weapon, and surprise was one of its few advantages. The men knew it must be kept secret. As fires raged across the city, they watched workers open the submarine's hatch—it had no ballast tanks—and let the murky water seep into its hull. Slowly *Pioneer* sank into a deep bend in the New Basin Canal between downtown New Orleans and Lake Pontchartrain. It had never even seen combat. Now it would never again resurface under its own power. But before *Pioneer* disappeared into the muck, the submarine did one very important thing for its builders: it proved they could do it—they could build a working submarine.

They would escape with that knowledge.

THE STRIFE THAT LED TO THE CIVIL WAR HAD BEEN building for decades, but when the fighting actually began, it felt sudden. No one was really ready. Eleven southern states had broken away from the rest of the country in the winter of 1861, as they believed was their right, ill will festering until war broke out a few months later. In many ways this was a conflict of agrarian versus industrial economies and lifestyles. For that reason the farmlands of the South may have been doomed from the start. In the world of the mid–nineteenth century, the South depended on the North to manufacture anything and everything it needed—from buggy parts and all-important farming implements right down to clothing. In some ways it was a one-sided relationship. Nowhere was that more apparent than on the water. The Confederate government had gone to war against the Union with a poor excuse for a navy. There simply wasn't time to assemble one and no economically feasible way to catch up. Hopelessly outnumbered, the Confederacy had only one hope to break U.S. president Abraham Lincoln's massive blockade of the entire southern coast: Confederate president Jefferson Davis called on privateer ships to do the work. Privateers were ships owned by regular, although usually wealthy, citizens with permission from the government to attack enemy vessels on its behalf. Their pay was on commission. For the Southern government, it was the only fiscally prudent way to handle things: it didn't have to ante up until a Yankee ship fell.

It wasn't a bad idea. Patriotism was perhaps the only thing not in short supply in the South during the War Between the States. There were thousands of men willing to take on the Union Navy in anything that would float and some things that wouldn't. The Confederate government and rich southern planters further enticed these men by offering ridiculously handsome rewards for every Union ship destroyed. Bringing down the *New Ironsides*, the North's seemingly indestructible warship, would net a little privateer $100,000—obscene money for the time. Businessmen were willing to put up a purse because the blockade had clogged the South's shipping lanes, killing their import/export business. The war was costing them a lot of money. Soon the whole Confederacy would be broke. Something had to give.

The South needed an edge.

This 1860 photograph is the only known image of Horace Lawson Hunley. (Courtesy Louisiana State Museum)

PERHAPS IT WAS PATRIOTISM THAT LED HORACE LAWSON Hunley to become a privateer. Or maybe it was the thrill, the notions of glory, that first attracted him. He certainly didn't need the money. At thirty-seven Hunley had more than most people ever would. He was an attorney, a former state lawmaker, and the deputy chief collector at the customhouse in New Orleans. He owned a plantation outside town and, by the time the war began, had started looking west for land investments. New frontiers were very much on his mind in 1861.

Like the fish-boat that would soon be swimming around in his head, Hunley operated on many different levels. On the surface he was polite, ambitious, and fastidious. He had lifted himself out of a childhood of poverty to the top of the social ladder in antebellum Louisiana. Heavily involved in the political scene, he made bets with friends on nearly every race—from the mayor of New Orleans to the president of the United States. Among his large circle of friends, Hunley's closest confidant and chief client was his brother-in-law, Robert Ruffin Barrow. Barrow was a sugar baron and one of the richest men in the South: he owned eighteen plantations. Barrow had married Hunley's younger sister, Volumnia, in 1850 and gained a good friend as well as a wife. Together the two men talked politics and looked for profitable investments. Because Hunley was a bachelor, Volumnia and Barrow were his only family. He kept Volumnia supplied with new books and watched out for Barrow's expanding business interests. He was a kind and devoted brother to the couple.

Beneath the surface, however, a somewhat different man lurked. Behind piercing dark eyes and a thick black beard, Hunley was driven by a hungry ambition to leave his mark on history. In a tiny ledger he kept in his pocket, Hunley wrote inspirational quotations meant to push him harder: "Procrastination is the thief of time" and "Attend to that which is most important and do not neglect business or duty." In his daily ledger—a gumbo of legal briefings, political thought, and points to make in letters—Hunley kept his days planned to the hour. He would jot down just about every grandiose scheme that came to mind: "Build in New Orleans an octagonal brick tower, three hundred to six hundred feet high." In his ledger he kept track of every bet.

Hunley also made notes to himself to read about Great Men. His preoccupation with the lives of historical figures seemed a vain exercise. What makes a Great Man? he wondered. What diseases do they get? He wanted to know everything that might help him succeed in joining their ranks: it seemed he yearned to be recognized as a Great Man. One notation, made less than a year before the war began, said simply, "Get book on the death of Great Men."

It was not surprising he was drawn to war; he had it in his blood. Hunley was descended from veterans of both the Revolution and the War of 1812. He was born in 1823 in Sumner County, a patch of rolling Tennessee farmland just north of Nashville. Horace was one of four children to come from the marriage of John and Louisa Lawson Hunley, and one of just two to survive childhood. In 1830 only Horace, seven, and his sister Volumnia, two years younger, would make the trip to the Crescent City with their parents. It was an odd move for the family: there was no real reason to go. Most people assumed John Hunley was drawn back to the city of his greatest glory, where he had fought alongside Andrew Jackson in the legendary Battle of New Orleans.

It was exciting for the Hunleys, moving from the rural countryside of Tennessee to a huge, beautiful—and decidedly European—city. But whatever joy they experienced was short-lived. Just a few years after the move, in 1834, John Hunley died following a long, lingering illness, leaving his family stranded in a town where they had no close friends or relatives. But they were too poor to attempt a trip back to Tennessee, so they stayed.

A few hard years later, Louisa remarried, this time to a wealthy planter from New Jersey. That set young Horace on a comfortable course. His stepfather provided Hunley's entrée into society. As soon as he was old enough, Hunley earned a law degree from the University of Louisiana (now Tulane) and served a session in the legislature as a representative from Orleans Parish. He set up a law practice a short distance from the French Quarter and took on additional work at the customhouse. It was a good, busy life. But until 1860 Hunley had yet to find the destiny for which he so longed. And then talk of war began. It seemed that Hunley, a fierce Southern patriot, had found his calling. That December, just one month before the Union would be dissolved, Hunley began to list in his little notebook the states he thought would secede. The gambling man was right about every state except Delaware.

This daguerreotype image of James R. McClintock was taken in the 1850s or early 1860s, just before he began dabbling in the design of submarines. (Courtesy Naval Historical Center)

BY SUMMER 1861 HUNLEY WAS COMPLETELY IMMERSED IN the war—to the detriment of his other businesses. Nothing else mattered: the War Between the States consumed him. In June that year, before the Battle of Bull Run, he led a blockade-running mission to Cuba for the Confederate Army aboard the schooner *Adela*. Hunley seemed to operate in a vacuum, not officially a military officer, but not exactly a privateer, either. Whatever his official status, the Rebels seemed not to mind. Usually Hunley got results. When he returned from Cuba, Hunley reported that he was convinced the army could break the blockade to bring in more ammunition and men. It was most likely wishful thinking. Already the Union fleet was strangling New Orleans, the largest and most important port in the South. It was also eating into Hunley's cotton-exporting business, just one more reason to hate the damn Yankees. In some ways Hunley felt he was refighting his grandfather's war, the Revolution. Southerners were being forced to rebel against an overbearing, overreaching government. Something had to be done. But Hunley had no more ideas left in his little ledger.

WHATEVER THE CIRCUMSTANCES OF THEIR FIRST MEETING in the summer of 1861, James McClintock turned out to be the perfect partner for Hunley. Where Hunley was full of ideas and had the money to fund his imagination, McClintock owned a machine shop and had a talent for tinkering. Just thirty-two when war broke out, McClintock had been one of the youngest steamboat captains on the Mississippi before going into business building steam gauges with Baxter Watson in a little shop near the French Quarter. Like Hunley, McClintock was eager to make a name for himself—and more money.

Even in the early days of the conflict, the submarine was not a unique idea. In fact, the notion of a "fish-boat" had become quite fashionable in both the South and the North. A stray letter printed in a Tennessee newspaper near the beginning of the war had urged Southerners to build the sneaky underwater ships to combat the superior Union Navy. For enterprising young Confederates, it seemed a worthwhile pursuit. The word was that one already had been built in New Orleans. But by late 1861 few Rebels, if any, had actually constructed one that worked. That fall Hunley, McClintock, and Watson decided to give it a try. McClintock, a native of Cincinnati, harbored little of the patriotic fervor that filled Hunley. He merely saw the idea of building a submersible boat as a challenge and possibly a good way to turn a

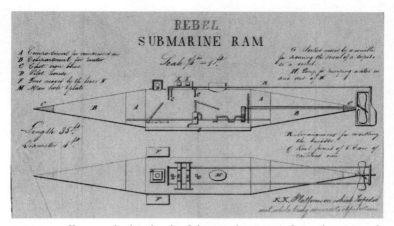

A Union officer made this sketch of the Hunley group's first submarine after finding it near New Basin Canal in December 1863. (Courtesy Friends of the Hunley)

profit—a better profit than he and Watson were making churning out bullets for the Confederate Army.

McClintock and Watson began their work late in 1861 with financial backing from Hunley, Barrow, and a few other wealthy investors whom Hunley had lined up. They built their submarine out of an old iron boiler, a quarter inch thick. It was 34 feet long, 4 feet wide, 4 feet tall. The boat carried a crew of three, two of whom would sit facing each other while cranking a handle to turn the screw propeller. It had one hatch atop a conning tower, where the captain stood and steered with ropes attached to the rudder. The submarine would pull a mine with a contact trigger at the end of a long rope. It had diving fins to make it submerge and surface. The fins worked on simple principles of water pressure: when they pointed down, oncoming water drove the submarine deeper into the water. When the fins pointed up, water flowing beneath them lifted the submarine. Those same principles, when applied to air a few decades later, would lift the Wright brothers into the heavens. The little submarine was, in some ways, well ahead of its time.

IN MARCH OF 1862, AS SPRING DESCENDED SLOWLY ON the South, naval warfare took a huge step into the future with the battle of the *Monitor* and *Merrimac*. The Confederates had salvaged the warship *Merrimac,* scuttled by Union forces fleeing Hampton Roads, and rechristened it the CSS *Virginia*. But they changed more than just the name. The Rebel engineers added iron plating to its side, a suit of armor for the ship. The South, the manufacturing underdog in the war, had created the ironclad. It changed the course of naval battles. In the Civil War both sides had resurrected an ancient battleship configuration called the ram. A ram was a steam-powered ship that would charge a wooden enemy ship, slamming an iron spike for a bowsprit into its side. It was a blow from which many ships never recovered.

The ironclad *Virginia* was impervious to such attacks, though, and also able to withstand the barrage of gunfire from Union ships. With the launching of the *Virginia*, the Confederates thought they had a way to break the blockade. But the North, having received word of the ironclad from spies, was working on similar technology. The USS *Monitor* sat less than 2 feet above the waterline with a single circular turret amidships. It wasn't perfect—it had some buoyancy problems— but it was enough. It was a shaky but deadly warship.

When the two ships met on March 9, 1862, they pounded each other for hours with cannon and gunfire while the crews sat behind their armor absorbing the concussion. The fight ended in a draw, but it began the escalation of the "ironclad" war along the eastern seaboard. It forced both sides to begin thinking about alternatives to conventional methods of naval warfare.

Roughly a month before that historic battle, the next generation of warship was launched. It was christened, appropriately enough, *Pioneer*.

The early tests were baby steps. Outside New Orleans on Lake Pontchartrain, a huge but relatively shallow body of windswept water that is often as rough as the open sea, *Pioneer* dove and resurfaced successfully but was wobbly in the process. John Scott, an acquaintance of Hunley and investor in the submarine, piloted the early missions. If the boat took on too much water, Scott could drop a few keel weights to increase its buoyancy. The sub would quickly pop up to the surface,

The first battle of ironclads took place on March 9, 1862, when the CSS
Virginia *(the former Union ship* Merrimac*) battled the USS* Monitor *off*
Hampton Roads, Virginia. Engraved in 1863 by J. Davies from a drawing
by C. Parsons. (Courtesy National Archives)

where Scott could replenish the crew's air supply. For a while everything seemed to be progressing nicely.

McClintock urged caution, however, and even though he rode
along on a few tests, would not declare *Pioneer* fit for actual battle. He
was a perfectionist and slightly nervous with the new technology. The
excited and anxious investors, however, could not be dissuaded. They
applied for and received one of the first privateering licenses issued by
the Confederate government. *Pioneer* would be the only submarine to
get official recognition in the war—and it wasn't even ready. McClintock was ordering still more tests when New Orleans's defenses fell.

There was simply no way to save the submarine. It would make
only 2 knots, not nearly enough speed to outrun Union ships, and it
certainly wasn't ready to take on Farragut. Nor was there any way to
carry the 4-ton monster across land. Facing the inevitability of the
situation, Hunley and McClintock chose to scuttle their invention. In
the chaos of the pending invasion and the exodus from the city, the

men took their boat to a deep gash in the channel outside of town and had workers from the machine shop sink it. But even as *Pioneer* sank, the men could not help but be encouraged by its progress. They wanted another shot at building a secret weapon for the Confederacy.

As people burned cotton—and anything else for which the Yankees might have use—in the streets, the men gathered their plans from the Front Street machine shop and headed east. Fueled by ambition, they felt sure they could help change the course of the war in Mobile.

MOBILE, ALABAMA, LOOKED LIKE AN IDEAL PLACE TO DEvelop and test submarine technology. The large Confederate port was one of the safest cities in the South. It sat on the western bank of a huge bay nearly 30 miles inland from the open sea. The mouth of the bay was small, just a shipping channel between Dauphin Island and Fort Morgan. From those two posts, Rebel soldiers easily kept the Union fleet out in the Gulf of Mexico until the final days of the war.

Mobile enjoyed a calm that was rare in the South during the war. Even if enemy ships could run the guns and get into the bay, they could not sneak up on the city. To stay in deep water, ships had to navigate up the eastern side of the bay and circle back to reach Mobile. There were no unannounced visitors. As a result of all that security, the Alabama port town became a recreation stop for troops. Sailors drank in Mobile taverns, met their sweethearts, or frequented brothels. Sometimes the relaxed troops even put on plays. The calm and confidence of the city were a welcome sight for the inventors. Hunley, McClintock, and Watson had barely escaped from Yankee-infested New Orleans before the Union flag was hoisted.

The men felt right at home in Mobile: even the architecture of the city was reminiscent of the Crescent City. Perhaps best of all, they felt the huge, protected bay was the perfect testing ground for their new submarine. As soon as the crew arrived, they reported to Confederate authorities. They told them of their plans, about *Pioneer*. This time they wanted to build a bigger and better boat for attacking the enemy fleet. Their tests in New Orleans had proved it would work. They asked only for a place to continue their work. Soon enough they had the government's permission and blessing: the Confederacy was in no shape to be turning away help.

In May 1862 Horace Hunley and James McClintock walked into the machine shop of Thomas Park and Thomas Lyons in downtown Mobile to build the secret weapon both men knew could mark their names down in history. McClintock was comfortable in his surroundings and with his new colleagues. They shared common immediate pasts. Park and Lyons were mostly doing government work in their shop these days, just as McClintock had been doing before Hunley came along. But the working conditions in Mobile were much better than they had been in New Orleans. Park and Lyons had a plethora of help, as the Confederate Army supplied skilled soldiers to speed along their work. On the day McClintock and Hunley came in talking grandly of fish-boats and secret weapons, two of the fascinated young men working in the shop were William Alexander and George E. Dixon. As they listened to the men from New Orleans outline their plan, neither of them had any idea their destiny had just walked in the door.

THIS ONE WOULD BE BETTER.

McClintock had charted every little flaw in *Pioneer*, determined to improve upon the design. *Pioneer* had been slow to dive—and in fact, just slow, period. The new submarine would adopt those features from *Pioneer* that were successful and discard those that weren't. It was mechanical natural selection, like the theory of evolution Charles Darwin had unveiled just three years earlier. McClintock wanted the new boat to dive more easily, so it would include ballast tanks. The crew could let in water for the weight needed to submerge and expel it with pumps when they wanted to surface. The new boat would be a little bigger but narrower. Water resistance had sapped what little speed *Pioneer* could manage, so the new submarine would be sleeker. McClintock gave his sketches for the body of the new boat to Park and Lyons, who in turn handed them to Alexander.

The submarine could not have been in more capable hands. Even at twenty-five, Alexander knew his business. The sandy-haired soldier had arrived in Mobile three years earlier to start his business as a machinist. He had been born in London to Scottish parents, but he loved the South. Soon after he arrived, Alexander had adopted Mobile as his home for life. When the war began, he immediately signed with the Confederacy. He was put in an artillery division of the Twenty-first Alabama Regiment and was soon at work on the construction of Fort Morgan, protecting Mobile Bay. When the fort was finished, the army decided Alexander's talents were best suited for the machine shop, where now the young man would be in charge of building the hull of the second Hunley-McClintock submarine. It was tentatively called *Pioneer II*.

The work began in the summer of 1862 and continued for months. The men fashioned the hull out of pieces of an old iron boiler. It wasn't perfect, but there wasn't exactly an abundance of raw materials in the South at the time. The submarine was built with diving fins and a screw propeller. Two hatches were affixed to the top of its 4-foot-tall hull. It was 36 feet long but only 3 feet wide, its ends slightly tapered. Two feet longer, but a full foot skinnier than *Pioneer*, it was aeons ahead of its predecessor.

McClintock busied himself with its propulsion. An inventor at heart, he thought the idea of men turning a crank to provide the submarine's power was ludicrous. For this new boat he wanted to build an electromagnetic engine, something as rare at the time as submarines. He tinkered with it for months, spending hundreds of dollars—dollars that came solely from Hunley. Working in a town without wealthy friends on whom to call, Hunley had decided to finance this new submarine by himself. He did not mind too much. Being the sole proprietor had its advantages: he would be the chief benefactor of any reward money—or glory—the new privateer earned.

Ultimately McClintock had to fit the new submarine with hand cranks. Alexander and his troops had finished the submarine, and Hunley and the Rebels were anxious for a launch. The time for experimentation had run out; none of McClintock's little engines could provide the power needed to turn the boat's propeller. Begrudgingly he rigged the new boat with hand cranks for four men. At least, he thought, the additional manpower should make it twice as fast as *Pioneer*.

The tests went wonderfully. The new submarine, which they eventually christened the *American Diver*, took to Mobile Bay like a fish to water—just as Hunley and McClintock had hoped. The submarine could submerge and surface much more quickly than *Pioneer*. It was still slow, but at least it was a consistent 2 knots.

The crew was made up of men from the machine shop: even though Mobile was friendly surroundings, the project was still top secret. The Rebels figured the fewer people who knew about it, the better. William Alexander and George Dixon were happy with the arrangement. They had built it; they wanted to pilot it. Dixon, particularly, was captivated by the craft. It had come along at a turning point in the life of the young Confederate soldier, recently promoted to the rank of second lieutenant. Hunley and McClintock had arrived in Mobile talking about their fish-boat at very nearly the same time Dixon had limped into the machine shop carrying the wounds—and nightmares—of Shiloh. Early in the fighting at that Tennessee battle, he'd suffered a severe wound to his leg. A bullet meant for his left thigh had instead hit a $20 gold coin in his pants pocket. It was unbelievable luck. The coin saved his life, but the impact left him with a painful limp. Submarine duty was, for Dixon, in some ways easy work—no walking. But there was more to it than that. Dixon believed more than anyone that the submarine might be the Confederates' salvation. Maybe he'd been spared for a reason.

EVER CAUTIOUS, McCLINTOCK ORDERED TESTS ON THE new submarine through the fall of 1862. The men didn't mind the daily tests, although the submarine was confining and uncomfortable. Dixon, 6 feet tall, had trouble fitting into the 3-foot-wide interior of *Diver*. There were other problems. The iron hull played hell on the magnetic compass; it never read correctly. And soon it became obvious that Mobile Bay was not the best testing ground after all. Where they practiced, it was sometimes too shallow to dive under the larger ships. It was difficult to gauge the submarine's true potential.

The first mission of the *American Diver* was launched on February 14, 1863. The Confederates had a Valentine to deliver to Farragut's Gulf Coast fleet—a torpedo mine at the end of the *Diver*'s 100-foot towline. The Rebels were full of optimism, sure that on that night they would raise the stakes in naval warfare.

The tiny submarine set out from Fort Morgan at eight P.M., its crew squeezing into the narrow hull by candlelight. The five men planned to travel underwater until they reached Sand Island, outside the bay. There they would come up for a bearing and make for the nearest Union ship in the gulf—and attack. But when the *Diver* surfaced to pick its target, the men found themselves well past Sand Island, out to sea practically, in a vicious current that was pulling them south. The crew had to cut the mine loose and crank like hell just to make it back to the protective waters of Mobile Bay. They'd been lucky. It was amazing the slender torpedo boat wasn't lost at sea that night.

HUNLEY WAS ABSENT FOR MUCH OF *DIVER*'S SHORT CAREER. He always seemed to be gone from Mobile, always traveling to get close to the action of the war. He would be in northern Mississippi one week, south Alabama the next. Some of the men thought he might be a secret agent for the Confederacy, or maybe he just fancied himself as such. But when it was time for his new submarine to go out on its next mission, Hunley was there.

The plan was to tow the *American Diver* to the mouth of the bay, near Fort Morgan, 20-odd miles away. If the submarine tried to make the trip from Mobile to open water itself, the crew would exhaust themselves before they got halfway to the mouth of the harbor. Better to let another ship do that work and have the crew board the submarine at the fort, where they could head into the Gulf of Mexico and attack the fleet, anchored about 4 miles south—safely out of the range of Rebel batteries.

The *Diver* was designed to drag a mine at the end of its long tow

Hunley and McClintock lost their second submarine, the American Diver, *within sight of Fort Morgan, which guarded the entrance to Mobile Bay. (Courtesy National Archives)*

line and dive under its prey, guiding the bomb along on the surface. On contact with the Union ship's hull, the charge would detonate. The *American Diver* would be nearly 100 feet away and insulated by the water when the blast went off. It was a fine plan, except for one thing: the Confederates never considered the weather.

The winter shows itself perhaps most fiercely on the water. Strong, cold winds turn the sea into a battlefield of whitecaps, and on an average day even the most seaworthy vessel is shaken as violently as a rag doll in a dog's mouth. The subtropical Gulf of Mexico was no exception. On the day the *Diver* was to get its first taste of battle, a vicious squall came up. On board the towboat, Hunley, McClintock, and the *American Diver's* crew held on to anything they could find as they were rolled from one side of the deck to the other. The towline, taut enough to squeeze any lingering water out of it, held on mightily to the tiny fish-boat dragging behind. If it was this rough in the bay, Mc-

Clintock thought, the boat would have little chance in the open water of the gulf.

But they would never know. One minute the *American Diver* was there, the next it was gone. Just like that. Mobile Bay swallowed their invention without a sound.

It was the one thing about his submarines McClintock would never be able to fix: they were heavy, quick to sink. It took little more than a few gallons of rough water to give the submarine negative buoyancy, which for the unmanned vessel was a one-way ticket to the bottom. Off Fort Morgan, Hunley and McClintock had lost their second submarine in less than a year, and neither had seen combat. As they stared at the hungry water in disbelief, it seemed as if their new technology was not meant to be.

Just over their shoulders outside the harbor, Union ships cruised by like sharks, still untouchable.

It cut through the water like a scythe, its black icebreaker bow slicing the chop as if it weren't even there. Diving planes hugged its tapered bow like comforting arms, and it dove and surfaced so quickly that it practically undulated. It had been built so hydrodynamically that even the conning towers had cutwaters. When it broke the surface of Mobile Bay on that summer day in 1863, Hunley and McClintock thought it was even more beautiful than the other two. It was perfect. They called it the *H. L. Hunley*. And it would be the Confederacy's new secret weapon.

The order had come from Charleston: Beauregard needed it. Fighting had escalated, and the Rebels couldn't hold out much longer. Nowhere was this felt more desperately than in South Carolina. The Union had a particular hatred for Charleston, where secession began, where the first shots of the war were fired. And the general was feeling the Yankee wrath. Dozens of blockaders were enforcing President Lincoln's Anaconda Plan, strangling the city. It was a one-sided fight; Beauregard's troops were demoralized. When Maj. Gen. Dabney H. Maury, in charge of the Confederate troops at Mobile, had mentioned the strange fish-boat to Beauregard, the commander of the Charleston military district knew that was what he needed. He asked Maury to send the *Hunley* to him, which was exactly what the Alabama general had planned to do. Maury felt he wouldn't be able to use a submarine against Farragut's fleet so far out to sea: the *Diver's* Valentine's Day performance had only cemented that opinion. Besides, Mobile was safe and secure, while Charleston was close enough to the open ocean that the city was in danger of shelling by the Union Navy.

Beauregard did not care that the test runs weren't completed. The sub had proved itself enough already, enough to give the desperate general hope. He sent orders to all rail stations between Mobile and Charleston to expedite the large iron package.

"It is much needed," Beauregard's short note read.

So much had happened in six months. Hunley and McClintock had grieved for the *American Diver* only briefly. It was odd, but with each failure they appeared to grow more encouraged, even more confident. They seemed completely assured that eventually they would succeed. McClintock was particularly eager to improve yet again on his design plans. Shortly after the *Diver* sank in late February 1863, work on the new submarine had begun at Park and Lyons's shop.

Hunley, however, was feeling the effects of the war and the loss of his exporting business. He had financed the *American Diver* alone, and now more than $12,000 of his money was on the bottom of Mobile Bay. This time he would take out insurance: he would sell shares in the new boat. Several investors jumped at the chance.

When the fighting began, most men of high ideas in the South had been on the verge of building the machinery that would one day industrialize their primarily agrarian economy. With the war they had to modify their ideas. These men were eager to join Hunley, as they had similar goals. Hunley quickly sold two-thirds of his submarine for $10,000 to four men in a secret Confederate engineer corps that was developing torpedoes. Among them were E. C. Singer, a member of the family that would make the sewing machine a household product, and Gus Whitney, a relative of Eli, inventor of the cotton gin.

Even though he was only one of a handful of shareholders, Hunley

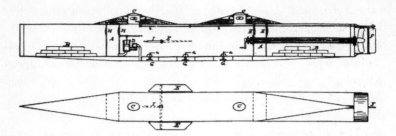

This 1870s sketch was made at the direction of James R. McClintock, who claimed it was the "vessel that destroyed the USS Housatonic." Among the features that match up with the Hunley are the ballast bars in the forward and after ballast tanks (B); the cutwaters guarding the hatches (C); the detachable keel weights (G); and the diving planes (E), called "vanes" in this sketch. (From the Eustace Williams collection)

In 1902 R. G. Skerrett made this apparently unfinished sepia-wash drawing of Conrad Wise Chapman's famous painting of the Hunley shown on the dust jacket. (Courtesy Naval Historical Center)

was still the man driving the project, the one person who made sure that there would, in fact, be a third submarine. They decided to name the new boat in his honor.

The inventors had returned to the Park and Lyons machine shop, to Alexander, to handle the construction. The new submarine was built from the keel up as just that—a submarine. A skeleton was formed, and ⅜-inch iron plates were attached to it. They riveted the plates to ribs and sanded off the outside edges to make the hull slicker. Noting the complaints about the tight crew compartment on the *American Diver*, they widened the *Hunley* to a relatively roomy 42 inches—3½ feet. Thick glass portholes, or deadlights, were mounted with O-rings in rows of two along the top of the hull for better lighting inside. Viewing ports were put in the two conning towers and another in the forward hatch, so the captain could tell when it was safe to open it. A mercury depth gauge was installed, and it proved relatively accurate. Determined to move quickly, McClintock was convinced to forget about engines and stick to the method of propulsion that had been proved. He built the *Hunley* to be hand-cranked but nearly doubled his previous cranking crew. The *Hunley* was 40 feet long and 4 feet tall. It could carry a crew of eight, seven of whom would sit on a wooden bench along the submarine's port side turning a crank with angled handles. The crank, in turn, rotated the submarine's propeller shaft.

It seemed the engineers had forgotten nothing. They took every precaution. A protective shroud surrounded the *Hunley*'s propeller to keep anchor lines from fouling it; there were little tabs mounted in front of the dive planes to deflect seaweed or rope that might jam the fins. The keel weights were hung on the outside of the boat and could be dropped from inside by twisting T-shaped bolts. The captain would stand with his head in the forward conning tower, working the dive planes and steering with a joysticklike tiller. The first officer would sit aft, cranking and working the after ballast tank pump with a long handle. A pine bowsprit was lashed to the top of the bow like a spar. In murky water it would give them a little warning before the submarine hit something but, being wooden, would not allow the submarine to act as a ram: it would splinter on impact. There was even a pair of snorkels leading to an air-exchange system, but it never seemed to work properly.

Regardless, this submarine had benefited from nearly two years of trial and error. The men who fashioned the fish-boat's parts at the Park and Lyons machine shop and assembled it at the Seaman's Bethel in downtown Mobile knew exactly what they were doing. The day the finished submarine was rolled down to the Alabama waterfront in July 1863, it was the most technologically advanced weapon ever built. The men who built her were confident that the *Hunley* could take naval warfare to a new level. They had no idea how far ahead of their time they were.

The submarine's early tests only stoked that optimism. On a test run for General Maury, the *Hunley* had slipped through Mobile Bay towing a floating mine toward an old ship, just as the *American Diver* had been designed to do. As it closed on the abandoned boat, the *Hunley* dove beneath the glassy surface and disappeared. Moments later the torpedo hit the underbelly of the ship and exploded. Pieces of wood flew nearly 100 feet in the air. A few minutes after the attack, the *Hunley* surfaced a good distance from her victim, its captain hanging out of the forward conning tower watching the old barge sink.

The glory of that great demonstration was just a fading memory in early August 1863 as Dixon and Alexander watched a crane in downtown Mobile load the *Hunley* onto two flatcars. The two young men had built the submarine, and trained in it. They were its crew. But only McClintock and one of the investors, Whitney, were making the trip to Charleston with it. A new crew would be assembled in South Carolina. Dixon and Alexander were being left behind.

They didn't watch long before the submarine was camouflaged. Scaffolding was built around the *Hunley* to hide its shape, and then it was covered with a tarpaulin. Armed guards kept a discreet distance on the train: Beauregard's package would not be lost in transit.

As the train carrying the *Hunley* steamed away from the Mobile station on that hot summer afternoon, Dixon and Alexander stood together, wondering if they would ever see their fish-boat again.

Chapter 2

MELANCHOLY
OCCURRENCES

I T WAS A RIDICULOUS COMMISSION, ENOUGH TO MAKE them rich from one night's work. But then, it was a mighty task.

When Gus Whitney and James McClintock arrived in Charleston with the *Hunley* on August 15, 1863, they were greeted with the promise of a monstrous first paycheck: $100,000 to sink either the *New Ironsides* or the *Wabash*, two of the most fearsome blockade ships in the Union fleet. The staggering amount of money—the early-twenty-first-century equivalent would be $1.6 million—suggested the enormity of the task. But the Rebels were so eager for victory, they sweetened the pot still more, lest any of the submarine's crew feel they might lose their nerve. Brig. Gen. Thomas Jordan promised the men that "steps are being taken to secure a large sum to be settled for the support of the families of parties" should they die or be captured in their efforts. Small comfort, but comfort nonetheless for dirt-poor Southern soldiers.

Fresh in from a trip that rambled for days through Alabama, Georgia, and South Carolina, Whitney and McClintock were stunned by the generous offer. But they didn't yet realize just how desperate the Confederate government was. When the *Hunley* arrived in Charleston, the city was in the noose of the Union Navy's South Atlantic Blockading Squadron, which was enforcing a simple edict: cut off Charleston's high-seas arteries to Europe, Cuba, and South America. The United States government knew that if the South's supplies from foreign trade were stopped, it would only be a matter of time before the Confederate government collapsed. The Southerners knew it, too. That's where the fish-boat came in.

Holding the 3,500 miles of coastline between Alexandria, Virginia, and Brownsville, Texas—a stretch pierced by 189 harbors, inlets, and navigable rivers—was an enormous task for the U.S. fleet. In the early days of the war, in fact, the South had enjoyed some wiggle room. The U.S. Navy had only ninety warships in 1861, and less than half of those were in commission. But by the time the *Hunley* arrived, the Union blockade had become viciously efficient. Charleston's lifeblood, its seaport, was cut off from the world. Beauregard and his troops were about out of hope.

So it was no surprise that McClintock, being his cautious self, soon wore out his welcome with the frazzled Confederate brass. When the submarine was unloaded, McClintock and Whitney assembled a crew of volunteers and immediately ordered more practice dives. The *Hunley* spent its first week in Charleston frolicking in the relatively safe waters of the harbor. The blockade remained unbroken.

HORACE LAWSON HUNLEY SOUNDED LIKE A WORRIED father. The *Hunley* had not even got wet in Charleston Harbor before its namesake wrote a desperate note to McClintock seeking a progress report.

"I have been extremely anxious about your experiment at Charleston," Hunley wrote to his partner on August 15, 1863, the day the submarine arrived in the city. "It is not at all on the question whether you will succeed in blowing up a vessel of the enemy for I think that is more than probable and of itself only a small matter. It is whether your success will be made available in effecting a real solid benefit for the Confederacy and conferring glory on its originators."

Hunley had great confidence in the new submarine. He knew it could sink an ironclad; he was just worried about getting the credit for it. In his visions of grandeur, Hunley imagined that the torpedo boat would be so effective it would scare the Yankees into stepping back from Charleston altogether, maybe even drive the Union troops from Morris Island at the mouth of the harbor, which they had just taken. He knew the existence of the *Hunley* had to be kept quiet for it to be effective. But if the important project were kept top secret, fame might elude him. When he wrote his letter to McClintock, Hunley was already 150 miles east of Mobile, headed for Charleston. He wanted to be there when the *Hunley* sailed into port after it sank its first Union ship. Hunley had no idea what he was walking into.

INITIALLY THE SUBMARINE WAS STATIONED BEHIND FORT Moultrie, a Revolutionary-era stronghold on the south end of Sullivan's Island that sat facing the rocky shore of Fort Sumter. From that perch the boat was within seeing—and striking—distance of the blockading fleet. Or so the Rebels thought. But a week after the sub's arrival, the ragged frontline troops had grown unimpressed by the secret weapon. The *Hunley* had been out on three trips but had yet to even try for a Yankee ship. McClintock ran the submarine through tests between Fort Moultrie and Fort Johnson on James Island, safely behind Sumter and out of sight of the blockade.

Gen. T. L. Clingman, the commander at Sullivan's Island, quickly lost patience with McClintock. On August 23 he sent word to the Confederate headquarters that he didn't think the *Hunley* would "render any service under its present management." Whitney tried to reassure him that all was well. He told the general the problem was McClintock. "He is timid," Whitney told Clingman, but promised the submarine would go out that night. That is, he qualified, unless the weather is bad.

*Confederate general P.G.T. Beauregard, commander
of forces at Charleston, was not regarded as a military genius, but he did suggest mounting the spar
torpedo on the bow of the* Hunley. *(Courtesy National Archives)*

After another week of excuses and inaction, Beauregard was livid.
The fish-boat had not been freighted to Charleston to put on two
shows daily. The Rebels were getting suspicious, wondering if there was
something wrong with the secret weapon that the investors weren't
telling them about. Finally Beauregard asked McClintock to allow a
Confederate Navy man to sail on the submarine's next trip. Just to ob-
serve, he said. When McClintock refused, it was the last straw for Beau-

regard. He seized the submarine and ordered it crewed with volunteers from soldiers and sailors already stationed in the city. The government took over the little privateer. McClintock was out, his invention taken from him.

GENERAL PIERRE GUSTAVE TOUTANT BEAUREGARD, commander at Charleston, was not a man with great patience at such a late date in the conflict. The War Between the States was taking its toll on him. The Creole son of French descendants in Louisiana was fiery and flamboyant, and certainly not accustomed to this manner of treatment. In the three preceding years, Beauregard had been promoted, demoted, and declared AWOL. He had begun the war in Charleston and, after a lap around the South, was back again. In September 1862 the Confederate government put Beauregard in charge of the South Carolina and Georgia district and soon added Florida to his troubles. The entire region was in a shambles, Beauregard felt. When he arrived in Charleston, he found his troops in "defective locations." It was so bad that the mouths of two strategic, nearby rivers—the Stono and the Edisto—were not even guarded. Beauregard had his work cut out for him.

Even though he had served as superintendent of the U.S. Military Academy at West Point before the war, some people thought that Beauregard, an engineer by trade, was not a perfect fit in the Confederate Army. He seemed to have little respect for his superiors and was not considered to have a great military mind. He had a reputation for preferring society to soldiering. And he liked Jefferson Davis only a little more than he cared for U.S. president Abraham Lincoln. The feeling was mutual. But Beauregard, Davis was forced to admit, had been there when it counted: he ordered the first shots fired at Fort Sumter, commanded the troops in the first battle at Manassas, led the Tennessee Army at Shiloh. And now, as his wife lay dying in Union-occupied New Orleans, Beauregard was stuck defending Charleston Harbor, and despite his best efforts, it was a losing proposition.

Heavily armed Fort Sumter guarded Charleston Harbor for the duration of the war and hid the Hunley's *trial runs from Union blockade ships. (Courtesy National Archives)*

Earlier in the year Beauregard had sent his two rams, the *Palmetto State* and the *Chicora*, out to engage the blockaders. It was an effective, if short battle that ended with two Union ships limping off over the horizon. The euphoria of that small victory was brief. Weeks later the Union retaliated and sent down more than a half dozen new ironclads impervious to the spiked bows of the rams. The Yankees were determined to choke Charleston. Lincoln badly wanted the town and the political victory that would come from taking it.

In reality, the city was no prize. By 1863 Charleston bore little resemblance to the suitor that had wooed the South into war two years earlier. It was the largest city in the Confederacy following the fall of New Orleans, but its grandeur had been mostly bled. The Union had forced most people to flee inland to escape what would become nearly six hundred days of bombardment from land and sea. For two years cannonballs would fall like hailstones, announced only by the terrifying whack of their crashing into wood, shingles, brick, or cobblestone. Charleston also still bore the mark of an accidental fire in December of 1861 that cut a swath of destruction through the city nearly a mile wide. In its wake the blaze destroyed trees and left the burned-out facades of mansions standing like markers in a graveyard. The resulting lack of shade made the city especially hot in summer, while winter winds howled down Meeting Street. It was almost a ghost town. The only residents on the southern tip of the city's peninsula were troops, many of whom camped in the backyards of those grand old homes within view of Fort Sumter. They were hardly living the good life. Often the soldiers passed time by melting silverware to make bullets.

The defense of Charleston was eating up precious Southern resources. Seventeen forts protected the inner harbor, and 240 guns and nearly six thousand men guarded the steeples of the Holy City. At the forts the wounded were operated on in full view of crowds, and the summer breezes kept uncovering the shallow graves of Union and Confederate soldiers. The people who remained in Charleston tried to lead normal lives during the blockade, going about their business amid the smells and sounds with a European gentility. They just had to be prepared to take cover a couple of times a day when the Union troops opened fire. It was demoralizing, but then it was meant to be. In one nine-day stretch, more than fifteen hundred shells would hit the city. Beauregard was commanding his own corner of hell. As a result of these many pressures, the general was in no mood for McClintock's plodding progress.

Lt. John Payne of the Confederate States Navy quickly volunteered to provide the results Beauregard demanded from the fish-boat. Payne, a sailor aboard the ram *Chicora*, was appointed the *Hunley*'s new commander. The eager Virginian recruited his shipmates from the *Chicora* for the submarine's crew and finished out its complement from the *Palmetto State*. Payne took only volunteers, and he had no shortage of them. Anything beat the spartan conditions on those ships. The loss of a few hands mattered little to those ragged old boats: they wouldn't be going out for combat anytime soon. The iron-clads patrolling outside the harbor were much too formidable.

At first turn the volunteer crew's handling of the *Hunley* was passable. They cranked well, and the submarine performed as promised. Even though it drew looks from many people, it didn't stand out too much in Charleston Harbor, where all manner of floating warships congregated, most notably the Davids. The Davids were also torpedo boats, a distant relative of the *Hunley*: they sat low in the water and attacked with stealth. In fact, the submarine would be mistaken for a David throughout its short career and for much of history. During the war there were a number—between three and ten—of the little boats in and around Charleston. Like the *Hunley*, they were privately financed. They were cigar-shaped, made of wood with a thin layer of iron covering their hulls. Their bows came to a point, where a long iron spar with a torpedo warhead was attached. They resembled an overturned boat with a tall smokestack sticking out of it. However, unlike their submarine counterpart, they had the luxury of being powered by steam.

The David would eventually beat the *Hunley* into combat. On the night of October 5, 1863, a David commanded by Lt. William T. Glassell attacked the Union's *New Ironsides* just outside the harbor. Glassell and a three-man crew rammed their boat into the much-larger Yankee ship and detonated a 70-pound charge in its side. The explosion crippled the ship but did not sink it. The Union troops were not so surprised that they couldn't fire back, and soon bullets were ricocheting off the David's iron-plated hull. As the boat rocked from the concussion of the explosion, water went down its smokestack and put out its fire. Soon the David was drifting. Glassell and most of the crew abandoned ship, diving into the cold, black Atlantic. The captain and one of his crewmen were fished out of the water by the Yankees and taken prisoner.

The David's engineer, James H. Tomb, swam back to the boat and found its pilot, J. W. Cannon, hanging on to its drifting hull: the man couldn't swim. Together they stoked the fire enough to start the engine and limp away. Both ships survived the short battle.

But in August 1863 Payne was pushing to have the *Hunley* sink a Union ship before one of the Davids did. He took the submarine out

Low-profile, steam-powered Davids were Confederate surface rams often mistaken for the Hunley. *This David was abandoned in Charleston Harbor after the city fell in 1865. (Courtesy National Archives)*

daily and, after just a few days, declared the *Hunley* fit for combat. But the crew had underestimated the submarine. McClintock had always warned that the submarine's machinery appeared so simple to operate that most people believed they could sail it with no practice. The Charleston troops didn't listen, and the engineer no longer had any say in the operation of the submarine. Disgusted and disrespected, McClintock eventually left Charleston. He would never see his creation again.

No one would ever agree on exactly what happened. The *Hunley* was moored at Fort Johnson, near the end of James Island, across the harbor mouth from Sullivan's. It was Saturday, August 29, and Payne was about to cast off. The rest of the men had already squeezed into their seats on the portside bench. Lt. Charles

Hasker sat at the first position behind the captain. He was filling in for Charles Stanton, a shipmate from the *Chicora* who was a regular member of Payne's crew. But Stanton's shift at watch on *Chicora* was not over when the *Hunley* was ready to go out. So Hasker, who had been eyeing the fish-boat with great interest, volunteered to take his place.

With all his men in position, Payne was climbing in through the forward hatch when a Rebel ship called the *Etiwan* came steaming by. The wake of the ship rolled over the *Hunley* and sent water pouring through the hatches into the crew compartment. In a panic the men tried to climb over one another to get out. It was no use.

The *Hunley* was an unforgiving machine. To keep its profile low on the waterline—and to maintain an even keel—the submarine was weighted heavily with lead ballast bars and iron blocks bolted to the bottom of the hull. That made it susceptible to the slightest change in weight or movement of its hull. The crew had to stay in their places on the water—as if they had any choice—or the boat would tip violently. A little water was all it took to send it sinking to the murky bottom of Charleston Harbor.

CHARLES HASKER, A NATIVE OF LONDON, WAS THIRTY-two and as accustomed to the water as anyone could be. As a teenager, he'd served in the Royal Navy. When he later migrated to the United States, Hasker joined its navy. He'd been in New York City when the war broke out and immediately left for Portsmouth, Virginia, where he joined the Confederate Navy. He had served on the *Merrimac*, or as he called it, the CSS *Virginia*. But nothing in all his training had prepared him for this. As the *Hunley* went down, Hasker was caught inside.

He lunged at the water rushing in through the forward hatch, tripping over the controls for the diving fins as he fought his way upstream through the waterfall. Hasker was more than halfway out when the hatch came down on him. The *Hunley*'s hatch covers weighed nearly 150 pounds each and were not easy to move even in ideal circumstances. In these conditions it proved impossible. Hasker was trapped like a seal in a shark's jaws.

Water rushed past Hasker, blinding him, choking him as he involuntarily rode the submarine to the harbor's bottom. Soon the water filled the *Hunley*, speeding its descent. The whole crew compartment had become a ballast tank. Hasker used all his strength to push against the water and wiggled out somewhat, until he thought he was free. But the hatch clamped back down on his leg. He was still struggling when the submarine crashed on the muddy floor of Charleston Harbor.

As the pressure inside the *Hunley* equalized, Hasker felt the hatch ease its hold on his leg. Working blindly in 42 feet of water, he pushed the hatch off his wounded leg and swam toward the light squeezing through the black water. When he broke the surface, he sucked down fresh air ravenously. The crew of the nearby *Chicora* plucked him out of the water.

Payne escaped without so much as a dunking, and the steamer *Etiwan* had picked him up. One man got out through the after hatch while Hasker struggled in the forward one. Five others drowned. The *Hunley* had claimed its first victims, and it still had not seen combat. Because the submarine was a secret weapon, most of the news had to be suppressed, or at least heavily edited. The sinking warranted only a short mention in the Monday, August 31, 1863, edition of the *Charleston Daily Courier*:

> *On Saturday last, while Lts. Payne and Hasker, of the C.S. Navy, were experimenting with a boat in the harbor, she parted from her moorings and became suddenly submerged, carrying down with her five seamen, who were drowned. The boat and bodies had not been recovered up to a late hour on Sunday. Four of the men belonged to the gunboat* Chicora *and were named Frank Doyle, John Kelly, Michael Cane, and Nicholas Davis. The fifth man, whose name we did not learn, was attached to the* Palmetto State.

THE MEN WHO SURVIVED THE *HUNLEY*'S FIRST SINKING would never set foot in her again. Payne told friends he'd lost his taste for submarine service and had "tossed in the sponge." This new secret weapon could remain at the bottom of the harbor for all he cared.

Years later Hasker would claim the accident was speeded along because of clumsiness. Payne, he said, got tripped up while climbing into the submarine and stepped on the controls for the diving fins. It went down immediately. Payne denied any wrongdoing for his remaining years, and Hasker—happy to be alive—made little of it. As an old man living in Richmond, he would occasionally tell his story.

"I was the only man that went to the bottom with the 'Fish-Boat' and came up to tell the tale," Hasker said.

WHEN HORACE HUNLEY ARRIVED IN CHARLESTON IN LATE summer of 1863, he half expected some sort of hero's welcome. Surely by now, he thought, the torpedo boat has sunk a Yankee ship. There would be reward money to split among the investors, and probably the government would bestow some sort of award on its builders. Finally there would be some hope in the Confederacy. Perhaps the shipping lines could be opened by the end of the year. Hunley, more than many, understood the importance of exporting goods. He knew that without open channels to other countries, the South was doomed.

The reality in Charleston was unfathomable to Hunley. Before he had settled into the city, the submarine was sunk in the harbor with five dead men inside it. He had lost a third submarine in less than two years and had yet to engage the enemy with any of them. Plans were under way to raise the submarine, however, if for no other reason than to retrieve the bodies of the sailors who had died on board. He knew the submarine had suffered no damage, sinking into the muddy floor of the harbor. The problem was that the men supplied by the government did not know how to handle the boat. McClintock had been right. It wasn't as easy as it looked. That miscalculation by the military had cost the lives of five good men.

Hunley sent word to Beauregard that he wanted his boat back. This government, of which he was growing decreasingly fond, had managed to sink his submarine in less than a week. Hunley felt he could do better, and he had rarely even dived aboard the fish-boat. In his terse note to the general, he said:

> *Sir—I am part owner of the torpedo boat the* Hunley. *I have been interested in building this description of boat since the beginning of the war, and furnished the means entirely of building the predecessor of this boat which was lost in an attempt to blow up a Federal vessel off Fort Morgan, Mobile Harbor. I feel therefore a deep interest in its success. I propose if you will place the boat in my hands to furnish a crew (in whole or in part) from Mobile who are well acquainted with its management and make the attempt to destroy a vessel of the enemy as early as practicable.*
>
> *—Very Respectfully, Your Obedient Servant H. L. Hunley*

Beauregard did not have to consider the request long. Within a week Hunley had requisitioned soap and brushes and was cleaning the smell of death out of his recently raised submarine—the bodies of the first crew having become so bloated, they had to be chopped in pieces to be removed. It was a grisly sight and a worse smell. But the scent—and image—of death would linger on the *Hunley*. Soldiers becoming wary of the submarine called it an "iron coffin." It was the first of many unflattering nicknames the boat would pick up in its short time in Charleston.

As was his nature, Horace Lawson Hunley became obsessed. This submarine was his last chance. It had to work. He telegraphed word to send what workers could be spared from the Park and Lyons Machine Shop in downtown Mobile to help. The men in the shop had been upset that they were not loaded on the train with the *Hunley* when it was shipped to Charleston. He knew they would be eager to come to South Carolina. As far as they were concerned, they were the submarine's crew. At the shop a handful of men were selected to go, among them Robert Brockbank, Joseph Patterson, Charles McHugh, John Marshall,

Henry Beard, and William Alexander. They were to ship out to Charleston as quickly as possible.

And then fate stepped in again. On the day the crew was set to leave Mobile, Thomas W. Park, the son of the shop's owner, begged Alexander for his spot on the crew. For whatever reason Alexander chose to stay behind and gave Park his seat. Although Alexander didn't know it, with that generous gesture he had saved his own life.

IT DID NOT TAKE LONG FOR RUMORS OF HUNLEY'S LATEST mission to reach Louisiana. His sister, Volumnia, worshiped her brother and tried to keep tabs on him, but it was a task she found nearly impossible. She spent a good part of her time wondering where he was. But by the first days of fall, news of his grand scheme reached New Orleans. The Barrows learned that Hunley himself planned to handle operations of the torpedo boat, perhaps even take it into battle against the Union fleet. They were terrified. Volumnia knew that her husband was the only person who had any chance of dissuading Hunley from such foolhardiness, and she asked him to intervene. In a letter written in late September 1863, Robert Ruffin Barrow pleaded his case to his brother-in-law, saying that he believed the federal government had overstepped its power, but he was strongly opposed to secession and the breakup of the Union. It's all Jeff Davis's fault, he said, an opinion Hunley seemed to share. But mostly Barrow was trying to talk Hunley out of playing war hero, out of piloting that damn boat. He didn't say it, but both he and Volumnia feared the submarine could be the death of Hunley.

"This is the place for you and you ought to be here and *you should be here*," Barrow wrote in his letter. "So come home."

The letter would not arrive in time.

OCTOBER 15, 1863, WAS A DREARY MORNING. IT WAS RAIN-ing, the haze too thick to see the fleet just offshore. The weather scrambled the surface of Charleston Harbor. Still, Hunley felt good. He had his Mobile crew, led by himself and Thomas W. Park, and they were ready. They had taken the submarine out a few times already, to get reacquainted with it, and it had performed well. As far as Hunley was concerned, this was all the fish-boat needed—a crew that understood how to operate it.

It was a quiet morning in Charleston, a rare day when the Yankee troops would not hurl a single shell at the city. Hunley had prepared a little show for the few curious people milling about in the foul weather on Adger's Wharf. He pointed out in the harbor, where the receiving ship *Indian Chief* lay at anchor between downtown Charleston and Mount Pleasant on the far banks of the Cooper River. Hunley told his crew they would charge toward the ship, dive under her, and come up on the other side to demonstrate how the submarine delivered its floating mine, dragging 100 feet behind on a towline. It would be almost like a dress rehearsal. Soon the *Hunley* would attack the blockade.

The black torpedo boat, which some people thought resembled a whale in the water, moved away from the dock slowly, churning water in its wake. Still on the surface, its course was set amidships of the *Indian Chief*. For ten minutes it slid across the water gracefully. As it got closer to its target, the *Hunley* slipped beneath the surface.

At Adger's Wharf the people who had seen the submarine dive before immediately knew that something was wrong. Normally the boat went under quickly, leaving little trace that it had been there at all. But this time the water was bubbling where the *Hunley* had submerged out near heavily fortified Castle Pinckney. Charles Stanton—the member of the submarine's first crew who was away on watch when it sank in August—observed the same scene from the deck of the *Indian Chief*. Perhaps before anyone else realized it, Stanton knew the fish-boat would not be coming back up.

SOMETHING HAD GONE TERRIBLY WRONG.

Nearly 60 feet underwater, Hunley and his crew fought death in the pitch-black interior of the sub. They tried desperately to make the boat surface. They turned the T-bolts to drop the keel ballast and cranked the propeller in reverse. But it was useless. The men could barely even hold themselves in place. The submarine's bow was buried in the mud, its stern floating, pointed toward the surface. Thousands of pounds of water pressure held the hatches down—the men couldn't get out. Panic setting in, Hunley pumped maniacally to empty the forward ballast tank and free the submarine from the harbor floor.

And then the water began to seep into the crew compartment.

At a 45-degree angle, the *Hunley* retained pockets of air but was mostly filled with harbor water spilling over the bulkhead walls from the open ballast tanks. It took only minutes for most of the men to drown. But Park and Hunley, their heads above water in the conning towers, their crewmates clawing at them from the dank blackness, had time to think about their fate as they suffocated. Perhaps Hunley even had time to realize that he could not pump the water out of the forward ballast tank because he had forgotten to close the seacock. But then, he was not thinking clearly. In his hand he held a waterlogged candle next to his head, its light forever extinguished. It would do him no good.

In his last moments, as the life faded from him, Hunley may have wondered, Is this how Great Men die?

On Friday morning, October 16, 1863, the *Charleston Daily Courier* carried this small notice: "Melancholy Occurrence—On Thursday morning an accident occurred to a small boat in Cooper River, containing eight persons, all of whom were drowned."

In Louisiana that November, Volumnia Hunley Barrow received the note she had feared most. It was from Gardner Smith, a friend of her brother's who had been called to Charleston for help. Smith had arrived on October 18, three days too late.

Madam, It becomes my painful duty to address you in relation to the decease of your brother, Horace L. Hunley. I was in his employ for several months previous to this bad event. He telegraphed me in Mobile to come to Charleston. . . .

We succeeded in raising the boat and recovered the body of Capt. Hunley on the 7th November. I had a coffin ready. The funeral took place on Sunday the 8th at 4 o'clock P.M. General Beauregard ordered a military escort. The funeral service was solemn and impressive, performed by the Rev. W. B. Gates, Episcopal.

I saved a large lock of his hair and his watch and a pair of sleeve buttons and two gold studs. The watch is ruined. I had them all cleaned and [they] will be prized as mementoes. I gave them to Mr. [Henry] Leovy, except for a small lock of hair, which I enclose to you. At the grave I could not refrain from tears as the casket of the spirit of a noble and generous man was being lowered, earth to earth, to its final rest.

AFTER ITS RECOVERY BEAUREGARD ORDERED THE SUB-marine grounded. He decided that it was simply too dangerous. It had killed thirteen men of the Confederacy and had not yet even come close to a blockader. It was an experiment before its time and would do Charleston no good. The secret weapon would be shelved before it ever saw combat. It seemed the *Hunley* was an idea that would die with its originator.

"It is more dangerous to those who use it than the enemy," Beauregard said.

NEWS OF HORACE HUNLEY'S DEATH HAD REACHED THE Park and Lyons Machine Shop by telegraph. Any of the men in the shop that day knew that they could have been among those entombed in the belly of the fish-boat, save for fate. There was the odd feeling of sorrow mixed with relief, the anguish of loss tempered by the natural instincts of self-preservation, the thoughts that "it could have been me."

George E. Dixon and William Alexander felt little of that, however. Their thoughts were with the submarine. They knew it would be raised to recover the bodies of Hunley, Park, and the other men. Both Dixon and Alexander wanted to be there when that happened, not only to bury their friends but also to save their submarine. Soon they left for Charleston.

When the two arrived in the Holy City, the *Hunley* was still at the bottom of the harbor. Angus Smith, one of the divers who had raised the submarine after its first sinking, had found it in 9 fathoms of water three days after the sinking. But he had not yet been able to salvage it. It was a violent October on the water. A northeast wind stirred the harbor like a washing machine and held rescue crews on land. The hoisting boats could not keep an even keel. For more than two weeks, the submarine hung with its nose buried in the silt 60 feet below the surface. It was Saturday, November 7, before Smith and his hard-hat diving partner David Broadfoot were able to sling enough chain and line around the craft so that it could be raised to the surface. When they had the *Hunley* on the dock at Mount Pleasant, only then did they realize the horrible death the submarine's benefactor had suffered.

Inside, the men lay contorted in their death poses. Some still reached for the hatches; a couple held candles. A few held on to each other on the floor of the submarine. Hunley's face was blackened by suffocation. It was a grisly sight, even for Beauregard, who knew war all too well.

"It was indescribably ghastly," Beauregard would write years later. "The unfortunate men were contorted into all kinds of horrible attitudes. After this tragedy I refused to permit the boat to be used again."

Beauregard's order to scrap the *Hunley* project devastated Dixon and Alexander. It had not even seen combat yet. The submarine was in working condition: they had examined it already. It sank only because the crew forgot to close the ballast-tank valves. It had simply flooded. To discard it would be a waste, and that was a luxury the South did not have. The two friends refused to give up and finally wangled an audience with the general himself.

Beauregard was quartered in a house north of Charleston's center. Earlier in the war he had been set up in a fashionable house on Meeting Street near the Battery. But when he found out that Union troops were close enough to land mortars all around the property, Beauregard discreetly retreated farther inland. When Dixon and Alexander arrived at headquarters, they found Beauregard's office full. His chief of staff, Gen. Thomas Jordan, was there, as well as Maj. Francis Lee, the engineer who had built the spar torpedoes for all the Davids in the harbor. Lee was on the general's staff, partly because of his skills and partly because Beauregard liked him. They had things in common. Before the war Beauregard had been an engineer in New Orleans—in fact, he had supervised construction of the customhouse where Horace Hunley had worked part-time. That day Lee was present because Beauregard needed him in on the meeting about the fish-boat.

Beauregard knew that Dixon would not easily give up his plans for piloting the submarine. Dixon had fought under Beauregard at Shiloh and, though he was injured early in the battle, soon returned to active duty. Beauregard considered the lieutenant brave—and determined. He proved the Charleston commander right.

Dixon was calm and resolute and, like the general, not afraid to speak his mind to a superior officer. He demanded another chance. The submarine he helped to build had killed thirteen men, and he had yet to share the danger. To his conscience that was untenable. He told Beauregard the *Hunley* was as fine as the day it was built. It would work; it just hadn't been operated properly. Putting inexperienced Confederate sailors on it had been a mistake; Hunley's piloting the boat had been another. The entire accident, Dixon said, could have been avoided. Hunley absentmindedly forgot to close the seacock to the forward ballast tank. Dixon said that Alexander and he, with a crew of their picking, could sink a blockader. He was certain of it.

Beauregard had to admire the young officer; perhaps he even noticed that Dixon shared some qualities with himself. Still, Beauregard's instinct was to politely turn down the request. In the bars around town, people had taken to calling the *Hunley* the "peripatetic coffin."

He could see his statement of the torpedo boat's being "more dangerous to those who use it than the enemy" coming back to haunt him.
But at the time Beauregard was under newfound pressure that may
have helped sway him.

Beauregard had just recovered from a three-day visit by Confederate president Jefferson Davis. Davis, through an endless parade of
pomp and circumstance, toured the war-torn town of Charleston with
his general in tow as kind of a morale tour. It was a strained few days,
given their contempt for each other. During the official visit, Davis had
seen the Davids and had been told about the *Hunley*. And then the
president, in a public speech in Charleston, promptly spilled the beans.
He told his people that Charleston would never fall, for even if the
Yankees got past their forts, they had "other means" of defending the
city. It was practically an endorsement of the stealth boats, which most
city residents had glimpsed at one time or another.

As a result of his president's endorsement, Beauregard felt he had
to at least consider Dixon's offer. Besides, he was in no position to be
turning away willing soldiers. Beauregard, at Jordan's suggestion, offered a compromise: if Dixon would fit the submarine with one of
Lee's spars and attack on the surface, he would give the fish-boat one
last chance. Lee objected at first, not wanting his new invention associated with what he felt was a death trap. But Beauregard insisted. Dixon
agreed, although if he had any intention of keeping that promise, he
didn't entertain it for long. The *Hunley*, he knew, was a diving boat.
And it would dive again.

THE WORK WOULD TAKE NEARLY A MONTH. AS WITH ITS
first sinking, the bodies had sat in the submarine for weeks. It took
lime, 21 pounds of soap, and ten men working for more than three
weeks to get the boat back in shape. The submarine was perched on a
dock overlooking the harbor in Mount Pleasant with its hatches
opened to air out the foul smell inside its hull. Dixon left the cleaning
to others while he and Alexander went out to recruit a new crew. At

first Beauregard refused to let Dixon solicit his soldiers. He had a bad feeling about the fish-boat and said if they were looking for fools, they could find them among civilians. Finally he relented—but only if the two made sure every volunteer knew what he was getting into. Literally.

They started on the *Indian Chief*, now moored safely up the Stono River. Dixon and Alexander explained that the mission would be dangerous; the submarine had already killed the better part of two crews. It was tough work. It might require twelve hours of hard labor at a time several days a week. They could not be claustrophobic or scared of the dark. It would be the only time they would have to make the speech. Dixon and Alexander had to turn away volunteers.

In the end the *Indian Chief* would provide most of the *Hunley*'s final crew, including Arnold Becker, Fred Collins, C. Simpkins, James A. Wicks, and Joseph Ridgeway. Most of these men were young or slight of build—definite advantages in the cramped interior of the submarine. Few of them had families, save for one.

James A. Wicks may have been chosen for the *Hunley*'s final crew because of his experience. He was an old salt, a veteran of more than ten years in the U.S. Navy; still, he was a son of the South: his wife and four daughters were living in north Florida when the fighting began. At the time Wicks had been serving on the USS *Congress* in Chesapeake Bay. He stayed at his post, but his sympathies lay elsewhere—a common personal conflict during the American Civil War. Early on in the fighting, the *Congress* was attacked and sunk by the CSS *Virginia*, the salvaged *Merrimac*. As his ship went down, Wicks swam ashore at Hampton Roads and joined the Confederate Navy. A year later he was in Charleston, serving at several posts before joining the *Hunley* crew. Dixon and Alexander were glad to have a seasoned sailor on hand. They would need all the expertise and experience they could get if they were going to do this.

DIXON AND ALEXANDER, NATURALLY, REFITTED THE *HUN-ley* themselves. With their new crew helping, the two men readjusted the submarine's machinery, restuffed its stuffing boxes, and prepared it to return to the water. As they were working one day, an unannounced visitor appeared on the wharf. He introduced himself as the rector of St. Philip's Episcopal Church, which displayed one of the finest steeples on the downtown Charleston skyline. The rector had sailed across the harbor to speak to the submariners, word of their mission having leaked out in town. He spoke privately to Alexander, asking the young man if he realized the danger of what he was attempting to do. The reverend invited him to attend the next church service. Alexander accepted the invitation—a devout Christian, he was moved by the pastor's concern.

The next Sunday Alexander left the King Street boardinghouse where he and Dixon were staying and walked the few short blocks to St. Philip's. Before the service he met privately with the rector. History did not record the conversation, but Alexander most likely calmly assured the man that he would be fine.

By early December 1863 the *Hunley* was almost ready to sail again when a twenty-year-old artist came upon the submarine. It was still on the dock in Mount Pleasant, its aft hatch open to air out the remaining scents of wet paint—and its financier. There was one man guarding it, minimal security for something that was supposed to be a state secret. The funny fish-boat inspired the man to pull out his sketchbook. Conrad Wise Chapman was the son of a famous Virginia painter. An Italian by birth, he'd come to America only when the war broke out and joined the Confederacy. A veteran of Shiloh like Dixon and Beauregard, Chapman had been severely wounded in the Tennessee countryside. Following his recovery, he was transferred to Charleston, where he made paintings of the war at the request of the government. The *Hunley* was something so odd, so out of place, the artist in Chapman couldn't resist it.

First he sketched the submarine and later based a painting on that drawing. Shown from the stern, the image of the submarine is so sleek, so long and tapering, that for nearly a century Chapman would be ridiculed as fanciful and inaccurate. There was no way, most people would argue, that the *Hunley* could be that hydrodynamic—not something built in 1863 by Rebels without resources.

But Chapman had captured the *Hunley* perfectly and, for his own posterity, painted himself into the scene, seated and holding a rifle, talking to the guard. It would become the classic image of the submarine, made just before it set out on its last tour of duty.

Just before it made history.

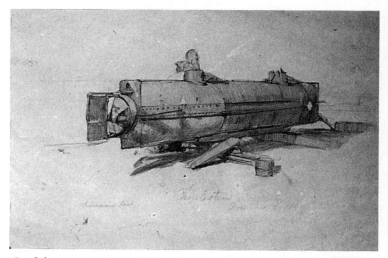

Confederate artist Conrad Wise Chapman made this sketch of the Hunley *in December 1863 as it was being repaired following its second sinking. Chapman used this and other sketches as the basis for his painting of the submarine shown on the dust jacket. (Courtesy Valentine Museum/Richmond History Center)*

Chapter 3

UNDER A
CAROLINA MOON

THE MOON HUNG OVER THE ATLANTIC LIKE A FLARE.
It was piercing cold on the beach at Sullivan's Island as the last flecks of daylight faded out of February 17, 1864. Lt. George E. Dixon cursed, but not necessarily about the weather. After three months of refurbishing the submarine, of training a new crew, of waiting for calm waters, it was time. Tonight the *Hunley* would attack the blockade. But Dixon was uneasy. There were complications. The bright moon shone like a spotlight on the water, possibly eliminating the tiny fish-boat's single advantage: surprise.

Still, there was no choice. Dixon knew he had tried the patience of the Confederate brass long enough. Since it had arrived in Charleston in August, the *Hunley* had spent more time at the bottom of the harbor than it had on patrol. When his latest leave from the Twenty-first Alabama Regiment was up in a few weeks, Dixon would be going back to Mobile. And that would be it for the *Hunley*—unless he could sink one of those blockade ships on the horizon.

As Dixon stood on the beach, tall and handsome, the sea breeze tousling his light-colored hair, he knew his time had come. The South Atlantic Blockading Squadron was strangling Charleston. The blockade could eventually threaten the entire Confederacy—unless, that is, he could do something about it. It was an enormous pressure on him. He was only twenty-four years old; he should have been nervous about the task before him. But as Beauregard had described him, Dixon was resolute. And he was confident. Above all else, Dixon had faith in the little submarine. He'd helped build it, tested it in Mobile Bay, and put it through more than two months of successful training in Charleston Harbor and the backwaters around Sullivan's Island. The submarine would work in the right hands. The previous accidents were the fault of the men piloting it. He and William Alexander had proved to Beauregard that the boat was not a death trap.

It was a temperamental piece of machinery, to be sure. Before the Lee spar had been fitted, when the submarine was still stationed in the harbor, there had been problems, even with Dixon commanding. One night the *Hunley*'s floating mine had got entangled in the David towing the submarine out to sea, nearly blowing both boats out of the water. That had been the fish-boat's last night in the harbor. After that the *Hunley* was moved to Sullivan's Island, a spit of sand on the north side of the harbor's entrance.

At the southern end of Sullivan's stood Fort Moultrie—which had battered Sumter into submission—and what few other buildings the island had. The *Hunley* was kept at the north end of the island, across Breach Inlet from Long Island (the modern-day Isle of Palms). It was a remote spot, away from the prying eyes of spies. Most important, it was close to the open ocean and was the only real departure point for the submarine to use and have any chance of reaching the Union fleet. It was when the *Hunley* was moved to Sullivan's Island that crew and submarine and environment jelled. The men fell into a simple pattern: they stayed together in an abandoned house in Mount Pleasant, 7 miles from the boat. Every other day they would make their way toward the ocean, take a rowboat or ferry over to Sullivan's, and walk along the beach to Battery Marshall, where the boat was moored. It was a long, dangerous walk, within sight—and firing distance—of the blockade, but it was much better than fighting the scrub of the barrier island. Besides, the view gave them more time to study the enemy.

The weather had been rough that winter, nor'easters chewing up the coast and turning the Atlantic into a mountain range of angry waves—no place for a submarine that could barely maintain buoyancy. On many nights they had contented themselves with practice and sailed the submarine through the safe water behind the island. Sometimes they would go out a few miles but only got close to the blockade ships occasionally.

One afternoon in January they had become comfortable enough with the boat to test its limits. Just off Battery Marshall on the inland side of the island, the crew took the submarine down and let it sink to the bottom. They wanted to know how long they could stay down without fresh air. After an attack they might have to submerge and lie still until favorable tides came around. Propelling the *Hunley* was hard enough work; fighting against the sea currents was nearly impossible.

Dixon believed they could hold out for about thirty minutes without refreshing their air; that was how long the candles lasted before expiring. But they would not know unless they tried, and on that day it was too rough on the open sea to venture out. After he filled the ballast tank, Dixon maneuvered the *Hunley* down softly in the mud. When the submarine settled into the muck, the men stopped talking and waited. It was daylight when the submarine went down, but very little of it filtered in through the submarine's ten deadlights—two rows of tiny portholes along the top of the hull. Within a half hour the candle flickered out, and the interior went blindingly dark.

The deal was that they would sit still until one crewman could not take it anymore. They had agreed that when the first man yelled "up," they would make for the surface. In the dark it seemed that time lost all meaning. Occasionally Dixon would ask Alexander "How is it?" but other than that, silence. No one wanted to be the one to end the test. No one wanted to seem the weakest among a crew of daring—some said suicidal—volunteers. So they waited, all of them trying not to be the first to give the word.

Perhaps there was a single second when the last bit of oxygen had been used, when their lungs screamed out and the men's bodies told them they were out of time. At the same time every man in the crew yelled "up" in unison and furiously began pumping and cranking.

Soon the bow of the submarine was rising, reaching toward the surface, but the stern sat stoically in the mud. Alexander pumped the after ballast tank madly but quickly realized nothing was happening. It had happened before, and the Scot needed little time for adjustment. Working blind, he took off the pump's cap and felt seaweed clumped beneath the valve. He threw it out, put the contraption back together from memory, and began pumping. Soon the *Hunley* broke the surface, where Dixon and Alexander threw open the conning tower hatches, greedily sucking down the fresh Carolina air, letting it fill the boat. It was now dark. The submarine had been on the bottom for two and a half hours.

On the island the crew had been given up for dead. Word had already been sent to Beauregard that the third crew of the *Hunley* had perished, again on test runs. Dixon would have to correct that. Later. After the men extricated themselves from their tiny ship, they stood on the dock and came to an agreement. They decided that if the *Hunley* ever became stuck, they would open the submarine's seacocks and end it. They would rather drown quickly at their own hand than suffocate slowly. It became the crew's pact, forged from shared experience. That day they'd been lucky. Alexander had saved their lives.

ALEXANDER. HE HAD BECOME ONE OF DIXON'S CLOSEST friends; together they had shared the *Hunley*'s entire history. But now Dixon was alone. Two weeks earlier Beauregard had ordered Alexander back to Alabama to build a new rapid-fire repeating gun for the Confederacy. Talent such as Alexander's was in high demand in the South as the fourth year of the war began. It was a tough separation for both men. The two had spent much of the Charleston winter together, Dixon the submarine's pilot, Alexander its first officer. Before going out in the evening, the two men would lie on the beach, a map and compass between them, and pick out targets. Their choices were limited; most of the Union fleet anchored farther than the crew could crank the boat's propeller. Or if they did get there, they wouldn't have enough energy to get back. In fact, fatigue had left them within hearing distance of the fleet on some mornings, the men turning the screw furiously while listening to some stupid Yankee singing to the rising sun.

Now, with Alexander gone, Dixon felt alone. He wrote letters to his old friend, keeping him informed as if he were still a member of the crew. In a couple of short messages sent to Mobile, Dixon told Alexander about weather conditions keeping the submarine docked, how the crew missed him. He let Alexander know about his replacement. Dixon wrote the notes in a void, during the time that normally he would have spent with his friend, scouting prey. Now that was one task he unhappily had to perform by himself. On this day he would write his last note to Alexander, telling him that the weather had finally cooperated. It was time.

As he silently watched the Union fleet, Dixon rubbed a bent coin he kept in his pants pocket. It was a $20 gold piece, and two years earlier it had saved his life. Now he fondled it constantly, rubbing it smooth with his thumb. He kept it with him always, took it with him everywhere. His girlfriend in Mobile had given it to him on the day he shipped out to the front lines. He had carried it into war. For a man in his early twenties, the gift meant much more than its monetary value. It represented his future. After the war he would be married and have a family of his own. He would settle in Mobile, where he'd been working on riverboats far from his native Kentucky before the fighting began. That's what he thought about when the coin was new and shiny and flat. And then came Shiloh.

Dixon's regiment stormed through the misty Tennessee predawn of April 6, 1862, eager to get the jump on the Yankees. It was a rare moment when the Rebels felt as if they had a good chance. But the Union fought back hard, its troops laying down a terrifyingly efficient spray of gunfire. The Twenty-first Alabama was hit harder than most regiments: five flag-bearers fell, one after another, that morning. Dixon was one of the first ones downed. The bullet smacked him high on his thigh. When he dropped, he thought he was dead—a fire sizzled in his leg. Soon the world went black.

When he awoke later, he found out just how lucky he'd been. The bullet had hit the coin, denting it, leaving it with a permanent warp. Twenty dollars had stopped the bullet and the gangrene that almost certainly would have followed. Queenie Bennett, his Alabama sweetheart, had saved his life from 400 miles away.

From that moment on, the coin was never out of Dixon's reach. He rubbed it absently sometimes, not realizing what he was doing. On other occasions he knew exactly what he was doing. The coin was his good-luck piece, if there was such a thing. Perhaps it represented something more to him, but he could not put it into words. Above all else, it was a comfort to him—a reminder of what was waiting for him, a sign that his work was not yet finished.

Dixon's unfinished business swung at anchor nearly 4 miles offshore. She was the USS *Housatonic*, a huge Union warship, steam-powered, triple-masted, and more than 200 feet long. She stood proudly on the horizon. But the *Housatonic* suffered from the luck of geography. Her place in the blockade was near Rattlesnake Shoal, at the north entrance of the channel, and her captain had a habit of coming in a little too close to shore to anchor. It was a mistake that would cost them. Perhaps Dixon smiled at that thought.

Nevertheless, he felt torn. His duty and honor were most important to him, and he'd told Beauregard he could do it. There was no backing out. But he longed for Mobile, for Queenie, and for his friends. Alexander's return to Alabama stirred those feelings. In addition, his comrades wanted him back. Capt. John Cothran of the Twenty-first Alabama—Dixon's regiment—had written to the young lieutenant, asking him to rejoin the company. Dixon politely declined. He was committed to the *Hunley*. Dixon wrote to Cothran on February 5, 1864:

> *I am fastened to Charleston and its approaches until I am able to blow up some of their Yankee ships. I have been here over three*

months, have worked very hard, in fact I am working all the time.
My headquarters are on Sullivan's Island, and a more uncomfort-
able place could not be found in the Confederacy. For the last six
weeks I have not been out of the range of shells and often I am
forced to go within close proximity of the Yankee battery. . . . If
you wish to see war every day and night, this is the place to see it.
Charleston and its defenders will occupy the most conspicuous
place in the history of the war, and it shall be as much glory as I
shall wish if I can inscribe myself as one of its defenders.

Dixon closed his letter to his friend with his most honest thought, an amazing display of candor: "I am heartily tired of this place." He knew what he had to do to erase that irritation. It was Wednesday, February 17, 1864. Time to go to work. Dixon walked around the end of the island to Battery Marshall for his appointment with history.

THE SUBMARINE WAS MOORED AT A WOODEN DOCK ON THE back of the island, very close to Breach Inlet, a rough stream rushing between Sullivan's and Long Islands. It took only minutes to reach the open water through the channel that the ocean—with the help of a hurricane—had cut between the two barrier islands. After months of trials, accidents, and bad weather, the submarine was ready. Earlier in the day Dixon had made final adjustments with the help of some of the troops stationed behind the earthen mounds of Battery Marshall. The spar system was working perfectly; the powder load had been increased to 90 pounds. When the David had had its first battle months earlier, 70 pounds had proved too small a charge to sink a Union ship. This, everyone was sure, would blow a hole in a warship big enough to drive a train through.

That evening it was cold, barely above freezing—to that point the coldest day of the year. The water was calm that night, almost glassine. The tide had turned sometime around six P.M., and the water followed its normal currents, rushing out through Breach Inlet toward the open sea. Within an hour the water was running swiftly, and what darkness the *Hunley* would enjoy that night had fallen. They would let the rushing tide carry the fish-boat out to sea.

Dixon gave the order to load up. It was not quite seven P.M. The men carried candles and a lamp into the submarine's dark, damp crew compartment. Even though it was cold, they would soon be working up a sweat that would leave them chilly, clammy, and uncomfortable. Among the crew, which had been together for three months, was Cpl. C. F. Carlson. A soldier from an artillery unit stationed in Charleston, Carlson had taken Alexander's spot on the crew. He'd had little training. In fact, he had scarcely been aboard the boat more than a half dozen times.

As Dixon climbed through the front hatch of the *Hunley*, he reminded Lt. Col. O. M. Dantzler, the commander at Battery Marshall, of the plan. Dixon would flash a blue phosphorus lamp when the *Hunley* had accomplished its mission. That would be the sign for the troops to start a signal fire on the beach, which the *Hunley* would use to steer home by.

And then Dixon closed the sub's hatch. It was the last time he was seen alive.

LT. GEORGE E. DIXON HAD NO IDEA THE YANKEES WERE expecting him. The only real surprise the *Hunley* had on its side was the exact date of the attack. The Union Navy knew about the fish-boat, had been on the lookout for it since January, when two Confederate deserters reported its existence and described its inner workings to Rear Adm. John A. Dahlgren.

The two men had been present, oddly enough, at nearly every turn in the *Hunley*'s path from Alabama to the blockade that night. They were George Shipp and a man named Belton, both of whom had been drafted into the Confederate Army against their wishes. Belton was a mechanic from Michigan who had worked his way south in the years before the war. When the South fired on Fort Sumter, Belton was running a train between Montgomery and Mobile, where the Rebels eventually put him to work. In the spring of 1863, he was laboring at Park and Lyons watching as the *Hunley* was built. Belton had seen nearly everything. In his report to Dahlgren, he mistakenly referred to the submarine as the *American Diver*, but he had everything else exactly right.

Belton had transferred to the navy and Charleston, believing that it afforded him a better chance to make his escape. He wanted to join the Union as a safe way of getting back to the wife he'd left in Ohio. In Charleston he served with Shipp on the *Indian Chief.* Shipp had been on the receiving ship for some time. In fact, he had seen the submarine's ill-fated dive with Hunley at the controls. Together the two men talked of escaping their miserable lives in the Confederate military. Soon a few others would join them. All they needed was the right break.

It happened on a foggy night in early January. Four of them took the captain's small launch and sailed away from the *Indian Chief.* But in their haste to get away, the men sailed up the Cooper River, not out to sea. They ended up in Shem Creek, a channel that ran through the middle of Mount Pleasant. In the rain, without food, the men hid in the marsh grass all the next day until nightfall, when they sailed the little boat out of the creek. The men sailed into the harbor and between the two forts, Moultrie and Sumter. They waved as they passed a Confederate picket boat.

As soon as the men met a blockader, they filed reports for Admiral Dahlgren. They told him about the Davids, about how strong Charleston's defenses were—everything the Union Navy needed to know. Dahlgren listened most closely, however, to the talk of this little boat that could submerge and plant an explosive charge on the belly of a Union ship. It, well, interested him.

On the deck of his flagship, the *Philadelphia*, moored off Morris Island, Dahlgren savored the information. Peering out over Charleston Harbor, where the church steeples spiked out of the landscape, Dahlgren marveled at how his life had turned around in a few short months. Just when it seemed that his career was over, salvation had come from the least likely source.

U.S. Navy Rear Adm. John A. Dahlgren, commander of the South Atlantic Blockading Squadron, learned of the Hunley from two Confederate deserters. He ordered the fleet to take defensive measures. (Courtesy National Archives)

A year earlier Dahlgren had filled his days sitting in a Washington office peering out at the Anacostia River. He was one of the most important men in the Union Navy, but with each passing day, his chance of seeing combat was evaporating. Dahlgren was chief of the Bureau of Ordnance, and had been for nearly twenty years. During that time he had designed the most effective weapons in the Northern arsenal, including the lethal 15-inch smoothbores currently being fitted in the Union's monitors. The new wonder guns, shaped like a soda pop bottle, would smash anything the South could float. But at a moment when he should have been enjoying his greatest achievement, he was stuck at the Washington Navy Yard awaiting a command. He was suffocating under the weight of navy bureaucracy. He wanted to be on the open sea.

Not even his friendship with President Abraham Lincoln could help. On February 14, 1863, just a year before the *Hunley* would attack his fleet, Dahlgren found himself making a second trip to the White House in one day. Lincoln was brooding. The president had recently issued the Emancipation Proclamation but could not get the secessionist city of Charleston and its damnable defenders out of his thoughts. For nearly two years a city built almost on the Atlantic coast protected only by sand forts, a few thousand men, and an armada of small, sometimes home-made boats had fended off practically the entire United States Navy.

Dahlgren walked in as Lincoln was getting a shave. "He let off a joke," Dahlgren scribbled in his diary later, "the first I have heard for a long while." But he added, "Abe is restless about Charleston."

President Lincoln needed the political victory that would come from capturing the city that had started all this. He confided to Dahlgren that the Union's commander of the South Atlantic Blockading Squadron, Samuel du Pont, had let him down. Du Pont had done little to destroy Charleston. He had focused too much of his attention—and his guns—on Fort Sumter, which by now was little more than a pile of rubble. Within a few months Lincoln stopped complaining and did something: he gave his friend du Pont's job and a mandate. Break Charleston's will.

From the deck of the *Philadelphia*, that's just what Dahlgren planned to do. In January 1864, after hearing the tall tales of deserters, Dahlgren had mixed feelings. The inventor in him was impressed by the ingenuity of his adversaries; the commander, fearful that it might actually succeed. But now the advantage had turned again: he knew everything Beauregard planned to unleash against him and quickly issued new orders to the fleet.

"I have reliable information that the rebels have two torpedo boats ready for service," Dahlgren wrote, "which may be expected on the first night when the water is suitable for their movement. One of these

A drawing of the USS Housatonic *made by R. G. Skerrett in 1902. (Courtesy Naval Historical Center)*

is the 'David,' which attacked the *Ironsides* in October; the other is similar to it. There is also one of another kind, which is nearly submerged and can be entirely so. It is intended to go under the bottoms of vessels and there operate."

Dahlgren, a crafty sailor, wasted little time in coming up with his defensive plans. He ordered his ships to put chain netting along their hulls in hopes of foiling any chance the torpedo boat might have to get close and plant a bomb. He told ships' captains to change their anchorages occasionally, to keep the enemy off guard and to keep the Rebels from picking off weak vessels. He ordered guns trained on the water at all times and increased lookouts, especially when the water was calm. And he told them to take one last precaution.

"It is also advisable not to anchor in the deepest part of the channel, for by not leaving much space between the bottom of the vessel and the bottom of the channel it will be impossible for the diving torpedo to operate except on the sides, and there will be less difficulty in raising a vessel if sunk."

That order would save more than a hundred lives.

THE CREW OF THE SLOOP OF WAR USS *HOUSATONIC* FOL-
lowed Dahlgren's instructions to the letter; they thought they were
ready. Besides, what little torpedo boat would dare take on such a massive ship? She lay at anchor just off Sullivan's Island, her bowsprit
pointed defiantly skyward. She was one of the newer additions to the
fleet, named after a New England river that emptied into the Long Island Sound just east of Bridgeport, Connecticut. The *Housatonic* had
arrived at its station in the blockade in late September 1862 and by the
winter of 1864 had proved itself a formidable warship. The *Housatonic*
was one of the Union ships that helped bomb the city's forts. Its crew
had captured, or assisted in the capture of, at least two blockade-
runners. Once, the guns of the mighty ship had run the *Chicora* and
Palmetto State back into Charleston Harbor.

From land she cut an impressive profile. Her masts towered
more than 100 feet above the decks, and she carried acres of sailcloth.
The sloop ran fast on steam, and since the torpedo boat scare, her
bunkers were kept filled with coal. She had a crew of 155 men—most
of whom had bedded down by eight P.M. on February 17, 1864. If
they didn't have the watch then, they would have to stand it early in
the morning.

That night the *Housatonic's* watch included six lookouts in addition to a handful of officers on deck. Even with that many men, on a
ship with a beam of 38 feet, they were barely within hearing distance of
one another. On the starboard corner of the bow, Robert F. Flemming,
a black sailor, had just settled in for his watch. It was scarcely 8:40 P.M.;
he'd been there little more than thirty minutes. It was a pleasant evening, and Flemming scanned the horizon quietly. Even though the
temperature was only a few degrees above freezing, many members of
the crew remarked that it felt oddly nice that night. Flemming was
looking in the direction of Fort Sumter 5 miles away, catching the re-
flection of the moonlight shimmering on the water, when he saw it.

It was nearly 400 feet away—two ship's lengths—and looked like a
log. A very big log. Remembering his briefing from a month ago,

Flemming ran to report to the petty officer on the forecastle. Flemming had heard the warnings about the torpedo boat and was almost sure the queer log was really a Rebel fish-boat. But Lewis A. Cornthwait, an acting master's mate, was unimpressed by his excited lookout's report.

"It's just a log," he said, and ordered Flemming back to his post.

But Flemming, who had a sharper eye, argued with his superior officer. "It's not floating with the tide like a log would, it's moving across the tide."

Flemming called over the port lookout, C. P. Slade, for a second opinion. Seeing his men support each other, Cornthwait saw the possibility that they might prove him wrong. This spurred him to look again, this time using his spyglass. Not wanting to lose face, the officer repeated his earlier claim, "just a log."

And then he turned and ran aft, in a panic, toward the bridge. But by then the ship was already moving.

JOHN CROSBY, THE SHIP'S ACTING MASTER, WAS ON THE *Housatonic*'s quarterdeck at 8:45 P.M. In the distance he could see the South Atlantic Blockading Squadron stretching along the coast, little lights from the decks flickering on and off. Just a mile away was the mightiest ship in the fleet, the *Canandaigua*, a ship that Crosby admired. It was calm, too much so. Peering toward the South Carolina coast, scanning for blockade-runners, Crosby saw something in the moonlight that registered oddly in his mind. He would later testify that at first he thought it looked "like a porpoise coming up to the surface to blow." It was less than 100 yards off the starboard beam. He called the quartermaster over. Do you see that? Is it a tide ripple? But when Crosby looked again, he realized that what he was seeing was no dolphin.

"Beat to quarters, slip the chain and back the engine," Crosby ordered, and went to alert the captain.

———

IN THE ENGINE ROOM THE HEAT WAS SWELTERING. JAMES W. Holihan, an assistant engineer, had been on watch less than an hour but was already drenched in his own sweat. The engine room was under strict orders: keep heavy banked fires and 25 pounds of steam from six in the evening until six in the morning. That would allow the *Housatonic* to move from a dead stop to 7 knots—screaming speed for the ship—in just a few minutes. That was how it had to be: everything ready to go at a moment's notice. But the *Housatonic* didn't have that much time left. When the bells rang to signal the engineer to start moving, Holihan repeated the order: open the stop valves, back the engine.

And that's when the explosion knocked the 200-foot warship violently on its port beam.

CAPT. CHARLES W. PICKERING HAD BEEN IN HIS CABIN working on the ship's charts when he heard the shouting. He thought a blockade-runner was coming. In his haste to reach the bridge, he had grabbed the hat of the ship's doctor, who was working with him. Realizing his mistake, he returned to the cabin for the proper hat. When he finally reached the deck, he repeated the order to slip the anchor chain and throw the engine in reverse: moving forward risked fouling the anchor chain in the ship's propeller. But going astern only gave the *Hunley* a better target.

The submarine was aimed straight for the mizzenmast of the *Housatonic* and moving at a steady rate of speed. On deck the crew could see an eerie yellow glow coming from little portholes in the fishboat, although they did not know what they were seeing. Pickering told his crew to open fire and then took his own double-barreled shotgun loaded with buckshot and aimed at the *Hunley*'s front conning tower—where the biggest yellow target was glowing. By the time the submarine had been identified, it was too close, too low on the waterline, to train any of the Union ship's big guns on it. Dahlgren's new gun would be of absolutely no use to the *Housatonic*.

At first no one put the two incidents together. First, there was the noise. *Thud.* Many of the crew would later say they believed the ship had run aground in its attempted getaway. But with the dull sound, the ship moved only a little. It was almost imperceptible.

At the same time the odd thing in the water had stopped moving. Briefly it became an easier target and was showered with bullets and buckshot. Small-arms fire clanked off the hull of the mysterious boat. Then it started backing away, slowly at first, then faster. Between the shouting and the sound of the tide lapping at their ship's hull, the crew of the *Housatonic* could not hear the rope spinning from a partially submerged spool on the side of the submarine, easing out as slickly as fishing line.

The last thing any sailor on board the *Housatonic* remembered about the submarine was that it was about 50 to 80 feet off the starboard quarter when their world exploded. Pickering was still shooting when he felt his feet leave the wooden deck; he was airborne and the world went oddly silent. Perhaps he was deafened temporarily by the explosion.

If the *Housatonic* had moved only a little faster, she could have avoided being rammed by the *Hunley*, but the engine had made less than five revolutions when the torpedo that was rammed into the ship's hull detonated. Water immediately rushed into the engine room, followed by the sound of crashing timbers and metal. The ship lurched heavily to port, and many of the crew were tossed across the deck and into the sea. Most of the men had been in their bunks when the side of the ship disappeared; the whole incident took place in just a few minutes.

When 90 pounds of powder detonated in the *Housatonic*'s starboard quarter, she heaved mightily, like big game recoiling from a rifle shot. Instead of righting herself, the ship's hull just kept rolling to port. There was never any question, never any hope. She was going down.

Black smoke filled the air, but there was no fire. The explosion played itself out more like a depth charge. Splintered wood rained down on the Atlantic, and dozens of the crew soon found themselves in the cold, dark ocean. The sailors who remained on deck could feel the water creeping up their legs. Soon the ship would be underwater. Some went for the lifeboats, gathering up as many shipmates as they could. Others, including Captain Pickering, found themselves clinging to the ship's massive rigging. John Crosby, who had reached a gig, heard Pickering calling his name. The captain told Crosby to get all the men he could out of the water and then come get him. Together they would row to the *Canandaigua* for help. But the mightiest ship in the fleet was now nearly 2 long miles away.

The *Housatonic* had been anchored in water that, at low tide, was barely 25 feet deep—shallow water, just as Dahlgren had ordered. That would save most of the crew's lives. When the ship hit the bottom, its decks were less than 15 feet underwater; there was plenty of room in the rigging for the crew. Which is where they all ended up, waiting in a light Atlantic breeze for rescue. Some of them were naked, others in night-clothes. In five minutes the ship had sunk. Out of a crew of 155, only 5 died. The rest would live to tell the story a few days later at a Navy inquiry.

When the ship settled onto the silty floor of the Atlantic the night of February 17, 1864, those men hanging in the intricate webbing of the ship's rigging were briefly unsure of their fate. They could do little more than call out for help. Among the survivors was Robert F. Flemming, the man who had first seen the *Hunley* coming. The blast had left him unharmed, and he quickly scurried up the foremast. About an hour after the attack, as the *Housatonic* filled with seawater and settled onto the bottom, Flemming could see the *Canandaigua* coming for them towing the *Housatonic*'s launch. It was a comforting sight: they would be rescued, he knew.

Then he saw it. Just ahead of the *Canandaigua*, off the starboard bow of the *Housatonic*'s wreck, Robert F. Flemming saw a blue light shining on the water. He was sure of it.

ON SULLIVAN'S ISLAND THE REBELS SAW THE LIGHT, TOO, although they had no idea what events had precipitated it. Even a light ocean breeze masked noises 4 miles out on the water, and there was little or no fire from the *Housatonic*'s explosion. All those cold soldiers knew was, that was the signal. Immediately they began stoking a bonfire on the beach that could be seen a dozen miles out to sea. Had the Union Navy not been occupied at the moment, the sight of the huge fire burning on the beach might have puzzled the sailors on watch that night. They might have thought it was a victory celebration.

On land, however, the Confederates were oblivious to the chaos playing out on the water just a few short miles away. Cpl. D. W. McLaurin, a member of the Twenty-third South Carolina Volunteers, was one of the men on the beach that chilly evening. Earlier in the day he had been among the troops whom Dixon had ordered aboard the boat for last-minute adjustments to its equipment. It was a day McLaurin would never forget, but that night he didn't realize it.

From the edge of Sullivan's Island, the young soldier watched frantic signaling between the blockading ships as he threw driftwood on the fire. But McLaurin didn't put the two things together. None of the men did. They weren't expecting the *Hunley* to actually succeed. They were simply following orders and trying to keep warm, continually stoking the fire.

Over their shoulders the blue light called to them, twinkling brilliantly in the blackness. It would be the last confirmed sighting of the *H. L. Hunley* for 131 years.

*B*ENEATH THE *A*TLANTIC *O*CEAN *A* RIVER OF SAND CHURNS *in a constant dance to the rhythm of rushing seawater. Along the Carolina coast tiny granules of pummeled coral, shell, and quartz migrate from north to south in a perpetually recycling pattern of erosion and accretion that moves with the ebb and flow of the tide. As it drifts away from the land, where it slowly builds the dunes that rise out of the waves to form the coast, the sand swirls, tumbling end over end along the seabed. It is an endless wrinkling blanket covering the clay earth below. Anything in the path of underwater currents with enough mass to avoid constant motion is eventually buried, pulled down by the tug of gravity and pushed by the relentless sweep of the sand. It is a timeless cycle. Nothing on the ocean floor can escape it. There is this old saying: The sea never gives up its dead.*

Chapter 4

ETERNAL PATROL

A RARE DUSTING OF SNOW WHITENED CHARLESTON ON the evening of February 18, 1864, briefly hiding the ravages of war the grand old town had suffered. It was a pleasant distraction for the doomed city—a city that would not stand another year.

As far as anyone knew, the flurries were the only remarkable thing about the date. On that winter night no one in Charleston had any idea of the battle that had taken place 4 miles offshore the previous evening. At that point not even the troops at Battery Marshall realized that the submarine *H. L. Hunley* and its crew were missing in action. No one could have guessed that the next day a century-long search would begin—a search that would not end until the lost torpedo boat made its way back into Charleston Harbor 136 years later.

WHEN THE SUN ROSE OVER THE ATLANTIC THAT MORNING, nothing had seemed amiss to the Rebels at the north end of Sullivan's

Island. The signal fire lit on Wednesday evening to guide the submarine home had left a mountain of ash that the breeze scattered across the sugary beach. From the low-lying barrier island, the soldiers could see the three masts of the *Housatonic* jutting out of the horizon line, just a few more trees in a forest of Yankee timber blocking the harbor mouth. The ship appeared to be in about the same position where it had been the night before. From their vantage point, the Rebels could not tell that the sloop's hull rested on the ocean floor, nearly 30 feet below the surface.

The commander at Battery Marshall at first assumed that Lt. George E. Dixon had taken the *Hunley* into the harbor or perhaps was even still stalking the fleet. It would not be the first time the sun had beaten the *Hunley* back to Sullivan's Island. The *Hunley*'s failure to make it back to port was not even mentioned when the shift changed at the outpost. The men coming on duty on the eighteenth simply assumed the fish-boat had returned. For that reason no report was sent to Beauregard until the following day, when Lt. Col. O. M. Dantzler sent the general a brief note of concern.

"I have the honor to report that the torpedo-boat stationed at this point went out on the night of the 17th instant (Wednesday) and has not returned. The signals agreed upon to be given in case the boat wished a light to be exposed at this post as a guide for its return were observed and answered. An earlier report would have been made of this matter, but the officer of the day for yesterday was under the impression that the boat had returned, and so informed me," Dantzler wrote to Beauregard.

This, the Charleston commander feared, was the news he had dreaded since giving permission to relaunch the *Hunley* three months earlier. After the initial report to headquarters, word spread quickly through the ranks. Later that same morning the Mount Pleasant commander, Gen. R. S. Ripley, sent a similar dispatch, saying what Beauregard was already thinking:

"Unless she has gone to Charleston the boat has probably been lost or captured. I have no reason to believe that the crew would have deserted to the enemy. I fear that it is more likely that she has gone down judging from past experience of the machine."

Beauregard was not quite ready to give up hope yet. He'd had a similar scare from Dixon in January, the day the crew tested their underwater endurance. The Battery Marshall troops had reported the torpedo boat sunk, not believing it could have remained underwater for nearly three hours. As he had in January, Beauregard responded this day with a simple, sad—but bureaucratic—note:

"As soon as its fate shall have been ascertained pay a proper tribute to the gallantry and patriotism of its crew and officers. G. T. Beauregard, General Commanding."

It would be a long, suspenseful week after its disappearance before the Confederates accidentally learned of the *Hunley*'s success. The Rebels had nowhere near the intelligence reports from inside the Union that the North had on them and had little idea of the drama playing out on the water within shooting distance of Fort Sumter. But on February 26 Southern troops captured a Union picket boat outside the harbor that carried interesting news.

The six Yankees on board the little boat informed the Rebels of the *Housatonic*'s sinking at the hands of their not-so-secret weapon. The men, having no idea that the *Hunley* had not returned, spoke freely, matter-of-factly about the incident, assuming the enemy troops already knew about their great naval victory. The Confederates played it cool, giving no indication to the prisoners of war that their new secret weapon was missing. Slowly they began to piece together what had happened that night. In a telegram Beauregard immediately reported the successful engagement and its sad aftermath to Richmond, the Confederate capital. "A gunboat sunken off Battery Marshall. Supposed to have been done by Mobile torpedo boat, under Lieutenant George E. Dixon, Company E, Twenty-first Alabama Volunteers, which went out for that purpose, and which I regret to say has not been heard of since." In another dispatch a few days later, Beauregard reported the name of the ship, the *Housatonic*, and gave Dixon credit for the sinking. He ended, "There is little hope of the safety of that brave man and his associates, however, as they were not captured."

The Confederacy made great propaganda out of the *Housatonic*'s sinking, using it to glorify their new technology. But while heralding the latest turning point in the war with their miracle weapon, the Rebels neglected to mention that the submarine's designer had been forced to abandon his creation, that it had killed its namesake, or that the *Hunley* had been lost in its first and only battle. On the front page of its February 29, 1864, edition, the *Charleston Daily Courier* reported that the crew had returned to port safely. It was either journalistic incompetence or war propaganda to keep the Yankees guessing—and scared.

"The glorious success of our little torpedo-boat, under the command of Lieutenant Dixon, of Mobile, has raised the hopes of our people, and the most sanguine expectations are now entertained of our being able to raise the siege in a way little dreamed of by the enemy," the paper said.

THE BLUFF WORKED, AT LEAST INITIALLY. A FEW MILES out in the Atlantic, the Union fleet was frantically preparing for what its commanders thought was the beginning of a stealth naval campaign. Admiral Dahlgren, whose ship *Philadelphia* was in Port Royal harbor near Hilton Head, 60 miles south of Charleston, heard about the sinking in a series of telegrams, one from an officer of the *Housatonic*, another from J. F. Green, captain of the *Canandaigua*.

Dahlgren feared that the worst was yet to come. He reported the sinking to Washington, sending along with it the precautionary orders he'd issued in January, warning the fleet of just this kind of attack. He described the torpedo boat to Navy officials and matter-of-factly requested that the government have a "number" of them built and "sent with great dispatch." Even though he made the request in all seriousness, the engineers must have realized how ludicrous a request it was. But Dahlgren was too worried to be thinking in those terms. He thought the attack meant the Rebels were taking this fight below the surface and would come again and again. After his telegram to Washington, he warned his fleet about the torpedo boats, urging them, even more strongly than before, to be ready.

"The success of this undertaking will, no doubt, lead to similar attempts along the whole line of blockade," Dahlgren wrote.

Dahlgren didn't know if the attack had come from a David or the strange craft he thought was called the *American Diver*. He didn't care, really. He only expected the worst. The blockade, he feared, was vulnerable.

A FEW MILES OFF CHARLESTON, THE FORMER CREW OF the *Housatonic* was miserable. Some of them had escaped with nothing but the nightshirt on their backs and now sat shivering in old blankets aboard two sister ships, the *Canandaigua* and the *Wabash*—one of the ships the Confederates had so desperately hoped the *Hunley* would sink. Weathering the brutal North Atlantic February, the men were waiting for Dahlgren and the inevitable inquiry that would follow. Despite all their precautions, they had been surprised. A little iron boat had taken down one of the newest ships in the United States Navy, and they would soon have to explain exactly how that had happened. No one was looking forward to reliving that night. Tallying their casualties, they found they had lost 5 men out of 155: Quartermaster John Williams; Fireman John Walsh; Landsman Theodore Parker; Ens. Edward C. Hazeltine; and Charles O. Muzzey, the captain's clerk.

John Crosby, the *Housatonic* officer who had been one of the first to spot the *Hunley*'s approach, scratched off two letters to his wife in the days following the disaster. The attack had taken a lot out of him. He'd served on the ship since it had arrived in Charleston in September 1862—most of the war—and he was without assignment. He'd lost all his money on board the ship and now was, as far as he knew, out of a job. Crosby had piloted the rescue boat that plucked many of the ship's crew out of the black ocean that night. The "pitiful sounds" of the injured, freezing men in the water had left their mark on him. He wanted the inquiry over with, he wanted warm clothes, and he wanted a new photo of his dear Irene. He wrote her to start saving the money she got and asked her to have him a new suit made. Like the rest of his shipmates, he'd lost everything he owned.

"I cannot describe to you the sceen, it was awfull to behold. . . . Be a good girl and don't worrie about me. I have lost all your pictures.

Send me one. . . . Telegraph to Father and Mother that I am safe & O.K.," Crosby wrote.

STILL MISSING HIS WIFE, CROSBY WOULD BE THE FIRST member of the *Housatonic*'s crew the court of inquiry called upon when it convened. The trial was held on the USS *Wabash* off Charleston beginning on February 26, the same day the Rebels captured the Union picket boat. Second Lt. James B. Young of the marine corps served as the judge advocate. For more than a week, surviving sailors from the *Housatonic* were grilled about their actions and those of the ship's captain, Pickering, the night the torpedo boat attacked. Navy officials needed to know whether the Navy's own people were at fault or the Confederates actually had a weapon that could inflict more damage on the South Atlantic Blockading Squadron.

The court called nearly twenty sailors, asking most of them the same questions: Was the ship prepared? How quickly did the crew respond to the sighting of the torpedo boat? What did the captain do? Could anything else have been done?

Most of the crew described the mysterious object slipping through the waves as a "waterlogged plank" or a "porpoise." They told of conning towers—they called them "bumps"—and the eerie yellow glow coming from small portholes along the top of the vessel. It moved sleekly, silently, and churned up little wake. Everyone on board agreed that, by the time the object was spotted, it was too late to train the big deck guns on it.

Ens. C. H. Craven, who had been in his quarters when the torpedo boat was sighted, told the court that when he arrived on deck, Captain Pickering and another officer were firing their guns at it—and he joined them.

"I fired two shots at her with my revolver as she was standing toward the ship as soon as I saw her, and a third shot when she was almost under the counter, having to lean over the port to fire it," Craven said.

Ultimately, though, the entire week of hearings came down to a single question from the court: "Was there anything . . . that could have been done to save the *Housatonic?*"

Craven, as a dozen officers and crewmen had already attested, gave a single-word response: "Nothing."

On March 7, 1864, the Naval Court of Inquiry finished hearing testimony and quickly released its findings, eight points that would officially settle the investigation of the short battle between the *Housatonic* and the *H. L. Hunley:*

First. That the USS Housatonic *was blown up and sunk by a rebel torpedo craft on the night of February 17 last, about 9 o'clock P.M., while lying at anchor in 27 feet of water off Charleston, S.C., bearing E.S.E., and the distance from Fort Sumter about five-and-a-half miles. The weather at the time of the occurrence was clear, the night was bright and moonlit, wind moderate from the northward and westward, sea smooth and tide half ebb, the ship's head about W.N.W.*

Second. That between 8:45 and 9 o'clock P.M. on said night an object in the water was discovered almost simultaneously by the officer of the deck and the lookout stationed on the starboard cat-head, on the starboard bow of the ship, about seventy-five or a hundred yards distant, having the appearance of a log. That on further and closer observation it presented a suspicious appearance, moved apparently with a speed of three or four knots in the direction of the starboard quarter of the ship, exhibiting two protuberances above and making a slight ripple in the water.

Third. That the strange object approached the ship with a rapidity precluding a gun of the battery being brought to bear upon it, and finally came in contact with the ship on her starboard quarter.

Fourth. That about one and a half minutes after the first discovery of the strange object the crew were called to quarters, the cable slipped, and the engine backed.

Fifth. That an explosion occurred about three minutes after the first discovery of the object, which blew up the after part of the ship, causing her to sink immediately after to the bottom, with her spar deck submerged.

Sixth. That several shots from small arms were fired at the object while it was alongside or near the ship before the explosion occurred.

Seventh. That the watch on deck, ship and ship's battery were in all respects prepared for a sudden offensive or defensive movement; that lookouts were properly stationed and vigilance observed, and that officers and crew promptly assembled at their quarters.

Eighth. That order was preserved on board and orders promptly obeyed by officers and crew up to the time of the sinking of the ship. In view of the above facts the court has to express the opinion that no further military proceedings are necessary.

That was officially the end of the matter. The court declared that captain and crew had acted properly. The U.S. Navy wrote the loss of the *Housatonic* off to the expected costs of war. Nowhere in the proceedings did anyone note the historic first of this event. Never before had a submarine sunk an enemy warship in battle. But at the time the Union Navy was not worried about the "first" such attack. It was bracing for the next one.

NEWS OF THE *HOUSATONIC*'S SINKING BY THE TORPEDO boat soon spread across the South with much the same enthusiasm as had been reported in the Charleston newspaper. In New Orleans the friends and family of Horace Hunley took the news with mixed feelings. Hunley's contraption had succeeded, just as he had promised. But at what price? Volumnia Hunley Barrow wondered. Her brother was not around to enjoy the success. Was the loss of a single ship and five Yankees a fair trade for her only living blood relative? She would grieve over that question for the rest of her short life. Volumnia Washington

Queenie Bennett, Lt. George E. Dixon's Mobile sweet-heart, in an undated photograph. Before he went off to war, Bennett gave Dixon a $20 gold coin, which ultimately saved his life. (Courtesy Sally Necessary)

Hunley Barrow would die almost five years to the day after her brother's funeral.

In Mobile Queenie Bennett first realized some-
thing was wrong when the letters stopped coming. Bennett, the oldest
of eight children born to Robert Fielding Bennett and Sarah Elizabeth
Skinner Bennett, knew the way of the sea. Her father was a steamboat
pilot, as his father before him had been. It couldn't have made Bennett,
wise beyond her sixteen years, any more comfortable with her sweet-
heart's station. George Dixon had kept in touch from Charleston,
sending her notes as often as he could. Over the course of the war, they
had grown closer than ever. Dixon's wounding at Shiloh had in some
ways been a blessing. He had been moved back to Mobile, where he
got to see her often. He stayed in town for a year and a half, until he
had left for the coast to take command of the submarine. When Bennett received word that the torpedo boat was missing, she knew her
first love was gone forever. His voice from far away, his letters, had disappeared as quickly and as quietly as the *Hunley*. The gold coin could
not save him twice. She would mourn his loss for years.

In the same town William Alexander did not hear
the news until weeks after the attack. Alexander, considered an engineering genius by the Confederate Army, had been called back to Mobile to build a breech-loading repeating gun, a precursor to the
machine gun, less than two weeks before the attack. When he first
heard that the *Hunley* had taken out the *Housatonic*, he cried out with
disappointment at having missed the battle he and Dixon had dis-
cussed so often. But he soon noticed that in the reports there was no
word from Dixon or the crew about the mission. In fact, no one said
anything about the men who had piloted the submarine. Alexander
wired General Jordan daily for information, but all he ever got back
was the same resigned response: "No news of the torpedo boat."

Alexander had spent many nights aboard the *Hunley* and knew
what the crew faced. For weeks he pondered several scenarios, trying to
figure out what could have happened to his missing comrades. Finally
he concluded that Dixon had gone too far, literally. From 4 miles out

the submarine must have been unable to overcome the tide. On several occasions fighting the current had taxed the crew to its limits. Every member of her crew knew that the men who sailed aboard the *Hunley* were cutting it close every time they went on the open ocean. It was a real fear, being swept out to sea. That is what Alexander decided had happened to his friend. The *Hunley* was lost. If he ever bothered to stop and think about himself, however, Alexander might have realized that his association with the torpedo boat alone was charmed. He had given up his spot on the doomed second crew to Thomas W. Park. And twelve days before the submarine appeared lost forever, he had been re-called to Mobile.

Twice fate had saved William Alexander's life. He would live a long life, well into the twentieth century, but he would never forget that. He was blessed, something the rector at St. Philip's in Charleston would have been pleased to know. As he grieved for his friend and shipmates in 1864, Alexander had no idea he still had one last duty to perform as the sole surviving member of the *Hunley*'s final crew.

IN CHARLESTON EARLY CONFLICTING REPORTS AND DELIB-erate misinformation begat the first wild stories and theories that would blossom into the *Hunley* mythology over the next century. For a long time many people refused to believe that the submarine had vanished. Its absence from the city was explained any number of ways. Some suspected it had just gone underground—or underwater—to keep the Yankees guessing. It was all just wishful thinking for an increasingly lost cause. In a March 1864 letter to her sister, Charleston resident Susan Middleton reported one of the more curious tales:

> *We can't get at the truth of the fish boat story—some say she has never returned while the generals believe she came ashore safe somewhere near Georgetown [50 miles north]. She is said to have sunk two vessels besides the* Housatonic*—one a transport loaded with troops. This time she did not dive but attacked the enemy on*

*the surface of the water—they seeing her all the time and firing
grape and canister without any effect. Torpedoes have been sent to
her at Georgetown to start another expedition.*

Those stories were not circulating among official channels, however.
Beauregard was dealing with the constant inquiries about the submarine,
and he uniformly reported it lost. Perhaps only the conspiracy-minded
believed he was intentionally releasing false information—a charge about
the general and his protectiveness of the submarine that would linger for
decades. In March 1864 Henry J. Leovy, a friend and business associate
of Hunley—and the executor of his will—wrote Beauregard asking what
had happened to the submarine. Hunley's death had left him part owner
of the fish-boat. He may have been genuinely interested in the fate of
Dixon, or he may have been hinting around about the reward offered for
sinking Union ships. The letter Leovy received back, from an assistant to
Beauregard, said that as of March 10 nothing had been heard from
Dixon or the torpedo boat. "It is therefore feared," the letter to Leovy
said, "that that gallant officer and his brave companions have perished."

ON FEBRUARY 17, 1865—THE FIRST ANNIVERSARY OF THE
Hunley's successful mission—Charleston fell. Amphibious Union
troops had gone ashore at Bull's Bay, 20 miles up the coast, and at
James Island, on the south side of the harbor. There were too many of
them; the Confederates had no chance. Hopelessly outnumbered, a familiar situation for the South, Beauregard reluctantly gave the order to
evacuate the city. But before leaving, the general ordered new flags
hoisted at Moultrie, Sumter, and Castle Pinckney to lead the Yankees
to believe there were still troops at them. The crafty old Creole was de-
feated but not beaten.

Taking Charleston was the victory U.S. president Abraham Lincoln had longed for, and in the end the Yankees got what was left of
the city without much of a fight. The harbor was nearly empty when
navy ships entered it: the Confederates had blown up what vessels in

the fleet they didn't sail away. A few Davids were all that was left of the stealth fleet. The underwater warfare that Dahlgren had feared never materialized.

One hundred miles inland on that day, Gen. William Tecumseh Sherman invaded Columbia, the South Carolina capital. In the preceding months the Union general had been on the warpath. He had secured Savannah—a Christmas present for Lincoln, he said—and burned Atlanta. Now he had led the march into South Carolina, the state where the secession movement—and the entire war—had begun. He promised to make the state that started it all pay dearly. As the town burned, however, he proclaimed his innocence: the Rebels, he said, started the fires. It mattered little. The Civil War was, in effect, just about over.

Two months later, the Union army took Richmond, the capital of the Confederacy. Within a couple of days, it was safe enough that President Lincoln visited the town, where he could still smell the smoldering Confederate warehouses burned by evacuating Rebels who wanted to keep their goods out of Yankee hands. It was a sad tradition of the war. As the Southern forces retreated, they could do little more damage than burn their own abandoned supplies.

On April 9, 1865—three days shy of the war's fourth anniversary—Robert E. Lee surrendered the Army of Northern Virginia to Grant at Appomattox Courthouse, Virginia. The war that had led to the creation of the first modern submarine was over. The secret weapon labored over in a Mobile machine shop had finished the conflict in a draw: it sank a ship and itself. In its short service to the Confederate government, it had killed its namesake, Horace Lawson Hunley; its last commander, Lt. George E. Dixon; and 19 other volunteers. For that price the South had taken out one blockade ship and five Union soldiers. When Lee laid down his sword to Grant, the *Hunley* was barely a footnote in the War Between the States. At the end of the conflict, few people even knew about the submarine, its historic battle, or its fate. But as the war ended, the search for the *Hunley* was just beginning.

IN 1869, FIVE YEARS AFTER THE *HUNLEY* DISAPPEARED, THE great French author Jules Verne took the notion of the submarine and submerged it back into the realm of science fiction. Even before the first serialized installments of *Vingt mille lieues sous les mers (Twenty Thousand Leagues Under the Sea)* were published, Verne already had a reputation for the fantastic. He had written stories about trips around the world in hot-air balloons, voyages to the moon. The sea was just about his sole unconquered realm. His account of a submarine patrolling the depths of the world's oceans would become his best-known work. Later most Verne biographers would credit a novelist who wrote under the pseudonym George Sand with the inspiration for Captain Nemo and the *Nautilus*. In 1865 Sand told Verne, "I hope that you will soon take us to the depths of the sea, and that you will have your characters navigate in diving vessels that your imagination will manage to improve."

But Verne may already have been thinking along those lines. He might even have known about the *Hunley*. European newspapers fed their readers a steady diet of sensational news from the American front. Like most of his countrymen, Verne was enthralled with the American Civil War. In fact, one of his earliest short stories, published in 1865, was set in wartime Charleston. "The Blockade Runners" depicted a Scottish sea captain who runs the Union blockade to sell European supplies to the Confederate government. He is won over by an American girl who is a passenger on his ship and whose abolitionist father awaits death in a Charleston jail. The captain risks his ship and cargo to rescue the father of the woman he loves.

Twenty Thousand Leagues Under the Sea shared some thematic qualities with that story. It was an antiwar tale centered on Captain Nemo and his quest to rid the world of injustice and slavery while aboard his huge submarine, the *Nautilus*. In the book the submarine circumnavigates the globe, buries its dead at sea, and sails under a polar ice cap, just as its American namesake would do nearly a century later. In the novel, set in 1866, people who spot the submarine at first assume it is a whale, as no man-made machine could sail beneath the waves. The narrator describes it as resembling a "huge fish of steel."

In the end the *Nautilus* disappears after sinking an American warship—ironically enough, the *Abraham Lincoln*.

Verne made the submarine a myth at a time when it seemed that anything was becoming possible. During the industrial age, the *Nautilus* was better known than any of the half dozen or so submersibles actually under construction or being tested in the waning years of the nineteenth century. It was certainly a more common name than that of the *Hunley*, which was nowhere to be found. Depending, that is, on who was telling the story.

ON OCTOBER 11, 1870, THE *CHARLESTON DAILY COURIER* carried a small item on an inside page that in later years would have commanded a streaming banner headline on the front page. The story proclaimed: "Death on the Bottom of the Deep. Discovery of Buried Torpedo Boat off Charleston—Nine Skeletons at the Wheel."

The story reported that in "past weeks" divers in submarine armor had visited the wreck of the *Housatonic* and found the *Hunley* lying beside its victim. "Within her are the bones of the most devoted and daring men who ever went to war."

The story was most likely a hoax, and not the last of its kind. In the years following the war, tales of *Hunley* sightings grew so frequent and so far-fetched that U.S. Navy officials told people not to believe everything they heard. The story of the *Hunley*, as fantastic as it was, seemed to invite embellishment.

The first searches for the *Hunley* were, as they would be for nearly a century, government-driven. Back in November of 1864—before the war had even ended—Dahlgren sent Navy Lt. W. L. Churchill to the waters off Sullivan's Island to examine the wreckage of the *Housatonic*. Even the powerful U.S. Navy had not been in good enough shape that it could afford to discard ships. Dahlgren wanted to know if the *Housatonic* could be raised. Churchill's report, dated November 27, 1864, provided the first glimpse of how thorough a job the *Hunley* had done on the Yankee sloop. He declared the warship, which had already sunk 5 feet into the sandy bottom, "worthless."

"The cabin is completely demolished as is also all the bulkheads aft of the mainmast. The coal is scattered about her lower decks in heaps as well as muskets, small arms and quantities of rubbish. The propeller is in an upright position—the shaft appears to be broken. The rudder-post and the rudder have been partly blown away. The upper parts of both are in their proper position while the lower parts have been forced aft."

The *Hunley*, for which Churchill was also actively searching on his expedition, had scored a direct hit.

Dahlgren had, by that time, learned that the torpedo boat had disappeared after its attack on the *Housatonic*, and he was curious to see it. The war, after all, was not yet over. But Navy divers found nothing of the little submarine, despite claiming to have dragged 500 yards—more than a quarter mile—around the wreck. Churchill never clarified, however, whether his search extended that distance in every direction.

Six years later the 1870 expedition that led to the fantastic claims of skeletons at the controls of the *Hunley* was not attributed to anyone but most likely came from divers surveying the Charleston Harbor channels for a planned demolition of wrecks. While many accepted the report as fact, some former Confederates were immediately skeptical. They assumed, probably correctly, that if the *Hunley* were found, it would be pulled up, if for no other reason than to bury the bodies. Moreover, during Reconstruction U.S. Army engineers might have enjoyed seeing how the little boat had actually worked.

The story also lacked credibility because of several claims by the anonymous divers. They said they had turned the *Hunley*'s propeller, which, six years after it sank, would have been half buried in the sand or frozen in place by coral-like growth. And most outrageous, they claimed they had looked inside and seen the crew. Off the Charleston coast, the water is so murky that it is rare for a diver to see his hand in front of his face. Without underwater lights, invented only decades later, it is practically impossible that, even if any divers had found the

Hunley, they could have seen inside its hull through tiny, but thick, deadlights.

Two years later Benjamin Maillefert won the bid to clear the wrecks of the *Weehawken*, *Housatonic*, and the torpedo boat to a depth of 20 feet. The wrecks, at least that of the *Housatonic*, had become a danger to navigation into and out of the once again busy South Carolina seaport. Using helmeted divers who planted explosives on the shipwrecks, Maillefert finished the demolition work by the summer of 1873. The Navy noted, in its final report on the demolition, that "the torpedo-boat . . . could not be found."

For years Southerners still mourning the loss of the *Hunley* and its heroic crew held on to various theories regarding their fate. Some believed that the divers working with Maillefert, mistaking the *Hunley* for a boiler from the *Housatonic*, had dynamited it. Others believed that the *Hunley* had been sucked into the hole in the *Housatonic* following the explosion and was lying under the massive ship. Some even suspected the Navy had raised the submarine and secreted it away to the North, where it was tested and eventually scrapped. Years after Maillefert's operation, a book claimed that he had found the submarine fouled in the *Housatonic*'s rudder chains. The stories attempted to fill in the gaps in the story of the *Hunley* because something had to have happened to it.

But oddly enough, one of the most important, and chilling, accounts of the *Hunley*'s discovery from the time went curiously unnoticed. The claim came from the diver Angus Smith in an 1876 letter to Beauregard. The old general was working on a book of his military operations and preparing speeches about torpedo service in Charleston Harbor during the war, and his assistant sent out letters to old contacts asking for help in refreshing his memory.

Smith, who lived on Sullivan's Island, said that following the war he had the contract to remove all Confederate wrecks and obstructions from the channel. That, he thought, included the *Hunley*. But while working in 1872–73, Smith said he had a run-in with Maillefert, who claimed that the fish-boat was in his salvage contract. Smith ignored his rival and went about his business. He also claimed to have had better luck in his hunt.

"I went to work to save the torpedo boat, and I got on top of her, and found out the cause of her sinking. The boat is outside or alongside the *Housatonic*. She can be lifted any time our people wish. Maillefert is bursted and out of the way. I have no more to say than that she can be saved, and my opinion is she is as good as the day she was sunk," Smith wrote to Beauregard.

Smith's credibility was unquestionable. For one, he was a member of the dive team that had raised the *Hunley* following its two previous accidents in 1863: he knew what the submarine looked like underwater, knew what it felt like to run his hand along its hull. Where other divers might have mistaken an old boiler for the fish-boat, Smith wouldn't. He was intimately familiar with the *Hunley*.

He did not describe "the cause of her sinking" but revealed one little fact that, had other shipwreck hunters noted it, might have led to the *Hunley*'s discovery before the turn of the century. Smith said the submarine was "outside"—seaward—of the *Housatonic*. For the next hundred years, men searching for the lost submarine would confine their searches to the water between the well-marked wreck of the *Housatonic* and the Charleston shore. For a century no one would ever think to look farther out to sea. It would be a mistake repeated by everyone in search of the *Hunley*.

By the time Smith wrote his letter several years after the fact, however, it may have been too late to find the *Hunley* again. In the late 1870s P. T. Barnum offered $100,000 to anyone who could salvage the fish-boat for his traveling show, which was growing into what would become the modern circus. That reward set off another round of searches.

Barnum was a controversial man, even more so in Charleston than in most places. He had secondhandedly caused an ink eruption between two competing newspapers in the city over one of his more infamous hoaxes. In 1843 Barnum's uncle traveled to Charleston with the then-famous "Fejee Mermaid," a dubious attraction that even Barnum feared (he would never commit to buy it; he only rented it from other owners for "display purposes"). Advertisements for the exhibit featured a classic, buxom female with a fish tail. When it arrived in town, the attraction turned out to be something very different. It was a blackened, fossilized orangutan with drooping breasts and its mouth frozen open in a horrific death scream impressively sewn to the tail of a fish. In the *Charleston Mercury*, a man who had worked with John James Audubon criticized the mermaid as a fake. The *Daily Courier*, meanwhile, defended the exhibit. An editorial writer for the paper wrote that he'd studied the mermaid himself and declared it authentic. Such has always been the expertise of newspapermen. By the time the mermaid exhibit left town, everyone was mad.

Barnum, a staunch Unionist during the war, could have had bragging rights in mind given the outrageous (even by his standards) reward for the *Hunley*. Barnum's New York museum had barely escaped an arson plot by Confederates in 1865, only to burn later that same year. One of the items lost in that fire was a Jefferson Davis mannequin dressed in petticoats, supposed to represent the alleged attire that the former Confederate president was wearing in an apparent escape attempt when arrested by Union troops. Barnum had little sympathy for the South. But ultimately he was a businessman, and he knew an attraction when he saw it. The *Hunley* would draw massive crowds of people to his traveling show, especially war veterans, who numbered in the hundreds of thousands. The fish-boat, he supposed, might lure more people than even Gen. Tom Thumb.

After Barnum's offer was publicized, Smith and his old diving partner searched more than 5 acres of the ocean floor around the *Housatonic*, trying in vain to find the little Confederate torpedo boat they had rescued twice before. For weeks they scoured the ocean floor in helmeted diving outfits, sifting through the murky seabed for some sign of the lost submarine, but they never found it. Their failure, ultimately, was heartbreaking because, of all the people desperately searching for the *Hunley*, they *knew* it was still out there.

Somewhere.

*I*N 1879 GOVERNMENT ENGINEERS BEGAN WORK ON STONE
jetties along each side of the channel leading into Charleston Harbor.
These 4-mile-long groins, which give the illusion of a distant horizon from
the beach on Sullivan's Island, have but one purpose—to prevent the natural migration of 2 billion cubic feet of sand every year.

As nature intended, sand flows south along the East Coast of the
United States, leaving behind a little every day to replenish what is washed
away. Patiently it fills in gashes in the ocean floor, smoothing things out
to level. The jetties were built to stop that, insurance against the constant dredging needed to keep the channel gouged deep enough for the ever-
growing size of the merchant ships.

While the jetties helped Charleston develop into one of the major ports
of the Eastern Seaboard, they disrupted the natural order. Fifty years after
they were built, Morris Island, to the south of the channel, had mostly disappeared, leaving a lone lighthouse standing in a treacherous inlet to hold
its own against the ceaseless onslaught of the tide. To the north there was

the opposite effect. Having nowhere else to go, sand began to build up above the jetties, engorging Sullivan's Island. The sand that was not beached was soon caught in a new pattern of tidal currents created by the jetties.

Ever since it had disappeared, the Hunley *had lain in the quiet shallows of the North Atlantic, the sea gently caressing its iron hull at 1 nautical mile an hour. By the time the jetties were finished in the 1890s, all that had changed. To the northeast of the harbor mouth, the underwater currents began to swirl at nearly 5 nautical miles an hour, churning up the sandy bottom. Slowly sand began to accumulate around the lost submarine. Soon any part of the* Hunley *still exposed was covered, hidden. The sea had swallowed it.*

Chapter 5

THE MYTHS
OF DIXIELAND

Gᴇᴏʀɢᴇ Dɪxᴏɴ ᴡᴀs ᴀʟɪᴠᴇ.

That news washed over the Reconstructed South like a tidal wave in the summer of 1885. Somehow the legendary submarine commander had survived the attack on the *Housatonic* and the subsequent sinking of his *Hunley*. Some thought this could warrant the rewriting of history. Dixon had to be found, if for no other reason than to tell his amazing story. The first underwater attack had taken one fewer casualty than originally thought.

Or had it?

A man named H. Pacha created the stir with an unbelievable tale he published in *Blackwood's Magazine* in June of that year. In recounting the torpedo scare during the Civil War, he told of two encounters he had with a brave young man in a Charleston pub. The young sailor was commander of a torpedo boat, which Pacha said might also be called a "submarine."

"I was at Charleston, meeting in a coffee room at that place a young naval officer (a Southerner), with whom I got into conversation," Pacha wrote. "He told me that that night he was going to sink a Northern man-of-war which was blockading the port and he invited me to see him off."

The man described his acquaintance's boat as being 40 feet long, shaped like a cigar, and able to move at a speed no greater than 5 miles an hour. It carried a torpedo at the end of a long, bow-mounted spar. Only a small piece of it stuck above the water as it moved away from the dock. Pacha watched the man and his ship disappear into the blackness and went back to Charleston.

The next night he claimed to have met the same man in the same pub:

> I found my friend sitting quietly smoking his pipe. He told me he had succeeded in making a hole in the frigate which he had attacked, which vessel could, in fact, be seen lying in shallow water some seven miles off, careened over to repair damages. But he said that, on the concussion made by firing the torpedo, the water had rushed in through the hatches of his boat, and she had sunk to the bottom. All his men were drowned. He said that he didn't know how he escaped himself, but he fancied that he came up through the hatches, as he found himself floating about, and swam on shore.

After reading that eerie account, many people believed that the man Pacha had met was Dixon. The story fit the *Hunley* legend almost perfectly. Almost. There were two facts in Pacha's account that suggested he had met the captain of one of the Davids, another kind of cigar-shaped, low-lying torpedo boat stationed at Charleston. The two ships were often confused with each other. Pacha said his friend's ship carried a crew of four, the exact complement of a David. And he described the cigar boat as having a funnel—the most striking, and the only above-water, feature of a David. It was a strong clue that this story was not about the *Hunley*. But for years people who wanted to believe that the mysterious captain was the heroic—and living—George

Dixon explained away the funnel as the author's erroneous description of one of the submarine's conning towers.

As the years passed, and Dixon never turned up anywhere, historians dismissed Pacha's story as a case of mistaken identity. He had met a captain of one of the half dozen or so Davids that were stationed in Charleston during the war. That is almost certainly what happened. But there was a single discrepancy that nagged at some men, a puzzling nugget of truth in the story that gave them the faintest hope. It was this irrefutable fact: no David ever sank a warship.

As the nineteenth century gave way to the twentieth, the stories of the lost Confederate submarine had taken on mythic proportions. No one could agree how many times—or even where—the submarine had sunk. In 1899 a former Confederate Navy lieutenant named John Grimball wrote in the *Charleston News and Courier* a moving tribute to the "thirty immortals" who had perished in the fish-boat. Some estimates put the death toll of *Hunley* crews even higher, closer to fifty. In a lecture to the Georgia Historical Society, Col. Charles H. Olmstead, who was stationed at Fort Johnson for part of the war, spread the oft-told tale of divers' supposedly having found the sub next to the *Housatonic* with "the bleached bones of her crew" inside.

Many Confederate veterans claimed that the fish-boat sank an astonishing six times—including once in Mobile Bay, on a trial run in the Stono River outside of Charleston, even off the docks at Fort Sumter. It mattered little that the stories were often contradictory or defied all logic. Occasionally even the people recounting the flawed history would note how crazy it all sounded—the same crew involved in two accidents less than a week apart. The tales would take stray details from one accident and weave them into another sinking. It didn't make sense, but it was almost as if the *Hunley* were so far outside the realm of reality that anything was possible. For a while some people even held on to the notion that there were two *Hunley*s patrolling Charleston Harbor at the same time. One old general, in his memoirs, even claimed that a black sailor had drowned on board the fish-boat during its first sinking in Charleston Harbor.

The most popular story, told countless times, was that the *Hunley* sank under Lt. John Payne's command twice inside a week. The tales alternated between which happened first—the sinking off Fort Johnson or another near the docks at Fort Sumter. Perhaps the confusion was so rampant because of the conflicting reports as to why the *Hunley* sank at all that first time. Some claimed the fish-boat became tangled in mooring lines and tipped over; others believed that Payne accidentally stepped on the dive-plane lever, plunging the submarine into the depths. The official reports adopted the third, and most widely accepted, story: the *Hunley* was swamped by the wake of a passing ship. The tales of two accidents continued to be passed down until late into the twentieth century. No one recounting these stories ever considered how such a series of catastrophes would be impossible: each of the first two times the submarine sank, it took three weeks to raise it and several more to refurbish it. The legend of the *Hunley* was being stretched so badly that the fish-boat's story was beginning to resemble a farce.

The growing number of sad but exaggerated tales surrounding the lost submarine stirred something in one old man living quietly in Mobile—a man who, at the beginning of the twentieth century, knew more than anyone alive about the story of the *H. L. Hunley*.

Bearded and gray-headed, William Alexander was living his sixty-fifth year as the city electrician for Mobile. The builder and former first officer of the *Hunley* had settled in his adopted city after the war, starting a family and making his living as a machinist and an engineer. He had helped the city usher in the modern conveniences of electricity and fretted over things unheard of during the war, such as fire alarms. But he had never forgotten the *Hunley*. He never, in all his years, forgot Dixon. Perhaps he carried a little guilt for having been called back to Mobile less than two weeks before the submarine disappeared. Regardless, he still felt a loyalty, a duty, to the *Hunley* and its crew.

The wild stories about the submarine seemed to dishonor his former crewmates. As the last surviving crew member, Alexander decided

A turn-of-the-century photograph of William A. Alexander, builder and former first officer of the Hunley, *who revived interest in the submarine with a series of articles and speeches in the early twentieth century. (Courtesy Museum of Mobile)*

to set the record straight. In June 1902 the *New Orleans Picayune* published the most complete history of the *Hunley* ever written, under the headline THE TRUE STORIES OF THE CONFEDERATE SUBMARINE BOATS. In a four-thousand-word essay, an amazing length for a newspaper article in those days, Alexander gave the twentieth century its first peek at how the mysterious fish-boat had actually operated.

Alexander was working from memories nearly forty years old and admitted as much, conceding that all his measurements were purely from memory. Even he did not have plans for the submarine. But he did not forget many details of his work on the *Hunley* in downtown Mobile in the spring of 1863.

They had cut an iron boiler in two, Alexander wrote, and inserted 12-inch-wide iron strips down each side. It was about 4 feet wide and 5 feet tall, and was lengthened by adding tapering ends fore and aft. It had ballast tanks, which, he noted, "unfortunately . . . were left open on top." He described keel weights, a mercury depth gauge, bilge pumps, seacocks, and a compass corrected for the distortion inside the iron hull. Most fascinating, though, was its primitive propulsion.

"The boat was operated by manual power, with an ordinary propeller. On the propeller shaft there were formed eight cranks at different angles; the shaft was supported by brackets on the starboard side, the men sitting on the port side turning the cranks," Alexander explained. "The propeller shafts and cranks took up so much room that it was very difficult to pass fore and aft, and when the men were in their places this was next to impossible. In operation, one-half the crew had to pass through the fore hatch; the other through the after hatchway."

Most interestingly, Alexander's article also included two diagrams of the *Hunley*, drawn from his descriptions. They were the first look the world had inside the submarine, but for years their accuracy would be questioned. They showed an odd, crooked propeller shaft formed with cranking handles at varying degrees and a rather boxy-looking submarine with no hint of where the spar attached. It bedeviled curious *Hunley* historians for years, his vague description of a "yellow-pine boom." He didn't elaborate enough for most people's taste. In some ways Alexander raised as many questions about the strange torpedo boat as he answered. But while they questioned some things, *Hunley* historians accepted as the gospel his estimates of the submarine's dimensions, even though Alexander had adamantly pointed out they were guesses. It was simply all there was to go on. For decades people would attempt to interpret nuances of Alexander's writings, trying to wring out a few extra facts.

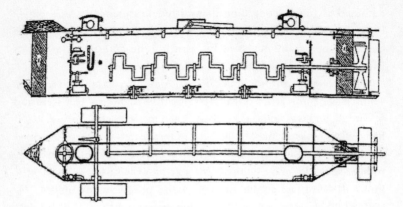

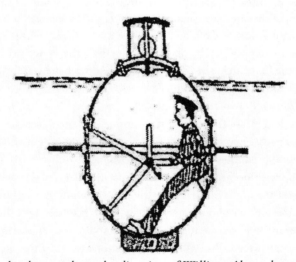

These sketches, made at the direction of William Alexander, accompanied his 1902 article on the Hunley. *Although many of the details in these drawings are correct, the overall boxy shape and dimensions are off, most likely clouded by forty-year-old memories. Note the crooked layout of the propeller-shaft hand cranks. (Courtesy Naval Historical Center)*

Ironically enough, Alexander himself furthered some myths about the submarine. Because he did not arrive in Charleston until after Horace Hunley had died on board, he knew little of its first months on the East Coast. Alexander accepted without question the story of two separate accidents at Fort Johnson and also the wild tale of the submarine's having been found next to the *Housatonic* after the war. He endorsed a theory that had been floated among Rebels for months after the attack—that the little submarine had been sucked into the hole it had made in the Union warship and was dragged down with it. He would correct some of those statements a year later during a series of public speaking engagements. Demand for him as a lecturer was sparked by his newspaper article, which was soon reprinted in Mobile, Charleston, and a number of other southern cities.

In front of the Iberville Historic Society in late 1903, Alexander criticized a world that had forgotten the brave sacrifice of the *Hunley*'s crew. He said the modern submarines just beginning to surface took most of their design attributes from the long-lost fish-boat. He quoted from an article in *Harper's Weekly* that breathlessly exclaimed, "Submarine navigation has arrived!"

"This is published as though it were some new thing," Alexander said to the members of the historic society, and continued:

> *The trouble with it, however, is in the implied date of its arrival. All of these operations had been successfully accomplished by the* Hunley; *if so then it would not seem to indicate but absolutely demonstrate that submarine navigation arrived with the* Hunley *forty years ago. . . . They were the first, so far as history records, in all the world to demonstrate the possibility of successfully operating a submarine torpedo boat. Years before much attention had been given to the subject but all experiments had proven failures. The* Hunley *accomplished the purpose for which a submarine torpedo boat is designed.*

Alexander, still proudly southern, was upset that the *Hunley* had not received its due as the first attack submarine. He took it, as people would for years after him, as a bias against the South. But there was more to it. Alexander, even though he was happy to be alive and had a wonderful family, felt he had missed something. As Dixon had been upset when two crews went to their death on *his* boat, Alexander in some small way felt the same. Also, he missed his friend. People who go through war together share a bond that others cannot understand. For as long as he lived, Alexander saved the notes Dixon wrote him from Sullivan's Island during that brief twelve-day span between his departure from Charleston and the *Hunley's* sinking.

Ultimately those letters helped Alexander reconstruct the history of the submarine, to keep the *Hunley's* memory alive. Of his final notes from Dixon, Alexander wrote simply, "What mingled reminiscences they bring!"

EVEN THOUGH ALEXANDER SPARKED MORE INTEREST IN the submarine for a few years, it didn't last outside of veterans' groups or submariners. The story of the *Hunley* was still largely unknown. Most historians of the nineteenth and early twentieth centuries considered the *Hunley* but a footnote to the Civil War, barely warranting mention. The War Between the States had been primarily a series of ground campaigns fought on the rolling landscape of the South; the naval skirmishes were merely a sidebar. For that reason the *Hunley's* sinking of the *Housatonic* was never listed alongside the great battles, never mentioned in the same sentence as Shiloh, Gettysburg, or Chickamauga.

The *Hunley* got more respect in fiction than it did in history. In his *Little Traitor to the South*, published in 1904, the famous historian and novelist Cyrus Townsend Brady dramatized the sinking of the *Hunley*. In a brief preface, he acknowledged that the "tragic interlude in this little war-time comedy of affections" had really occurred. He listed the names of the *Hunley's* crewmen and wrote, "These names should be written in letters of gold on the rolls of heroes. No more gallant exploit was ever performed." Despite Brady's praise, the *Hunley's* story was not weathering history well.

Just as the submarine had suddenly disappeared, the memory of it was fading. In the early years of the 1900s, the wreck of the *Housatonic* was again becoming a hazard to navigation into Charleston Harbor. As the size of ships grew, they drew more water and therefore needed more clearance. In 1908, when divers made another expedition to the wreck of the *Hunley*'s sole enemy victim, news accounts of that work didn't even mention the fish-boat. A year later, after the Union sloop's wreck was dynamited and sunk even lower into the Atlantic muck, an Army Corps of Engineers report mentioned the *Hunley* only in passing. Perhaps, the report noted, the contractor mistook the submarine for a *Housatonic* boiler and blasted it. Another scenario floated about that time was that the submarine could have lain in the path of the jetties and been buried under the rock groins. Whatever the case, the submarine was nowhere to be found. But then, it didn't appear anyone was looking.

Still, the story of the *Hunley* was so powerful, so mysterious, that it would not disappear completely. In the pages of magazines such as *Confederate Veteran*, where the men who had served during the war recounted their exploits, some of the *Hunley*'s secrets were being revealed to the twentieth century. Men such as D. W. McLaurin and C. L. Stanton—both of whom had witnessed important moments in the submarine's brief history—gave largely accurate accounts of the *Hunley*'s machinery, its first two sinkings, and Lt. George Dixon's final hours at Battery Marshall on the afternoon of February 17, 1864. But the accounts went largely unnoticed. The world's attention, in 1914, was elsewhere.

THE *HUNLEY*'S HISTORICAL FEAT STOOD AS A LONE ACCOMplishment for fifty years. In the half century between the end of the Civil War and the first shots of World War I, the descendants of the fish-boat were slowly developed—submersibles that could travel much farther, stay underwater much longer. These new submarines carried crews of two dozen and ran on steam or gas power. They were light-years ahead of the *Hunley* technologically. The United States Navy had been nurturing its own submarine fleet for years. In the waning years of the nineteenth century, two men—John P. Holland and Simon Lake—were working furiously, and separately, to build the first submarine for the U.S. Navy. They were attempting to build the successor to the *Hunley*. Lake especially had a keen interest in the *Hunley*. He had dreamed of building a submarine since he'd read Jules Verne as a child. The forward-placed diving fins of the Confederate fish-boat appealed to him—they jelled with his own ideas. In 1898, as he was finishing his *Argonaut*, Lake became friendly with Charles Hasker, briefly a member of the *Hunley*'s first crew—the "only man that went to the bottom with the 'Fish-Boat' and came up to tell the tale."

Even at his advanced age, Hasker, who was retired and living in Richmond, Virginia, still had great interest in submarines. Whoever contacted the other first is not known, but Lake and Hasker eventually became friends. Lake quizzed Hasker on the submarine, which he had seen only briefly but had, of course, never forgotten. Hasker remembered few details, although he did recall rows of deadlights along the top of the hull and how cramped it was with everyone sitting on the single bench mounted along the port side of the hull. The "father of the modern submarine," as Lake would eventually come to be called, could not believe that the entire crew had sat on one side of the hull. Surely, he said, there must have been water ballast on the other side of the boat to offset this weight, but Hasker didn't know. As was the case with almost everyone else, his memories of the fish-boat were fading.

Going on Hasker's description, Lake made a sketch of the *Hunley* and its inner workings that he published in *McClure's* magazine in 1898. And later Hasker traveled to Baltimore, where Lake gave him a ride on the *Argonaut*. It was Hasker's only peaceful trip aboard a submarine.

DESPITE LAKE'S PERSISTENCE AND ADVANCES IN THE DE-velopment of submarines, in 1900 the United States government bought its first submersible boat from John Holland. The USS *Holland* was commissioned on October 12 that year. Still, for more than a decade, the *Hunley* would remain in a class by itself as the only proven attack submarine. The new boats could navigate underwater, but until World War I no submersible proved that it, too, could sink an enemy's ship. That changed on September 5, 1914, when the German Unterseeboot *U-21* slammed a torpedo into the forward magazine of the 3,000-ton British cruiser HMS *Pathfinder*, blowing off the ship's bow and killing 256 men as the ship sailed the Firth of Forth. The follow-up to the *Hunley*'s sinking of the *Housatonic* was a deadly incident, heralding the new role of the submarine in warfare.

After the *U-21*'s success, submarine attacks became common in the war—the most famous of which may have been the sinking of the Cunard Line's *Lusitania* on May 7, 1915. That attack helped draw America into the war. By the following year Lake was routinely building submarines for the United States Navy, and his design standards—particularly dive planes forward of the conning tower—were remarkably reminiscent of the *Hunley*. Lake ultimately set the standard for underwater boats. By the time of the Second World War, the United States had nearly 250 submarines. They had become one of the—if not *the*—most effective tools in the Navy's arsenal. And still, the boats followed the basic formula designed by James McClintock in a little southern machine shop.

As the size and importance of the submarine fleet grew, the *Hunley*'s role was slowly gaining modern notice. In October 1937 Lt. Harry von Kolnitz, a Charlestonian, published an article titled "The Confederate Submarine" in the U.S. Naval Institute *Proceedings*. Von Kolnitz declared that the *Hunley*'s attack on the *Housatonic* was "the debut of the underwater craft as an actual factor in naval warfare." The article helped bestow historical legitimacy on the story of the Confederate submarine, which seventy years after the fact was still largely unknown outside the South. Drawing from Alexander's 1902 article and McClintock's scrapbooks kept by a grandson, von Kolnitz had models built to illustrate the submarine's exterior and interior. The models were based entirely on Alexander's sketches and became the basis for debate, discussion, and, years later, plastic hobby models. Von Kolnitz also put forth a theory on the *Hunley*'s fate that had not yet been considered.

"It is this author's humble opinion," von Kolnitz wrote, "that the cause of the sinking was due to the fact that the *Housatonic* had started to back and that the side drag on the lanyard caused a premature explosion of the torpedo before the submarine had reached a safe distance. Since she was so close, the force of the explosion may have capsized the little craft and allowed the water to run from her tanks into the hull where it would have been beyond reach of the pumps."

It was just the latest theory in a long line of scenarios thrown out in an attempt to explain something that made no sense. It had been missing for nearly a century, and still, no one could understand what happened to the *Hunley*.

IT WAS A COINCIDENCE ABOUT WHICH, IF ANYONE NO-ticed, little was said. But with the emergence of the Cold War, Charleston became, fittingly, a submarine base. For decades submarines would slip in and out of Charleston Harbor, becoming a familiar sight to South Carolinians. Often the descendants of the *Hunley* would sail out of port on the surface, their conning towers slicing through the water as the ships navigated under the Cooper River Bridges. From there they followed the river to the mouth of the harbor, past Fort Sumter to the open sea, following a runway defined by the jetties. The seamen on board those submarines had no idea as they cleared the rock barriers that the grandfather of the vessel on which they sailed lay less than 2 miles away. Sometimes those modern submarines even practiced anchor-dropping dangerously close to where the undiscovered wreck lay beneath the sand. Nobody had any idea how close they were to the *Hunley*'s wreck site.

Robert Bentham Simons, however, was certain the Confederate fish-boat was out there somewhere. Simons, a native Charlestonian, was a war hero in the twilight of his career in the 1950s. A 1911 graduate of the Naval Academy in Annapolis, Simons had risen to the rank of rear admiral following his command of the cruiser *Raleigh* at Pearl Harbor on December 7, 1941. When the Japanese attacked, Simons had been in his bunk growing nostalgic for home by reading the *Charleston News and Courier*. Grabbing his helmet, he managed to get the *Raleigh* under way despite its being hit by a bomb. Before the surprise attack was over, the *Raleigh* downed five Japanese fighter planes. In 1946, after the war, Simons had returned home to Charleston to run the ammunition depot.

More than a decade later, in 1957, Simons suggested to Charleston Navy officials that they should search for the lost Civil War submarine. At the time the *Hunley* was enjoying some new but relatively modest notoriety following the publication of F. van Wyck Mason's novel *Our Valiant Few*, which dramatically—and fictitiously—recounted the story of Horace Hunley, George E. Dixon, and the fish-boat. Simons knew that the U.S. Atlantic Mine Force would soon begin its spring training exercises in the same choppy patch of sea that for years he had calculated was where the *Hunley* sank. Simons had methodically studied the harbor, the location of the *Housatonic's* wreck, and tidal patterns, until he came up with a few areas that he thought were the most likely resting places of the lost submarine. He turned that information over to the minesweepers and said, in essence, see if you can find this. It was, in military circles, as good as a dare.

By late spring they actually thought they had it. The minesweeper *Adroit* had picked up a large anomaly on its sonar just about where Simons said the *Hunley* should be. It was in about 24 feet of water. Divers had tried looking, but the water was too murky, the weather uncooperative. Simons was elated and consulted with metallurgical engineers about the likely condition of the submarine after nearly a century in seawater. After a little more study, he was confident the submarine could be raised.

The Navy, however, never got back out to the site. After several delays, with the Navy always promising to resume its search later in the summer, a spokesman for the Charleston base said the hunt would have to proceed "at some future, indefinite date," as "time and official assignments allowed."

A year later, when the world's first nuclear-powered submarine, the

Nautilus, made its historic voyage beneath the North Pole, it carried on board a nondescript three-ring binder collecting all known documents relating to the lost Confederate torpedo boat.

But despite that ceremonial nod to the past, there appeared to be no real interest in salvaging the lost fish-boat. Soon the *Hunley* was officially forgotten again.

IN 1961 THE SOUTH CELEBRATED THE CENTENNIAL OF THE War Between the States. Nowhere was that more pronounced than in South Carolina, where the war had begun. As more histories of the war were being published, including the second volume in Shelby Foote's masterful narrative of the Civil War, the South grew transfixed by tales of the conflict. People made pilgrimages to Fort Sumter, around Charleston they sold small Confederate battle flags, and at the state-house in Columbia, they hoisted a naval jack atop the dome that would stay there for the remainder of the twentieth century. Lawmakers said it was to honor the war dead.

As the Civil War revival reached its crescendo, the Charleston Museum received a strange gift. Built by students at a local technical college, the life-size model of the *Hunley* was based entirely on the Alexander drawings and the von Kolnitz model. A cutaway in the hull showed the strange hand cranks of the mysterious submarine. Museum exhibitors sat mannequins at the cranking positions and put the model in a hall dedicated to the submarine. Soon few people passed through Charleston without learning something about the *Hunley*. After-school television specials on the submarine would follow as well as the first books on the fish-boat. Some tourists even thought the model was the actual *Hunley*.

Between the unveiling of the new model and growing interest in the Civil War, the *Hunley* had reentered Charleston's consciousness. The legend of the missing torpedo boat was perfect to glorify the Lost Cause: it was a tale of brave men making the ultimate sacrifice for their homeland. Because the tale had never been widely told, it was a new story to many people.

In the century since the *Hunley* disappeared, Charleston had turned into a midsize American city with a major port and military base in its backyard. No longer a formidable political power, its appeal as a tourist destination was nonetheless growing. In some ways Charleston had changed little since its antebellum heyday. It was still a quiet, proper town with old English traditions and a very structured social order. From the water the city's skyline looked much as it did when strange ironclads patrolled the harbor during the blockade. Its monstrous mansions, many going back to colonial days, had been preserved for generations. Tourists could wander onto back streets and feel as if they had stepped back in time. History was becoming, along with the military, the city's lifeblood.

It was in this environment, hearing romanticized stories of the Lost Cause along with the first strains of Carolina beach music squeezing through tinny AM radios, that a generation would grow up. They would love their homeland, celebrate their heritage, and revere their history. Among these southern baby boomers were the children who were quickly growing into the men who would raise the *Hunley*.

PART TWO

*T*HE ATLANTIC SEABED IS A JUNKYARD, AN UNDERWATER DESERT
   cluttered with centuries of maritime refuse. Mingled among the
sunken hulks of ancient warships are slipped anchors, abandoned buoys,
fishing tackle, even barrels of trash. Mostly the ocean buries its dead, suck-
ing down the discards into its sandy belly. An outboard motor that breaks
off a skiff in 10 feet of water can vanish in an instant. Most things that are
dropped into the sea disappear forever.

   Caught up in constant tidal patterns, this trash is reshuffled, moved
around by the unstoppable force of the ocean. What is uncovered one day
can be covered the next. The jetsam fouls anchors and fishing lines, collect-
ing more scrap for the sea to digest. It all conspires to make the ocean floor
a minefield of targets for radar and ground-penetrating sonar. The identity
of most radar hits remains a mystery until a diver with suction tools and
the ability to "see" with his hands uncovers what is there. And even then, it
is often impossible to determine exactly what it is. The sea is a cloak of
anonymity.

Chapter 6

"THIS COULD BE IT"

O N A FALL DAY IN 1970, THE 42-FOOT TRAWLER *MISS Inah* was chugging along in calm seas a few miles outside of Charleston Harbor. It was a Sunday, and Capt. Joseph Porcelli and a few friends were spending a leisurely afternoon collecting blackfish traps he'd set out earlier. The bottom feeders were easily lured into baited boxes that resemble the chicken-wire cages used by most East Coast crabbers. Once inside, the fish become disoriented, unable to find their way out. It is almost too easy to call it fishing.

As *Miss Inah* glided along the glassy surface, Porcelli searched for the buoys that marked his traps. As he found them, the captain pulled the cages from the water and threw them on the deck. But as he reeled in one cage, the line suddenly snapped taut. Stuck. The trap had snagged something on the ocean floor.

It was a common occurrence, one that many fishermen solved by simply cutting the line, sacrificing both their catch and tackle to the ocean. Porcelli was debating what to do when one of his passengers stepped forward and offered a hand.

Edward Lee Spence, named in part for the greatest Confederate general of all, had come along that day for a relaxing cruise, nothing more. He didn't have swimming trunks or a wet suit, but the soft-spoken, amiable twenty-three-year-old volunteered to dive down and pull the trap free. It was an unenviable task. November is one of the cruelest months for diving, when the water off Charleston is a bone-chilling 60 degrees. Spence, a professional diver, was used to the water in any condition: he didn't think it was a big deal. But this dive would change his life.

Spence stripped to his skivvies, collected what stray gear he could find aboard *Miss Inah*—two air tanks and Porcelli's scuba mask, which was too small—and flopped over the side. Absorbing the shock of the frigid water, Spence used the trap line to pull himself down into the murky water. It guided him through the darkness toward the snarled trap waiting below.

In 1970 Spence was a young man ready to make his name in the world of underwater treasure hunting. Born in Munich, Germany, where his father was stationed at a U.S. Army base, Spence later moved with his family to Sullivan's Island, outside Charleston. It was a sleepy, rural barrier island when the Spence family arrived, home to both fishermen and city lawyers. The island's past appealed to the history buff that Spence was becoming. The guns of Fort Moultrie, which had fired the first shots of the Civil War, sat aging at the island's south end. Near the fort African slaves had been quarantined after their long journey across the Atlantic. But it was the story of the ships that sailed during the Civil War that called to Spence. When he was growing up on the island in the 1960s, some of the wrecks could still be seen at low tide, half-buried in the sand.

From Sullivan's Island Spence launched his exploration of these underwater treasures and soon found that he had a voracious appetite for diving and exploring. By the time Spence boarded the *Miss Inah* that day in 1970, he had logged hundreds of hours underwater and, by his count, touched more than fifty shipwrecks littered off the coast. Earlier in the year he had announced in a newspaper article that he would lead an expedition in search of the lost Confederate submarine *H. L. Hunley*. He hadn't found the wreck, but he had proved again his mettle as a treasure hunter. Unsnagging a fish trap, he figured, would be easy work.

The trap that Spence was pursuing could have been hung up on an old wreck, an abandoned buoy, or an anchor—just about anything. Spence realized he was near the Civil War–era sloop *Housatonic*, which had been blown up and scattered twice to clear the channel leading into Charleston, leaving a mess of debris on the ocean floor. He wanted to see if the trap was stuck on the wreckage. Whatever the trap was, Spence figured he'd be on the bottom only long enough to give it a yank and then follow the line back to the *Miss Inah*.

SHIVERING, SPENCE SOON REACHED THE SANDY BOTTOM 27 feet below. He navigated toward the trap using its buoy line as a guide, that being easier than actually seeing his way. Charleston water is perpetually murky; visibility is rarely more than 2 feet. Spence was coping with the nearly opaque water and yet another problem: Porcelli's mask wasn't a perfect fit; water leaked in through the sides. It was aggravating, and if the salt water hit his eyes, it stung bitterly. Still, Spence could see well enough to find the trap. When he did, he was puzzled. It was caught on what appeared to be a ledge. But he knew there weren't any natural ledges on the notoriously flat ocean floor off the South Carolina coast. The closer Spence got, the easier it was to make it out. Soon he could discern vague shapes in the water. He could tell one thing for sure: whatever had caught the trap was man-made.

As he jiggled the trap line, Spence started studying its features, trying to figure out what it could be that he was standing on. It looked to be about 20 feet long and rounded, although only one side of it was exposed. Most of it was buried in a huge drift of sand. It was lightly corroded but still smooth. He would later write that he ran his fingers along its raised rivets and pulled off a sea whip growing on it. It appeared to be a solid, black iron tube.

Then it hit him like a tidal wave. The *Hunley*. It had to be.

Spence knew the legend of the *Hunley* well. He had read about the doomed Confederate submarine since he was a child. Only six months earlier, his own expedition to find what he considered the greatest archaeological treasure ever had ended in defeat. Now, ironically, he had stumbled on it purely by accident. There wasn't a question in his mind—this was it.

Forgetting the cold, Spence was flooded with emotions. First, it was euphoria: he believed he had just made the greatest Civil War find of all time (the *Monitor* had not yet been found), the kind of discovery for which most archaeologists spend their entire lives waiting. The salvage of the *Hunley*, he believed, could be the most important excavation of the century.

Just as quickly as those thoughts appeared, dread and fear crept in. While Spence had struggled to loosen the fish trap, he had stirred up the bait inside, the nautical version of ringing the dinner bell. He was afraid it would not be long before the chum would attract sharks. In the poor visibility, wearing a mask filling with seawater, he realized that a man-eater would be on him before he ever saw it. Spence knew he had to go. Reluctantly he touched the iron hulk one last time and followed the trap line to the surface.

When Spence broke the surface, he began to scream about his discovery before he was even able to spit out the mouthpiece of his air tank: "The *Hunley*! The *Hunley*! I've found the *Hunley*!"

Or had he?

Spence had just been on the object for a matter of seconds, and it would be the only time he ever touched what he found that day. He had taken no photographs, and he had left with no real proof. After he broke the surface, Spence treaded water while he scanned for the *Miss Inah* and, with a few strong kicks, was back aboard the boat. There he went to work to make a record of his find.

First, Spence threw a buoy over the approximate place where he thought he'd spotted it. Then he scratched out a crude record of its position on a stray piece of paper. Still dripping wet, he lined up a channel buoy with the Sullivan's Island Lighthouse, the most visible landmark. At the point where two imaginary lines of longitude and latitude intersected, he drew a large *X* on a map. Spence felt he had enough evidence to make a claim. It was the *Hunley*, he thought, and it was right there, his *X* marking the spot.

And there began a long, strange trip.

FOR THE NEXT THIRTY YEARS, LEE SPENCE WOULD TRY TO persuade the world that he had, in fact, found the *Hunley*. Trying to convince people he had found the lost fish-boat—and not an abandoned Coast Guard buoy near his coordinates—would become his life quest. It would become just another mystery in the long history of the submarine.

Spence began his work quietly in the early 1970s, writing letters to the state of South Carolina, the General Services Administration, the U.S. Navy, and a number of other agencies, but nobody showed an interest. The short, polite replies to his letters offered little. Some included congratulations, some commended his feat, but none gave him salvage rights or a license for an archaeological expedition.

Spence became a man obsessed, voraciously collecting materials on the submarine, filling one filing cabinet after another. Sporting long hair and a thick beard he would keep most of his life, Spence also continued to visit the site, more than twenty times over the following years. He would take friends along and, like a tour guide, boast about his unseen discovery resting below them on the ocean floor. He had even told a friend about his discovery the day after his trip aboard *Miss Inah* in 1970, and his friend later claimed he found the *Hunley* just where Spence had said it was. But Spence accused the man of losing his buoy on the site, and they didn't speak for years.

As time passed Spence's plight grated on him: no one gave him the credit he felt he was due. But then, most people said they couldn't give him credit because he couldn't produce any proof. As often as Spence went out to the site, he never again saw what he said he had touched in 1970. He didn't find it odd that it had been uncovered only that one time: he attributed it to the random patterns of the river of sand. Spence would claim to easily relocate the supposed *Hunley* with electronic equipment. He never exposed it, he said, out of fear of being charged with an archaeological crime—the equivalent of grave robbing. But for some people his lack of proof-in-hand raised huge questions about his story.

Even if he didn't find it, Spence perhaps did the next best thing to salvaging the *Hunley*: he kept its legend alive. He told everyone he met that it was out there, that he'd found it. Over time he became a popular speaker at various Civil War conferences, often introduced as "The Man Who Found the *Hunley*." Spence had everything but the elusive proof.

After four years of trying to get official recognition for his discovery, a frustrated Spence went to the press. On June 13, 1975, the *Orangeburg (S.C.) Times and Democrat* published a front-page story titled "Archaeologist Claims *Hunley* Remains Found." To get his story out, Spence had called a reporter he knew at that newspaper in a small town 70 miles inland from Charleston. Soon other newspapers picked up the story. Spence was trying to provoke the government into taking him seriously, into giving him a license to salvage the wreck. Mostly, though, he wanted recognition for finding it, whatever it was. He described his find carefully, even the depth of the water—27 feet. He said he had previously believed the *Hunley* was 40 feet long, but now he thought that length perhaps included the spar. What he'd found, he believed, was 20 feet in length. Spence gave great details, but because he didn't want the site looted, he kept the location a secret—for a while.

IN 1980, AFTER FIVE MORE YEARS OF LITTLE PROGRESS, Spence filed a claim on the *Hunley* in federal court in Charleston. He cited two legal principles—the law of salvage, giving him the right to take possession of the submarine; and the law of finds, which said the *Hunley* was his under rules of lost and abandoned property. In court documents Spence said the submarine rested in about 30 feet of water, not too far from the wreck of the *Housatonic*. He drew a half-mile-wide circle on a map and said the sub was somewhere inside.

The case was never heard. A federal judge in Charleston opted not to get involved, saying the bench had no jurisdiction over any shipwreck outside the United States's recognized 3-mile territorial limit—as Spence's find apparently was. Spence left the courthouse claiming victory. He interpreted the judge's lack of action as confirmation that the submarine indeed belonged to him.

Despite Spence's confidence, in the following years no major expedition was launched to recover the submarine, nor did any of the world's leading archaeological scientists ever come to verify his find. As the years passed, Spence reported deals with some big names in the field, but nothing seemed to pan out. He still insisted to everyone he met that he had found the *Hunley*.

Meanwhile, Spence was having more luck elsewhere—exploring, hunting, and diving on other shipwrecks. In 1987 Spence announced plans to search for the *Central America*, the famous "Ship of Gold" that had sunk off the Carolinas while bringing deposits from the California gold rush to the East Coast. He even appeared on the *Today* show to talk about his efforts, worrying the men who were searching—and would actually find the ship. But he couldn't put the proof to what he considered his greatest find. Eventually other hunters of antique submarines began to sail into Charleston, including one old salt who seemed to have the Midas touch.

AT THE AGE OF THIRTY-SEVEN, CLIVE CUSSLER WALKED out of a secure and comfortable job in advertising and took a seat behind the counter of a southern California dive shop. Beside him he plunked down an IBM electric typewriter. It was 1968, and he had one purpose in life: to write.

Cussler dreamed of creating a literary figure who would hunt lost treasures in a series of books. He would be dashing, educated, deadly, and brave. Cussler wanted a kind of archaeological Sherlock Holmes mixed with the tough-guy bravado of Matt Helm. Working in the slow pace of the dive shop was perfect. In between helping the occasional customer, Cussler could tap away on his IBM, creating his own adventure-filled world.

The dive-shop location was no accident. Not only did it suggest the world of his fictional characters, it reflected the author's own interests. Cussler was an early pioneer of sport diving. He had picked it up in 1951 while stationed in the Pacific as a sergeant in the Air Force. Cussler was a member of one of the crews that shuttled supplies to the U.S. armed forces fighting in Korea. On the return leg they'd come back carrying wounded GIs. Skin diving in Guam and Hawaii—with equipment ordered from French diving pioneer Jacques Cousteau—became his release after hours on board a plane with the wounded.

At the dive shop the gregarious author-in-training brought to life the stories of his hero, named in part for his son, Dirk, and a onetime prime minister of England he'd found in an encyclopedia, Pitt the Elder. Dirk Pitt stormed onto the American literary scene in the 1970s, finding sunken aircraft and raising the *Titanic*. And soon the dive-shop clerk was a very rich man.

By 1977 Cussler had accumulated enough money to follow his fictitious hero into underwater archaeology. He, too, began looking for the world's great shipwrecks by establishing the National Underwater and Marine Agency in Austin, Texas—a real version of Dirk Pitt's outfit, tasked with the hunt for lost maritime treasures. NUMA's first big search, launched in 1978, was for the *Bonhomme Richard*, the flagship of Capt. John Paul Jones.

The *Bonhomme Richard* had gone down off the northeast coast of England in 1779 after sinking a much stronger British warship during the American Revolution. It was believed to be somewhere in a 400-square-mile area of the North Sea, but that was as close as accounts could put it. The ship sank after drifting for thirty-six hours—

which meant it could be almost anywhere. Cussler didn't care how hard it would be: he desperately wanted to find it. The *Bonhomme Richard* was one of two ships that had filled his imagination since childhood.

Cussler and his NUMA team soon found that shipwreck hunting was much more difficult than Dirk Pitt made it look. The search for the *Bonhomme Richard* was a disaster, an exercise in beginner's folly. They found nothing of the ship—but the search bug had bitten him. As Cussler grew from best-selling author to cultural phenomenon, his time and money for exploration grew with him. After the initial *Bonhomme Richard* fiasco, Cussler and NUMA branched out and found success at almost every turn. His part-time hobby led to the discovery of more than sixty vessels lost in the ocean's muck. Other wreck hunters could only watch with envy.

In 1980 Cussler set a course for Charleston. A self-described Civil War buff, Cussler had been enchanted with the world's first attack submarine while growing up in the Midwest. When Cussler was a child, the Conrad Wise Chapman painting of the sleek Rebel submarine on the dock at Mount Pleasant spoke to him. Once he became an adult, it sent his million-dollar imagination into overdrive. He dreamed of the *Hunley* often, wondering what it would have been like inside the mysterious fish-boat.

With NUMA at his disposal, Cussler vowed to make the *Hunley* and the *Bonhomme Richard* the two ships he'd find before he died. No excuses.

CUSSLER'S FIRST VENTURE IN THE WATERS OFF CHARLESton went about as well as his first expedition for the *Bonhomme Richard*. Most expeditions, centered far offshore, were all business on the crowded confines of search vessels. But with the search for the *Hunley* concentrated within 3 miles of the coast, it was easy enough to go ashore at night and scout out the diversions of the little tourist town. Perhaps as a result, the expedition turned into more of a vacation than a true search. Most of the men involved brought their wives or girlfriends. There were beach parties at night that led into long, hot days on the water off Sullivan's Island. Cussler made it fun for everyone involved. Part of the time he walked around in a T-shirt that read "Clive Who?"—a self-deprecating nod to his growing fame.

In fact, the entire search was more fun than anything else. There was too much manpower for the small expedition, too many people to coordinate, and no real focus. The search centered on the area around the *Housatonic*, one of a half dozen shipwrecks the NUMA crew stumbled over that summer. The team eventually surveyed a good bit of territory between the Union wreck and the beach, but the entire operation was defined more by its disasters. Cussler's son rescued three boys struggling in the surf off the beach at Sullivan's, and a cabin cruiser that Cussler was on got stuck on the harbor jetties as its captain tried a shortcut to the open water. A couple of weeks of this kind of "fun" was about all any of them could take. The novelist came to call the expedition "The Great Trauma of '80."

The next summer, NUMA in tow, Cussler was back in Charleston for a second look. This time the expedition would be more serious. For nearly two weeks his team dragged electronic scanners across 16 square miles of ocean. They hit sunken Confederate blockade-runners, lost Union ironclads, and previously charted obstacles, but nothing that appeared to be the cigar-shaped submarine that had stirred Cussler's youthful imagination. They mapped a handful of anomalies beneath the ocean floor but didn't have time to excavate them all. At a posthunt press conference, Cussler said he couldn't imagine why they weren't making contact.

"We don't know where the *Hunley* is," he said, "but we know where it ain't."

Cussler was becoming convinced the *Hunley* was not anywhere within 2 miles of the *Housatonic*. His NUMA team boat had painstakingly scanned the submarine's most likely routes home and found nothing of merit. But his imagination would not allow him to be stumped. With a writer's mind, he plotted the course of all the various scenarios, coming up with a handful of theories. The submarine might have gone down after a panicky scramble back to shore, he reasoned, forcing the crew to take a more radical course. If that were the case, the *Hunley* might be buried in shallow water, maybe even near the surf line or within eyeshot of the beach. The scariest plotline, though, caused him to shiver. What if the *Hunley*, with its crew injured, limped un-piloted toward the deep abyss of the ocean? It filled him with a feeling of defeat that he hadn't felt since the first search for the *Bonhomme Richard*. If that was what happened, the odds of finding it were microscopic.

"If it floated out to sea," he said woefully, "we may never find it."

After Cussler left Charleston in 1981, he resumed his other career writing best-sellers. Meanwhile, other searches took him around the world, and for a decade he made no plans to come back to Charleston, even though he had a list of unidentified targets. Still, the *Hunley* mystery continued to nag him. But for a while he would be able to ignore that little piece of unfinished business. For a while.

FINALLY.

After a decade of work at the South Carolina Institute of Archaeology and Anthropology studying the rice culture and industrial history of the state, after years of digging up the grounds around old plantations under the hot Carolina sun, Mark Newell was going on his own hunt for the *Hunley*.

It was what he'd always wanted to do.

Newell was a wandering Englishman who grew up near a submarine base on the craggy coastline of his homeland. Ever since he was nine, when he roamed the decks of a Royal Navy submarine, he'd been fascinated by the sleek vessels and the undersea adventures of the men who wore two dolphins over a crown on their chests. He found the American Civil War equally alluring. For Newell part of the draw was the story of the world's first attack submarine. The legend of the *Hunley* was especially popular in Britain, where the submarine force is heralded as a special branch of the fleet.

As Newell reached his twenties, he did not forget about the lost fish-boat, but his life initially took a different turn. He became a journalist, left England, and worked his way through the warm climes of the Caribbean, sometimes freelancing stories as he went. It was in the tropical waters around those islands that he picked up sport diving as a hobby. He marveled at the world beneath the surface of the sea—the world of a submarine.

In 1972 Newell made his life-changing move. He left the Caribbean for the Carolinas, landing in Aiken, South Carolina, a small horse-country town that churned out thoroughbred champions just across the state line from Augusta, Georgia. There Newell quickly joined up with a unit of the Sons of Confederate Veterans, and his passion for the Civil War was stirred once again. With the help of his new friends in the SCV, Newell began making plans for a nonprofit organization that would search for the elusive submarine. His research, Newell thought, would help him find the *Hunley* when no one else could.

Newell was convinced the submarine had survived its attack against the *Housatonic* and was lost while trying to ride the tide back into the safety of Charleston Harbor—not the north docks of Sullivan's Island, where it normally moored. His research indicated the *Hunley*'s third crew was well acquainted with the course into the harbor. To prove his theory meant looking away from the wreck of the *Housatonic*—where all other searches had focused—and toward any possible point between the Union boat and the mouth of the harbor. He drove to Charleston and searched on the weekends, always coming up empty-handed.

In 1984 Newell's diving experience and interest in archaeology helped him land a job at the South Carolina Institute of Archaeology and Anthropology. SCIAA was the state's lead agency responsible for locating, studying, and recovering historical artifacts. The operation was run from the University of South Carolina in Columbia, and it had a powerful hold over all shipwreck hunters: it issued the permits that allowed treasure hunters and archaeologists to search and excavate anything in South Carolina waters. When Newell landed his new job, he had high hopes for continuing his quest for the *Hunley* as a government employee.

IT WAS 1992 WHEN NEWELL AND CUSSLER FIRST TALKED about a joint expedition. Cussler was finally planning a return to Charleston and another search for the *Hunley*. He was sixty-one, and finding the submarine was one of those nagging unachieved goals, but he had the means to do something about it. He contacted SCIAA for the permits he'd need to come back. That's when he met Mark Newell. Newell, however, later claimed he was the first to contact Cussler about their joint venture when he dangled the lure of state resources before the adventurous novelist. Whatever the case, they agreed to team up. Both sides saw benefit to the merger: SCIAA could use Cussler's purse, and the author would not have to worry about troublesome government paperwork.

They agreed to meet in the waters off Sullivan's Island late in the summer of 1994. With a small fleet of boats, a dozen divers, and the latest high-tech sensing gadgets that money could buy, it would be the biggest and most advanced expedition ever launched to find the submarine.

It would be a disaster.

AT FIRST THE ANTICIPATION OF THE SEARCH SENT NEWELL into a frenzy. He was optimistic, infectiously so. He had followed Cussler's exploits for years—even wrote an article about the 1981 *Hunley* expedition for a sport-diving magazine. This upcoming dive, Newell knew, would far outshine the one he had covered a decade earlier. The growing popularity—in fact, cult status—of Cussler's Dirk Pitt novels had elevated the author to true superstar status. His decision to join the SCIAA expedition was akin to having John Grisham defend you in court. At the time Newell—like most people—found the writer pleasant and charming.

On paper the joint operation looked simple enough. Cussler and his team would use their notes and coordinates to relocate eleven possible sites they had come across during the 1980 and 1981 searches. Once they had the sites, they would mark them with buoys. The SCIAA boat would follow behind and send divers into the water to probe whatever was there.

Cussler's boat, manned by NUMA and Ralph Wilbanks, a former SCIAA archaeologist and veteran of the 1980s searches, would use a magnetometer to find the targets. The tiny, torpedo-looking sensor device was dragged behind the boat on a line, much as the *Hunley's* first mines had been towed. The magnetometer monitored slight changes in the earth's magnetic field. Those changes, measured in a scale of gammas, mark the presence of metallic objects below. The gadgets, made to float a few feet below the surface, were quite handy.

On August 6, 1994, the two boats left shore for the most extensive search for the *Hunley* in history. It was supposed to be the best chance yet to reach the elusive submarine. But by the time the boats were beyond the protective waters of the harbor, the tension on the expedition threatened to put an end to the search before the magnetometer was wet.

For starters, Newell suspected Cussler and his group weren't sharing all their information. He particularly had a personality clash with Wilbanks, whose job he had taken at SCIAA. Cussler and Wilbanks, a friendly bear of a man who appealed to the writer's jovial nature, had become good friends over the years, and that made Newell suspicious. He figured Wilbanks would try to poison his relationship with Cussler.

Cussler and Wilbanks had their own misgivings about the expedition unfolding before them. They immediately sensed that Newell didn't have the experience or expertise to lead an underwater search, and neither man suffered fools well. The SCIAA team leader did little to allay their fears, especially when they first saw Newell's accompanying band of "divers."

Aside from a bright young archaeology graduate student and experienced diver named Harry Pecorelli III, Newell had invited mostly a handful of amateurs, some of whom were members of the Sons of Confederate Veterans, to take part in the search. The trip was meant to appeal more to the men's sense of heritage than to their diving skills. He billed the expedition as a chance for them to be the first southerners to touch the *Hunley* since the war. On the first morning several of these volunteers arrived at the docks suited up in an array of diving gear, silver knives at the ready. One wore red cotton sweatpants bought at Kmart as his wet suit; another was outfitted in gear that had been stored in a garage for fifteen years. Practically none of them were certi-fied, or even experienced divers. But they were eager. One showed up carrying a Confederate battle flag he hoped to rub on the *Hunley*'s hull. Pecorelli found it comical. Carl Naylor, SCIAA's dive-safety officer, took one look at the ragtag bunch and refused to take responsibility for anyone in Newell's crew.

Naylor had good reason for concern. Diving off Charleston is complicated. Currents are exhausting, and visibility is often near zero. Divers have to "see" with their hands, feeling along blindly in bottom conditions that become even more clouded during excavations, when silt is constantly kicked up by dredge hoses stirring up the sand. It is a dangerous business. But Newell's divers didn't seem concerned. They showed up with Dirk Pitt–like confidence, as if expecting an easy find.

Cussler's group was no more reassured by what they saw from Newell's group once they were on the water. As the Wilbanks boat relo-cated their old magnetic anomalies, they dropped peanut buoys— small, white Styrofoam balls—and moved on to locate the next site. Newell's boat constantly called them back: they couldn't find the buoys. It was the first of many annoyances to the author.

Newell's team had also left equipment Cussler bought for them back at the hotel and lost the antenna to their boat's loran, which would have helped them find their position on the water. The SCIAA divers also forgot underwater jet probes—rods that shoot water and make it easier to push through sand—and had to borrow them from Cussler's team. Then they lost some more equipment. When the pilot of Newell's boat accidentally snagged a buoy line, an expedition video camera picked up Wilbanks berating the SCIAA team as a bunch of in-competents. Newell didn't seem to notice the comedy of errors playing out before him.

Slowly the teams fell into a working pattern. The plan for the expedition was first to explore the targets Cussler had dis-covered a decade earlier. During the first five days of the search, at least four targets were probed to varying degrees. If the divers found wood, the site was immediately abandoned, since the *Hunley* was purely an iron vessel. One promising site near the *Housatonic* was rejected after a thick layer of oyster shells prevented divers from getting closer. Newell's field notes recorded that the magnetometer reading for Cussler's "target 1" was simply not in the right gamma range. For a little while Pecorelli had tried to worm through the mess, but Newell called him off. The divers moved elsewhere.

NEWELL BEGAN THE SEARCH WITH A GOOD IDEA OF WHERE he thought the *Hunley* was. At the outset he had wanted to direct the search toward the shores of Sullivan's Island in an area known as Maffitt's Channel. It was there that he hoped to test his theory about a harbor return route for the *Hunley*.

During the war Maffitt's Channel was a particularly daring route for blockade-runners. Only a few hundred yards off the beach, the deep channel marked the northern approach to Charleston Harbor, a weak point in the North's attempt to bottle up the city. To make sure the blockade was effective, the Union Navy had sunk a fleet of obsolete ships filled with rock ballast near the channel entrance as an underwater obstacle course designed to foil any cargo-laden ship sneaking in along the beach. But it didn't work. Confederate blockade-runners sailed freely through Maffitt's Channel anyway, sometimes painting their ships a light tan so they would blend in with the sand dunes on shore. It was camouflage to throw off chasing Union gunners during the frantic final sprint into the harbor.

Newell felt that if he could prove the *Hunley* made it back to within 2 miles of the shoreline but somehow was lost in the depths of the old channel, the mystery of what happened to the submarine would be solved. He finally got the chance to test his theory on August 13, the last day of the expedition. Newell had already taken his boat in for the day when a call came over the radio from Cussler: they were over the now filled-in Maffitt's Channel, and the magnetometer had detected something—something big. Cussler's boat had turned off its motor and had simply drifted over the spot when the reading came. It appeared to be about 40 feet long, according to the gadget, and the gamma reading was in Newell's range. He thought he had his match. He loaded up his divers and raced back to the site, quickly dubbed target 8.

Newell was encouraged by the logic of his theory. He believed the crew of the *Hunley*, riding low on the water, would not have been able to see their way home to Breach Inlet after the attack and would have steered for the harbor mouth. Likewise, he believed the troops on shore would not have seen the blue lamp signal from very far out to sea. A field test done with a blue carbide signal lamp—just like the one the *Hunley* supposedly carried—proved the light could only reliably be observed from shore at a distance of 2 miles. To Newell all those facts added up to one thing: Maffitt's Channel.

THE LAST DAY OF THE SEARCH PROVED TO BE A BAD DAY to be on the water. Offshore conditions had not cooperated throughout the expedition, making it that much more dangerous. Throughout the week Newell's passengers were seasick and cranky because they weren't allowed to dive—as if they wanted to. The jellyfish migration had started, a bigger hazard to divers than sharks. The gelatinous creatures stung anything they came in contact with. Pecorelli was the only one prepared. He wore a pair of women's panty hose over the exposed skin of his face, its legs flopping behind his head like sheer dreadlocks. Even though it was purely for safety, it drove Newell up the wall. He would turn off the camera he was using to film the dive every time Pecorelli showed up in the frame dancing around like a happy Rastafarian bank robber.

On that last day Newell decided to let some of his SCV crew dive on the site with Pecorelli just to give them a chance to feel included. He sent one man down to operate the sand dredge deep in Maffitt's Channel. But the man didn't get his mask on quite right and, while fiddling with it, allowed seawater to pour in, blinding him. Soon he started to drift off. He wasn't really in great danger at that point, but he had panicked.

Pecorelli swam after the man, who was being pushed away by the current. At the end of the line connecting him to the boat, Pecorelli let go to catch up to the foundering diver. He soon closed the distance and caught the wayward swimmer, calming him down. But by that time, the two men had drifted well out of range of Newell's boat and were floating south down the South Carolina coast. After a while Cussler's boat happened by and picked them up.

By then, however, Naylor, the SCIAA dive-safety officer, had had enough. Newell wasn't watching out for the rookies, Naylor said. This search was plagued with mishap after miscue, and soon someone was bound to get hurt. Naylor radioed to Cussler's boat trying to hail Newell, who had temporarily moved there. Cussler inadvertently caught the receiving end of Naylor's angry tirade over the radio announcing the dive was over.

Newell could do little but write derisively of the event in his diary: "Carl Naylor in panic. Using foul language over air to RW. CN aborted work w/out authorization."

BACK ON SHORE NEWELL TRIED TO PERSUADE CUSSLER TO fund at least two more days of diving. He felt he only needed a little more time to verify that target 8 was the *Hunley*. He was so close. It would be a monumental fiasco to stop now, he argued. But it wasn't to be. Cussler and Wilbanks were sick of Newell and SCIAA, so they packed it in. Forget target 8. Forget the joint venture.

In the days after the expedition, Newell began to blame Cussler for its failure. It was the writer's fault, he said, that the NUMA group took so long to search Maffitt's Channel, where he had predicted from the very start that the *Hunley* would be. Cussler, he felt, wasn't serious about archaeology; he was just a "glory-hunting millionaire." He fumed in his little diary: "Time up to last day largely wasted—no anomaly even close to profile. Last day Target #8 only worthwhile hit. Could have identified if Cussler had cooperated early in project."

A few weeks later the SCIAA team went back to Maffitt's Channel to probe target 8 again. Although divers didn't expose the object for fear of introducing artifact-destroying oxygen to the site, they more accurately mapped and measured it. "It" was 35 feet long, 6 feet wide. That, Newell said, was close to the size of the *Hunley*. It only made him more confident in his research and instincts. All he needed now was a little more time and a better-organized recovery plan, and perhaps he could solve the mystery of the *Hunley*'s disappearance.

"Too old to be dredge pipe (!!!)" Newell wrote in his notes. "Satisfied this could be it."

But as a precautionary note, he added "80 percent."

Newell planned to wait until the following spring to return to the site when more sophisticated sonar mapping equipment could be brought in. But he was too excited to sit still, and he couldn't keep quiet any longer. In January 1995, three months after the search had ended, Newell gave a story to *The Post and Courier* in Charleston saying that the *Hunley* possibly had been found. He was identifying the iron hulk at the bottom of the sea even though no diver had yet touched it. The object was buried 12 feet under the sand—3 feet deeper than his boat's vacuums could go. Still, he said, it was a "provocative" find.

WHEN HE HEARD ABOUT THE NEWSPAPER ARTICLE, CUSSLER was furious. Newell's announcement killed whatever was left of the fragile union between NUMA and SCIAA. From his home in Colorado, Cussler called Newell and let loose on him for making such an unqualified leap. It was unprofessional and flat-out wrong to get people's hopes up over an object that was still buried in the sand, Cussler argued. Friends said they'd never seen the easygoing author so "pissed off."

But Newell didn't listen. By that time he was convinced that Cussler had fouled up the 1994 expedition when he'd been so close. Finally.

Cussler thought Newell was obsessed—there was no getting through to him. Exasperated, he hung up the phone.

Half a continent away, Cussler regretted his decision to work with SCIAA. He was disappointed. It was his third search for the lost submarine, and everything had gone wrong. It was most frustrating because, more than ever, he was convinced the *Hunley* was out there, waiting for him.

But after all this, he wondered if he'd ever find it.

Chapter 7

VENI, VIDI, VICI, DUDE

H ARRY PECORELLI WATCHED THE BEACHFRONT MAN-sions drift through his peripheral vision as *Diversity* arced around the north end of the Isle of Palms. It was just after dawn on Wednesday, May 3, 1995, and as the 25-foot diving boat angled toward the open sea, he gulped down his daily fix of coffee.

Pecorelli could barely believe where he was, setting out on this unexpected expedition. The call had come just twelve hours earlier—an invitation to make history. The man on the other end of the line, an old acquaintance, made him an offer that had knocked him flat.

"Do you want to help us go find the *Hunley* tomorrow?"

For a brief second Pecorelli was apprehensive. He had suffered through the horrors of the 1994 SCIAA/NUMA search for the Confederate submarine and had not forgotten the mishaps and tense atmosphere surrounding it. That was not an experience he ever wanted to repeat, but he felt sure this time would be different. He completely trusted the man on the other end of the line.

Ralph Wilbanks had explained that he and his partner, Wes Hall, had quietly continued to look for the *Hunley* at Clive Cussler's request on and off through the winter of 1994–95. Fed up with government interference, they wanted to try to find the submarine on their own. The two men went out whenever they had a free day, taking their marching orders from maps the author faxed them. He'd mark where he wanted them to search and then send them handsome checks for doing it.

Wilbanks told Pecorelli that they'd hit a promising new target. It was the right size, the right shape—it could be the *Hunley*. But they needed an extra hand to help probe. It wouldn't be easy. Mostly it was grunt work: as the junior member of the team, Pecorelli would be the first into the water to check out any target. Whatever happened, Wilbanks promised he would be paid for a full day's work. Cussler himself would sign the check. They would sail from the Wild Dunes Marina at dawn. He repeated the question.

"Do you want to go?" Wilbanks asked.

Pecorelli thought about it for nearly a full second.

"Hell, yeah!" he yelled into the phone.

Now Pecorelli found himself soaking in the morning sea breeze as Wilbanks steered for a point a few miles off Sullivan's Island. Pecorelli felt good. He was relaxed. He felt like having another cup of coffee.

IN THE EIGHT MONTHS SINCE THE SCIAA/NUMA DIVE had ended on a bitter note, Wilbanks and Hall had continued the search for the *Hunley* to no avail. Despite Cussler's persistence, both men were becoming convinced it was a waste of time. They'd run hundreds of miles of surface scans, dragging electronic equipment through the swells, through hundreds of search lanes. And found nothing.

They felt guilty about sending Cussler dive bills for what they considered a fruitless search. Maybe the word around the diving community was right, the author was just chasing a Confederate ghost. But from his home in the Rockies, Cussler pressed his team to keep going. Wilbanks would call every few days with updates about the routes they'd run. Cussler, in turn, would go to his map of the South Carolina coast, study what had been charted, and fax back new lines for them to follow, sometimes including a note of encouragement. The author was thoroughly convinced the *Hunley* was still out there, even if Wilbanks and Hall were not.

Still, Cussler was baffled over why the submarine hadn't been found. After three trips to Charleston and the occasional searches by Wilbanks, he had nothing to show for his efforts—except $130,000 in bills. He was beginning to believe that, after the *Hunley* sank the *Housatonic*, it had drifted out to sea. "That's the thing about shipwrecks," Cussler often said. "The damn things are never where they're supposed to be."

It was a sea hunter's rule of thumb his crew was about to prove correct.

SITTING AT THE HELM OF THE *DIVERSITY*, WILBANKS explained the new target to Pecorelli on the way out. As he talked, Hall stood nearby studying the boat's electronic gear.

The target, Wilbanks said, was in moderately shallow water and within cannon shot of the *Housatonic* wreckage. They were going to expose what was there, no matter how much time it took. It would definitely be a multitank day. After his spiel Wilbanks grinned and told Pecorelli to relax. If things went right, he said, the whole world would be talking about the Italian-American from California who found the legendary lost Confederate submarine.

Wilbanks's sense of humor was one of the things that Cussler liked so much about him and why the author trusted the barrel-chested diver to carry on his search. In fifteen years, through countless hours on boats, they had joked, drunk, and shared life stories. Cussler described Wilbanks as "humorous, with a sly smile fixed beneath a Pancho Villa mustache." Wilbanks liked Cussler simply because he was eccentric, not some stuck-up rich guy.

Born in the tiny farm town of Clinton, South Carolina, Wilbanks moved to the Isle of Palms long before anyone thought of remodeling the Charleston barrier island as a gated resort. Like many of his generation, he fell in love with the old *Sea Hunt* television show and wanted to spend his days the same way, diving beneath the waves. But unlike most, he did something about it. In short order scuba diving became both Wilbanks's career and his hobby. He boasted that every week he sucked down eleven tanks of oxygen—five on Saturday, five on Sunday, and one on Wednesday night.

Wilbanks enjoyed an active career. He visited lost treasure ships and riverboats. He found beautifully preserved Spanish olive jars left by early explorers of South Carolina. And he found prehistoric shark teeth by the bagful in Charleston's Cooper River, left behind by leviathans from the dinosaur ages.

In the 1970s Wilbanks landed a job at the South Carolina Institute of Archaeology and Anthropology administering the state's Underwater Antiquities Act—the legal statute covering all artifacts found in its abundance of freshwater and salt water. That's how he met Cussler. By the early 1990s, several years after leaving his job at SCIAA, Wilbanks was a respected freelance diver and underwater archaeologist. He spent an ever-growing amount of his time working for Cussler and the National Underwater and Marine Agency (NUMA).

Wilbanks—with Hall as his copilot and magnetometer operator— would take *Diversity* out to search for the *Hunley* nearly two dozen times during the winter and spring of 1994–95. Most days neither man would ever get in the water. They'd simply run cornrow search patterns back and forth across the ocean surface, dragging their magnetometer and looking for anything registering big enough gamma numbers to indicate a *Hunley*-sized object below. It was like mowing the yard in the ocean.

Unbeknownst to SCIAA and Mark Newell, during one of their searches, Wilbanks and Hall dove on his "provocative" target 8 in Maffitt's Channel. They had gone back to the site unannounced two weeks after the 1994 expedition ended. Since Cussler was paying the bills, they figured he had a right to know what was there immediately. They dug up something rusty, nautical, and metallic. They weren't sure what it was, but it definitely was not the *Hunley*. They covered it up and left but never told Newell what they'd done or what they uncovered. If Newell wanted to blindly tell the world he'd found the submarine, Hall and Wilbanks were content to let him.

Now, on the morning of May 3, 1995, they had anchored over an anomaly in the deep ocean they prayed just might be the hiding place of the lost Confederate submarine. A few bottles of Corona beer had been iced down, just in case an early morning toast was warranted. They were ready to make history.

IT WASN'T THE *HUNLEY*.

Pecorelli had thrown on a single air tank and dove in by himself. When he reached the bottom, he immediately spotted something protruding from the flat seabed. Wilbanks's anomaly was rusty and mechanical, with a length of chain trailing from it. Junk. It was a ship's windlass—an anchor crank used during the early part of the twentieth century—not the Confederate torpedo boat. For Pecorelli it wasn't that big a setback. It was the first dive of the expedition, and he hadn't expected to find it so soon anyway. But Hall and Wilbanks had thought the target was a good bet, and their disappointment cast a pall over the group. It wasn't ten A.M., and they already seemed spent. They were no closer to finding the submarine than they had been months ago. They felt like setting course back to the Wild Dunes Marina.

But Cussler paid by the day—the full day—and Wilbanks felt guilty enough taking his money; he wasn't about to cheat the man. They would keep looking. As they passed around pickled okra, they tried to devise a new plan. Wilbanks began to quiz Pecorelli, who had been on Newell's boat during the 1994 expedition. He wanted to know how carefully they had probed all the targets the NUMA boat had buoyed.

Not very, Pecorelli said. Most of the sites were probed but not opened for fear of introducing oxygen into them—air being the lighter fluid that fueled corrosion. Wilbanks, having nothing better to do, decided to wipe a bunch of question marks off his chart. They would explore every one of Cussler's targets.

"Dammit, if they are not the *Hunley*, let's put them on the map for what they are," Wilbanks said.

Wilbanks turned on *Diversity*'s mapping computer and scanned through the list of targets. He decided they would probe them all until they could say for sure exactly what they were. If it was a bunch of ballast, or just sea junk, he wanted a label for it. He looked at the dozen or so targets and pointed at target 1. It was kind of out there by itself, farther out to sea than the other sites. They would start there and work their way in.

"Let's go find out what it is," he said.

PECORELLI HAD DIVED ON TARGET 1 THE PREVIOUS AU-gust. During the SCIAA expedition he had briefly poked around at the site with a diver's hand rod but wasn't able to touch what was buried there. A thick layer of oyster shells deposited nearly 2 feet into the sand strata had created a coat of armor over the top of it. Newell believed the site's magnetometer reading was too low to be the submarine, so the SCIAA team had abandoned the site, dismissing it based on a technical assumption.

Wilbanks steered *Diversity* to the site easily, relocating target 1 without difficulty. It was near the *Housatonic*, about 1,000 feet seaward of the old wreck. Most people would have passed over it. There was no reason to believe the *Hunley* would have gone out to sea after the attack, but Wilbanks had a feeling about it. He was curious. He wanted to know what it was, even if only to write it off for good.

When *Diversity* was over the spot, the men dropped the anchor line and hoisted the red-and-white flag that signaled a diver down. Pecorelli suited up, stepped to the gunwale, and pitched over the side, into the emerald water.

THE OYSTER SHELLS THAT HAD BLOCKED HIS WAY LAST summer were now gone, and Pecorelli found he could probe into the sandy bottom with ease. He started poking in the sand, working from a center point and moving in a circle, following normal underwater archaeology procedure. He pushed his stainless steel probe through the sand. In less than five minutes, he made contact with something.

Whatever it was, he soon deduced, it was at least 10 feet long and probably cylindrical. Beyond that Pecorelli couldn't tell what he had. He shot back to the surface for *Diversity*'s sand dredge—a 4-inch vacuum hose. He was going to clean out a hole and take a look.

Back on the bottom, where he'd marked his spot, Pecorelli began to work a cone-shaped hole about 3 feet wide over the target. He pushed the vacuum hose deeper, stirred it in an ever-growing circle to expose more. The work turned the water into a cyclone of silt. He was working nearly blind in the underwater storm. Soon he thought he glimpsed something metal peeking through the murk.

Pecorelli reached down and laid his hand on the find. It was corroded but fairly smooth, almost in immaculate shape. Whatever it was, Pecorelli made an educated guess, was in much too good a condition to have been down there a century. Maybe, he thought, it's an old pipe, discarded after the channel was dredged. He kicked back to the surface.

"I don't know what it is, but it's not the *Hunley*," he reported.

That's not what Wilbanks wanted to hear. He sent Pecorelli back down to figure out exactly what it was. The boat wasn't leaving until they knew for sure what they had. Meanwhile, Hall suited up to go down and give Pecorelli a hand.

SWAMP DIVERS AND RIVER EXPLORERS LEARN AN ART FORM that separates them from others of their kind. Spending hours underwater in dark muck, they learn to see with their hands, much as a blind person reads Braille. They decipher texture, measure width, and determine shape with their fingertips. The best among them can feel something in total darkness, pop back up to the surface, and report the size of their find to within a fraction of an inch.

Wes Hall was a master of the art.

Hall followed Pecorelli to the bottom, and together they began to

e *H. L. Hunley* breaks
e surface just after 8:30 A.M. on
ugust 8, 2000. The submarine was raised
om the Atlantic floor by the *Karlissa B*
ck-up crane. (Courtesy Friends of the *Hunley*)

Oceaneering engineers guide the *Hunley* onto its transport barge for the ride back into Charleston, 136 years after it departed on its final mission. An armada of boats watches nearby. (Courtesy Friends of the *Hunley*)

The *Hunley*'s twisted three-blade propeller is just as it was depicted in the Conrad Wise Chapman painting. Scientists were curious as to why half the propeller shroud was missing. (Courtesy Friends of the *Hunley*)

The *Hunley*'s bow is shaped like an Arctic icebreaker and comes to a knifelike edge, nothing like the blunt, boxy shape depicted in later drawings and replicas of the submarine. (Courtesy Friends of the *Hunley*)

Wes Hall, Ralph Wilbanks, and Harry Pecorelli III pose a few hours after finding the *Hunley* on May 3, 1995. (Photo by Phil Bazen/courtesy of NUMA)

Best-selling author and NUMA chairman Clive Cussler on lift day, August 8, 2000. (Photo by Carole Bartholomeaux/ courtesy of NUMA)

The interior of the *Hunley* just aft of the forward conning tower. The hand cranks for the propeller shaft are in the foreground and the wooden bench the men sat on is mounted along the portside wall. Note the exterior port dive plane at top. Braces hold unexcavated sediment in place beneath the bench. (Photo by Cramer Gallimore/ courtesy Friends of the *Hunley*)

Friends of the *Hunley* chairman Warren Lasch, *Hunley* Commission chairman Glenn McConnell, and commission member Adm. William L. Schachte Jr. at the *Hunley* lab on lift day. (Courtesy Friends of the *Hunley*)

Dr. Robert Neyland, project manager for the recovery and excavation of the *Hunley*, at the Warren Lasch Conservation Center. The *Hunley*'s preservation tank is in the background. (Photo by Schuyler Kropf)

Hunley senior conservator Paul Mardikian with the candle used to light the *Hunley*'s interior. Mardikian came to the project after working on artifacts recovered from the *Titanic* and the Confederate raider *Alabama*. (Photo by Schuyler Kropf)

Chief archaeologist Maria Jacobsen sits in the *Hunley* shortly after finding Lt. George E. Dixon's gold coin among his remains on May 23, 2001. The dive plane control lever Dixon used to set the submarine's depth is in front of her. (Courtesy Friends of the *Hunley*)

(Left) Dixon's good luck piece was an 1860 U.S. $20 gold coin that had deflected a Union bullet at Shiloh. The indention made by the bullet is visible just below the bun in Lady Liberty's hair. *(Right)* After the coin saved his life, Dixon had it engraved with the phrase "My life Preserver" along with the date he was wounded at the Battle of Shiloh. Legend told of the coin, but historians were unaware of the inscription the *Hunley* commander had added to it. (Courtesy Friends of the *Hunley*)

Among the crew's belongings found inside the *Hunley*, archaeologists recovered numerous buttons, including a Confederate artilleryman's jacket button and this rubber U.S. Navy coat button stamped "Goodyear" on the back. Scientists found a twelve-sided medicine bottle on the crew bench, several pairs of shoes, and pipes. The X ray shows the famous blue lamp Dixon used to signal the *Hunley*'s successful attack to Confederate troops on shore. (Courtesy Friends of the *Hunley*)

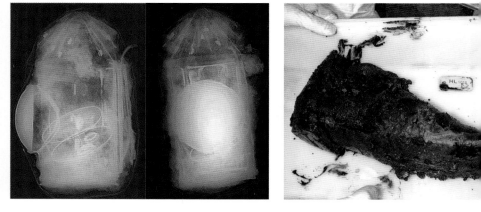

This dog tag from a Union soldier was perhaps the most surprising find in the *Hunley*. The medallion from Connecticut infantryman Ezra Chamberlin was found around the neck of one of the *Hunley* crewmen. No one knows how Chamberlin's identification found its way into the Confederate submarine. (Courtesy Friends of the *Hunley*)

work their dredge pit wider, rolling the hose in a concentric circle. After they had opened up the hole more, Hall dove down and began to *feel* his way around what they had exposed. Through the murk it looked like an iron pipe with a tree stump growing out of it. Hall touched the pipe in a few places, then reached out and hugged the stump.

Pecorelli watched Hall and wondered, Man, what is he doing?

FOR HALL, TAGGING ALONG ON WILBANKS'S *HUNLEY* SEARCHES was just good fun, even when he had to put up with the occasional outbursts of Wilbanks's famous temper. Hall had his own archaeological surveying company, but he still enjoyed working with his old friend. They'd been part-time partners for nearly twenty-five years, beginning when Hall arrived in Charleston as a young Marine. The two first paired up while diving in South Carolina's famous blackwater swamps. That's where the underwater archaeology bug bit the soft-spoken Hall. It was a different, fascinating world from the flat, endless Kansas farmland where he'd grown up.

After leaving the Marine Corps, Hall had picked up his archaeology degree at the University of Arkansas and then hightailed it back to the East Coast, where he studied under the tutelage of Gordon Watts, the man who led the investigation of the famous Civil War ironclad the USS *Monitor.* During the 1994 SCIAA/NUMA search for the *Hunley,* Hall had taken a backseat role. Hanging out with Wilbanks and Cussler was good work and good fun, but at the time Hall also felt he needed a career boost, something that would recharge his batteries. The politics of archaeology could be cutthroat, and Hall didn't like that part of it. He'd seen it when he was accused of stealing guns from a sunken blockade-runner off Wilmington, North Carolina. Hall carried a box of Enfield rifles ashore after some previous looter had left them behind near the wreck. A couple of days later, before he could get them to state officials, he was branded a thief. Although the charges of historical robbery against him were eventually dropped, the allegations left him soured.

He'd also seen the politics of high-stakes archaeology firsthand during the *Monitor* project, when the thin egos of the multiple academics involved clashed over how to preserve and study the decaying ironclad. Watching the *Hunley* search during the 1994 SCIAA dive, Hall saw the same sort of sparring. He was grateful the SCIAA crew was not along on this dive. They would have been just one more headache. He preferred to work in a smaller group, just as he was doing this day with Wilbanks and Pecorelli.

At first Hall suspected they'd found a ship's boiler, probably off the *Housatonic*. It could have easily been left behind during any one of the postwar salvages and dumped in the ocean, since it had no value in the aftermath of the Civil War. But as he hugged the stump, feeling his way completely around it, his hand landed on something odd sticking out of one side. It felt like a hinge. He was almost sure of it—he could see it with his hands. Hall was a calm man, but his mind nevertheless began to race. Boilers, he thought, don't have hinges.

He reached out and grabbed Pecorelli's arm and began to communicate in undersea sign language, clasping his hands like a clam, open then closed, just inches away from the other diver's mask. He was telling his partner what he'd found.

But Pecorelli watched, uncomprehending. What the hell is he doing? the younger man wondered. He pointed up, and they headed for the surface. Hall's mind worked quickly, and while he rose out of 27 feet of water, he came to a singular conclusion.

As he surfaced, he pulled the regulator out of his mouth, looked up at Wilbanks on the deck of *Diversity*, and calmly announced his find. Wes Hall identified target 1 as the lost Confederate submarine, missing for 131 years.

"It's the *Hunley*. That's it. That's all it can be," he said, almost nonchalantly.

———

PECORELLI HAD OPENED A HOLE RIGHT ON TOP OF THE submarine's forward conning tower. If he had dug 3 feet in any other direction, he would have found only curved iron. Somehow, miraculously, he had landed on the *Hunley*'s most identifiable feature. In the water Pecorelli's heart pounded through his wet suit, but Wilbanks stood on the deck, oddly silent. As Hall and Pecorelli submerged and went back to work, the captain of the expedition felt oddly ambivalent. Once he took in what his crew had told him, Wilbanks's first thought was, *Oh, shit.*

SOON WILBANKS JOINED THE OTHER TWO ON THE BOTtom, the three of them working together to make the dredge hole larger. They worked like salivating gold miners who'd spotted their first glimpse of ore. The submarine was resting on its side, listing 45 degrees to starboard. Just aft of the conning tower, they found the submarine's breather box, which housed the two snorkel tubes used to draw in precious air for the crew. Working their way down the side of the hull, they found the portside diving plane. It was arched in an up position. An eerie thought came to them all: *they were trying to surface.* Its bow was pointed for Sullivan's Island, toward home.

The submarine itself was quite a sight. It was solid, covered with a thin layer of corrosion that seemed to protect it. Realizing the location of the submarine, the men immediately understood why the *Hunley* had been so elusive. It was about due east—seaward—of the *Housatonic* wreck. That simple fact alone explained why no one had found it before. Everyone else had been looking between the *Housatonic* and shore, assuming the men had gone down on their way back. They would have had no reason to go farther out to sea. Perhaps the sub had drifted out with the tide as it sank slowly, or maybe Dixon had lost his bearings—the compass didn't always work inside the iron hull of the *Hunley*. Whatever had happened, it effectively kept the *Hunley* hidden for more than a century. Cussler had been right: shipwrecks are never where they are supposed to be.

WHEN THEY TURNED THE DREDGE HOSE OFF, THE SILT BE-
gan to settle gently, falling like snowflakes on the ocean floor. As the
water cleared, the men had a better look at their find. On the forward
conning tower, they felt glass still in the portholes where Lt. George E.
Dixon would have peered out to spot the *Housatonic* at her anchorage.
They also found a hole in the front conning tower, a jagged perpen-
dicular tear the size of a grapefruit. They speculated it might have been
caused by small-arms fire from the crew of the *Housatonic.* Historical
accounts said the Yankees had fired on the *Hunley,* aiming at spots that
glowed yellow from its interior light.

The men worked for two hours, excitedly exposing parts of the
submarine and then covering it back up. Finally the weight of the moment hit them. Until then the *Hunley* had been Clive Cussler's
dream—a quest that had occupied a good part of their lives, but really
just another job. It had been an almost mythical beast they were chasing through the enchanted sea. And now they had it. It was no longer
an abstract artifact, a fanciful Holy Grail. Standing on top of the iron
torpedo boat from another time, the ocean swirling around them, each
independently began to think of the *Hunley* as something entirely different. There were men dead inside.

It was a tomb.

BACK ON BOARD *DIVERSITY,* WILBANKS DECIDED TO GET
out of there quickly. Anybody who spent time on the water around
Charleston knew his boat, and he didn't want visitors dropping by to
say hello—or ask questions. It was the beginning of the spring shrimp-
ing season, so the waters could be full of trawlers at any time. They had
covered the submarine back up and marked their spot. And then they
headed for the marina. Except for the occasional clinking of Corona
bottles, the return trip was silent.

The postdiscovery ride home was unlike anything Pecorelli expected. There was no dancing, no screaming, no high-fiving. On the
ride back it suddenly came to him that he'd dived on the *Hunley* during the 1994 NUMA/SCIAA expedition. The thought hit him like a

sucker punch to the gut. That was the oyster-bed site, the one he'd been pulled off of before he could penetrate the ocean floor. If he'd had just a little more time that day, Pecorelli might have found the *Hunley* eight months earlier. He pushed the thought out of his mind.

As it was, the mood on *Diversity* was more funereal than celebratory. Pecorelli could sense something in the body language of Wilbanks and Hall, but he wasn't sure what it was. Each of the older men knew that finding the *Hunley* created a whole new set of problems. From previous discoveries Wilbanks and Hall both knew that a war over ownership would begin as soon as the find was publicized. The United States government, scientists around the world, and armies of Confederate reenactors would stake a claim to the submarine. There were a half dozen people they knew alone who would want to raise the boat. It would be a mess. But there was no way around it. The genie was about to come stomping out of the bottle, and it would not go back in easily. In some ways finding the *Hunley* caused more problems than it solved.

BACK ON SHORE THE TENSE ATMOSPHERE DISSIPATED A bit. Without tipping their hand, the crew convinced someone to take a ceremonial picture of them together on the docks. Then Wilbanks tried to phone Cussler, but the author wasn't home. So Wilbanks sent his partners home to clean up. He was going to take them out for a steak dinner.

A few hours later they ended up at Breck's Place in North Charleston, where they dined over uncomfortable conversation, talking about anything except what each of them was thinking. They gave great orations on the weather, the restaurant's wallpaper, and cocktails from the bar. They had sworn a blood oath not to say anything. But Wilbanks's wife could tell something wasn't right. She badgered them to tell her what was going on, and when they wouldn't, she figured it out. "You guys found the *Hunley,* didn't you?"

LATER THAT NIGHT, WITH WARM ALCOHOL COURSING through their blood, they drove downtown to the Charleston Museum on Meeting Street, where a life-sized replica of the *Hunley*, built by college students in the 1960s, decorated the front lawn. It was around eleven P.M., and the streets were empty. They walked around the submarine, sizing up the model. They were the first men ever to be able to compare it to the real thing. It was the end of a long, emotionally and physically draining day, and they were almost giddy with fatigue.

Wilbanks studied the boxy model—slightly bigger than the real thing, with squarish hatch covers and bulging rivet heads—and began his critique.

"That's wrong, that's wrong, and that's wrong," he said excitedly. "And we're the only people on earth who know it!"

EARLY THE NEXT MORNING WILBANKS FINALLY REACHED Cussler. It was six A.M. at the author's home halfway across the country, and he wasn't happy to be answering the phone so early.

"Clive, we're going to send you the final invoice for the work we've done."

It struck Cussler wrong. They were giving up, he figured.

"What, you guys don't want to search anymore?" he baited.

Wilbanks had set him up perfectly.

"We don't need to," he said. "We found it."

It didn't sink in at first—Cussler was still groggy.

"Are you sure?"

"It's a done deal," Wilbanks said.

Thirty seconds after the call ended, Wilbanks's phone rang. It was Cussler. He wanted proof. He'd seen too many instances of people making claims and then being shot down for lack of documentation. He told Wilbanks to go back to the submarine again, this time with a video camera. He wanted the type of cast-iron evidence that Lee Spence, or anyone else, couldn't produce.

THREE DAYS LATER THE DIVERS MET EARLY ON BOARD *Diversity* and made for the site. It was a Sunday morning, and the water would soon be covered with recreational boats. They hoped no one would notice a few adventurous divers slipping over the side for a dip near the wreck of the *Housatonic*. And they hoped no one would spot the video camera. The film was for the media. It would document their find and go a long way toward establishing that all-important burden of proof. Later Wilbanks would be mystified when Cussler told him to have a dozen copies of the tape made. He didn't know how to make multiple copies. But Cussler said to find someone who could. When Wilbanks took the tape to a shop and asked for a bunch of clandestine copies, he nearly froze. The guy behind the counter, noticing Wilbanks's nervous demeanor, innocently said, "What have you got on here, the *Hunley*?"

While they filmed some of the submarine's most identifiable features, the divers took another step to ensure there would be no question about who had reached the *Hunley* first. The calling cards of the world's great explorers generally tend toward flags: Sir Edmund Hillary left one at the peak of Mount Everest; Neil Armstrong planted one on the moon. But that seemed a pretty generic gesture for someone of Cussler's personality and wit. The divers thought they could do better.

It was Hall who came up with the idea of using Wilbanks's constant habit of butchering Julius Caesar. After a good day's work, the captain would call it quits by mispronouncing, in his raspy southern twang, "*Wenni, weedee, winky,* dude!" to honor the ass-kicking they had done that day in the ocean. From the Latin it translated to "I came, I saw, I conquered." Most of the people who worked with them thought it was hilarious. Hall thought it perfect.

He scratched a note on a piece of NUMA stationery, then cut Cussler's signature off another letter and pasted it on. The three divers then added their business cards for posterity, so that history would record that it was they who had found the *Hunley*. The note was laminated and placed inside a watertight plastic box. When they dove back down to the site, Hall stuck the note deep inside the hole in the forward conning tower. Then they covered the lost fish-boat in the muck once again and left.

When the note was found a year later by a team of National Park Service divers sent to verify the claim, it read:

Today May 3, 1995, one hundred
thirty-one years and seventy-five days
after your sinking.

Veni, Vidi, Vici!,
Dude
Yours respectively,
Clive Cussler
Chairman, National Underwater & Marine Agency

WEEKS LATER, AFTER THEIR DISCOVERY WAS ANNOUNCED to the world, Hall, Pecorelli, and Wilbanks tried to hide from their newfound celebrity. They wanted all the limelight cast on Cussler, who had paid the bills and pushed the search onward. To them the *Hunley* pursuit was over. Now it was someone else's problem. But they couldn't escape it: Cussler insisted on giving the men credit, always introducing Pecorelli as the first man to touch the *Hunley* in the twentieth century.

Late one afternoon the trio got together once more to finally, privately celebrate their find. They piled into a single car and drove up Meeting Street away from downtown Charleston, packed with tourists for the annual Spoleto music festival. As they drove north, Meeting turned from main thoroughfare to a path through the industrial heart of the city leading to the old Navy base.

Off Meeting, on a narrow road, they came to the gates of Magnolia Cemetery. Wandering past the war memorials and hauntingly beautiful tombstones of Charleston's oldest families, they drove on a dirt path that meandered toward the graves on the outskirts of the property near the Cooper River.

They stopped the car and got out, carrying a bottle of Gosling's Black Seal Bermuda Black Rum and searched for the grave of Horace Lawson Hunley.

When they found the old captain's burial mound, they mixed a drink appropriately dubbed Dark 'n Stormy—a mix of Gosling's and Blenheim Ginger Ale dressed with a wedge of lime. It was the divers' favorite grog. Beneath the shadow of a giant live oak, the three men saluted one another and their find, peacefully recounting sea stories among the headstones. As they toasted the submarine once more, they each poured a little bit of their drinks into the earth at their feet, inviting Hunley to take a drink in honor of his long-lost submarine, its final resting place discovered at last.

Chapter 8

THE WAR
BETWEEN THE STATES

NEWS OF THE *HUNLEY*'S DISCOVERY SEEPED INTO THE AR-chaeology community within a week of the NUMA find, and when it did, Mark Newell was livid. He had been planning a June expedition to uncover the target he'd identified as the submarine in newspapers nearly five months earlier. Now he'd been beaten to the punch. He thought he'd had his claim jumped.

Newell marched through the halls of the South Carolina Institute of Archaeology and Anthropology in Columbia to the office of Chris Amer, the director of the agency's underwater projects. When Newell burst through the door, Amer noticed that his face was ashen and he was noticeably shaken.

"The worst possible thing has happened," Amer recalled Newell saying. "*They* found the *Hunley*."

Amer was dumbstruck. Who were *they*? And how could this be a bad thing? Wasn't finding the *Hunley* everybody's goal? The news of the historic discovery did not even sink in at first: he was trying to make sense of what he was hearing from Newell. Amer didn't understand because he had been out of the country during the 1994 expedition, so he had not witnessed the breakdown of trust between SCIAA and Clive Cussler's National Underwater and Marine Agency. He didn't know about the falling-out between Newell and Cussler. Now Amer was witnessing the beginning of the strife that Ralph Wilbanks and Wes Hall had feared from the moment they first realized what they'd found.

Newell told Amer about the call he'd just taken. *The New York Times* had phoned about the *Hunley* and Cussler's press conference in Charleston, scheduled for May 11. The *Times* and *The Post and Courier* would carry advance stories on the day of the press conference. The call had caught Newell cold, like a death in the family. He realized the lost submarine had been found without him. He'd dreamed of finding the *Hunley* for so long. Now it had been located, and it was a nightmare. Newell imagined that Cussler's divers had reneged on the joint agreement to find the submarine together. He decided the only way to get the answers was to confront the one man he felt owed him an explanation: Cussler. Newell set a course for Charleston and the press conference he felt should have been his.

NEWELL FOUND CUSSLER AND HIS DIVE TEAM IN A HOLIday Inn in Mount Pleasant, an upper-middle-class bedroom community across the Cooper River from downtown Charleston. Mount Pleasant was where the submarine had sat in dry dock when Conrad Wise Chapman painted the scene that had captured Cussler's imagination as a child. Cussler, Wilbanks, Hall, and Pecorelli were in a festive mood, partying in the tight confines of the hotel room until it was time to make their announcement. "His Authorship," as Hall called Cussler, could barely contain himself. He'd made big finds before, but none as special to him as the *Hunley*.

It was during this celebration that Newell arrived, and the divers felt the tension go off the scale. They played Newell the tape they would show at the press conference, a grainy film that clearly showed the submarine's front conning tower and hatch cover. Newell had a very short critique of the film.

"Provocative."

The comment sent Wilbanks's famous temper fuming. It was a word that he and Cussler remembered Newell saying often, and he didn't like the implication.

"Provocative?" he growled. "That's the *Hunley* and we found it."

On May 11, 1995, Cussler met the press in front of the iron replica of the *Hunley* outside the Charleston Museum. He played the tape and graciously answered questions about the fantastic discovery. The assembled media ate it up. Cussler knew what they wanted to hear and told great stories. In reporters' parlance Cussler gave good quote.

"This is without a doubt the greatest underwater find since the *Monitor* was located," he said.

To throw off treasure hunters, Cussler was vague about the *Hunley*'s location. He said it was "far" from the *Housatonic* wreck and was lying in only 18 feet of water. He just shrugged when reporters asked him why it sank.

"I think they paddled like hell and just didn't make it. The snorkel was up, so they were trying to get air in."

Lee Spence showed up to congratulate the author on the find, all the while claiming that he had found it first. He conceded, however, that if the submarine was in 18 feet of water, he probably was wrong. His discovery had been in water closer to 30 feet deep. Cussler dismissed Spence's claim. "If Lee could have come up with some proof, he would have the *Hunley*. Unless I can prove that I went to the moon, what good is it?"

Officials with SCIAA attended Cussler's press conference, too, and asked for the coordinates to the submarine. Cussler refused. He was fed up with the agency, which had issued threats to have his divers arrested for allegedly searching without permission. SCIAA had even suggested to Cussler that they put a buoy on the site. The novelist thought that insane: it would be flagging the helpless, unguarded submarine for every treasure hunter in the world. Cussler, a man not used to being pushed around, dug in quickly. He vowed to give the coordinates only to the submarine's rightful owners—whoever that might be. Cussler was becoming increasingly wary of the South Carolina archaeologists, especially Newell. He told reporters flat out that, for the time being, the submarine would stay lost to the rest of the world.

"I didn't spend fifteen years looking for it only to have it broken up by amateurs. Until I see a comprehensive plan put together by qualified people, they won't get any cooperation from me."

Cussler had drawn his line in the sand.

ON THE DAY THE *HUNLEY*'S DISCOVERY WAS OFFICIALLY announced, South Carolina state senator Glenn McConnell was 100 miles away at the capitol in Columbia. The General Assembly was in its final month of meetings, when most of the state's business gets done—and all sorts of other suspect legislation slips through the cracks in the massively clunky system. It is a busy time, a time when it behooves politicians to pay attention.

But as someone droned on at the podium or the clerk read messages from the House of Representatives across the rotunda, McConnell, a Charleston native, sat behind his handsome desk on the Senate floor, oblivious to the noise in the ornate chamber. He was enthralled by a small story from his hometown paper, *The Post and Courier*: "Submarine *Hunley* Found off Coast, Explorer Says." He could not believe it. McConnell remembered visiting the Hunley Museum in downtown Charleston as a child, when the iron model was kept in a dark little room with dusty mannequins sitting along its crankshaft. It was an eerie sight, but one that had captured his imagination.

The submarine had a lot more significance for McConnell in 1995 than it had had when he was a kid. In the last ten years, he had gone from being just another of the state's rising young star lawmakers to one of its leading champions of heritage issues. He had fought to bring home the remains of a forgotten South Carolina Confederate found by developers in Virginia and had become a darling of the Sons of Confederate Veterans. The men of that heritage group sparked an interest in McConnell that had lain dormant most of his life. When the history bug bit, it bit hard. McConnell eventually quit his law practice to take over an art gallery that peddled romanticized images of the war and the Old South. Now he was acknowledged as one of the staunchest defenders of the Confederate battle flag flying atop the capitol dome— put there during festivities marking the centennial of the War Between the States. The flag was just another in a long line of targets of the political correctness movement, McConnell thought. Now the *Hunley* had been found at the apex of that movement. He feared for the future of the submarine and the men who were entombed inside it.

McConnell leaned over and showed the article to another Charleston senator, Ernie Passailaigue. We've got to claim this for the state, McConnell told his colleague. Passailaigue agreed. They quickly decided to do what they were best qualified to do: pass a law.

McConnell read the article again. He was strangely drawn to it; he couldn't put it down or stop thinking about it. It was funny, he thought, but it was as if a bell were going off in his head. As if the *Hunley* were out there, waiting for him to come and get it.

When the *Hunley* was found, Glenn McConnell was in a unique position to protect it and make sure that, if it could be recovered, it would return to Charleston—its final departure point. It would not be an easy task: there would be a fight for control and for the money it would cost to salvage the lost submarine. But McConnell had a better chance of success than anyone else in the state. He knew how to work the system—and that's exactly what kind of person it would take. Because the *Hunley* was now lost in a tangle of red tape.

When Clive Cussler announced that the *Hunley* had been discovered, bureaucrats and politicians began a mad scramble to claim it. Technically, under the rules of war, the lost submarine was war booty; the United States government owned all Confederate vessels. South Carolina, however, considered it abandoned property in its territorial waters. And Alabama believed the submarine should be returned to the town of its birth. In short order all hell broke loose. In the summer of 1995, just a month after it had been found sitting on the continental shelf off Sullivan's Island, the *Hunley* sparked another war between the states.

As is its custom, South Carolina fired first. McConnell and Passailaigue rushed through a resolution asking Congress to give title of the *Hunley* to the state. In Washington, Congressman Mark Sanford of Charleston filed legislation to do just that. He barely got his bill registered before the Alabama delegation staked the same claim for their state.

In Mobile people were frenzied over the news. Perhaps even more than Charleston, the coastal Alabama town where Horace Hunley and James McClintock built two submarines had kept the history of the fish-boat alive. Newspaper polls gauged strong support, and the director of the city's museum offered the *Hunley* a warm, happy home. The local congressman, "Sonny" Callahan—who shared his first two initials, "H. L.," with Hunley—said that Mobile should have a fair chance at the submarine.

The wrangling went on for months, with Charleston and Mobile taking potshots at each other in the press. One man from Mobile argued that the submarine should be shared between the two historic old cities. It could be kept on a railcar and moved back and forth every six months—just as it had been moved from one town to the other during the war. But that solution ignored the truth of civics: politicians don't like to share.

The problem with all of Alabama's and South Carolina's posturing was that neither had the upper hand—the Navy did. The General Services Administration legally owned the submarine and could do whatever it wanted with the wreck. The southern politicians were worried because there were rumors that the artifact-hogging Smithsonian Institution had its eye on the world's first successful attack submarine.

By June of that year, McConnell was ensconced as chairman of the

Hunley Commission, a state agency charged with the responsibility of the submarine. In the final weeks of the 1995 General Assembly, McConnell and Passailaigue had strong-armed through a bill creating the body. And then, leading an army of lawyers, they went to Washington to straighten the mess out.

The first meeting with Navy officials did not go well. The sit-down was scheduled to take place in U.S. senator Strom Thurmond's office. Thurmond, the longest-serving senator in history, was still, in his early nineties, a fiery presence on Capitol Hill. The former governor, presidential candidate, and Dixiecrat once had petitioned the Navy to name a nuclear submarine after Horace Hunley. He got a sub tender instead. The old man was not used to waiting, which is what the Navy made him do. The officers supposed to be in the meeting had another dilemma on their hands and arrived nearly forty-five minutes late. Thurmond would hear none of their excuses, berating them in the outer office of his suite. Very little was accomplished at the meeting, except that South Carolina pulled a rabbit out of its hat. The federal government was proceeding on the assumption that the *Hunley* was the spoils of war, a Confederate ship. After all, many people called it the "CSS"—Confederate States Submarine—*Hunley*. In truth, though, it was no such thing. The *Hunley* was built to be a privateer. Although never officially recognized as such, it was only briefly seized by the Confederate Army and then returned to its owner, Hunley. From there the submarine operated in something of a vacuum, only partly directed by military officials. For proof South Carolina lawyers produced papers from the estate of Henry Leovy, a partner of Hunley's from New Orleans. Documents from Leovy's estate showed that he had inherited Hunley's one-third ownership of the submarine. It was, the South Carolina contingent argued, private property abandoned a lot longer than the year-and-a-day provision of state law, giving them the rights to it.

Their other argument was even more inventive. Federal jurisdiction extends 3 miles into the ocean, and the U.S. government can claim anything inside that zone as its own. Beyond that the water is considered international territory. The *Hunley* was nearly 4 miles out, just over that invisible line. The South Carolina lawyers representing the *Hunley* Commission argued that the state's property extended to the seaward end of the harbor jetties, which stretch miles into the ocean, and the *Hunley* was within 2 miles of those rock walls. Therefore, the submarine was out of federal reach, but well within the legal borders of the state of South Carolina. In a town known for slick politics, it was an admirable maneuver. But as the men from the Palmetto State knew, one battle didn't win the war. They left the capital still at a stalemate.

THE TROUBLE WITH THE NEGOTIATIONS BETWEEN THE states and the federal government was that they were trying to secure title to something they could not find. Cussler had been ready to turn over the coordinates the day he made the announcement. Trouble was, he didn't see anyone he trusted. Newell, he thought, was unqualified as an archaeologist, and the state's early ideas for salvaging the *Hunley* were sketchy at best. He decided to hold back his numbers.

Archaeologists at SCIAA continued to search for the *Hunley* out of fear Cussler would never turn over the coordinates. The author had the agency over a barrel. He told SCIAA officials he would give them the numbers only when he saw their plans for the *Hunley*. About this he was adamant. He trusted no one with his greatest find. The state archaeologists suspected Cussler might never be satisfied, so they continued to look. In South Carolina the author was practically vilified. Newell claimed his "competent research was preempted by a glory-hunting millionaire." In one report SCIAA said that Cussler's "unwillingness to release the coordinates of the alleged site to the legal agency with whom he had agreed to work is the primary obstacle to the project." And it got worse still. Friends of Newell announced a Cussler book burning in North Augusta to protest the author's bullheadedness.

Newell eventually quit SCIAA in disgust. The submarine, he kept wrongly insisting, was in Maffitt's Channel. Twenty-three years' worth of research points to that site, he contended. "If I'm proven wrong," he said, "I'm proven wrong."

Cussler was dumbfounded by the wild claims hurled at him from the carnival atmosphere of South Carolina. Did these people think he wanted to stick the submarine out in his front yard? Newell, he said, had contributed little to his research—just a letter about Charleston tides in 1864. In September of that year, after being cussed for months, the author responded with a letter published in *The Post and Courier*.

"I've been accused of ransoming the sovereign state of South Carolina, the Sons of Confederate Veterans wanted to burn my books and I was charged with desecrating the tomb of our glorified dead," he wrote. "If that's the cost of saving the *Hunley* for future generations of Americans then, by gosh, it's worth it."

By then a frustrated *Hunley* Commission and SCIAA had contacted Lee Spence. Spence had spent the entire summer studying the situation, and something didn't add up. There was one thing about the Cussler story that didn't make sense to him: the depth of water where the *Hunley* allegedly rested. He was sure he'd found the submarine in deeper water, and despite Cussler's claims, the Coast Guard's no-anchor protection zone was farther out to sea than most areas off the coast with water that depth. When Cussler later admitted he'd thrown out the number to mislead looters, Spence took the admission for more than it was. Spence figured that the author's divers had found the submarine using a map he'd published in a book in early 1995. He decided to ask the *Hunley* Commission to credit him with the submarine's discovery.

Even though the commission at one of its first meetings asked Spence if he would relinquish his claim to the state—which he readily did—there was little chance it would name him the *Hunley*'s discoverer. But the treasure hunter had one final chance. Since Cussler had not turned over the coordinates, state officials asked Spence to lead them to his site. If he could take them to the submarine, he might prove he'd found it, and the state would have its numbers, with Cussler or without. Spence was ecstatic, in his mind certain he could lead them to the *Hunley*. Before that expedition was launched, however, Cussler gave the submarine's coordinates to the Naval Historical Center in Washington. It was November 9, 1995—six months after the discovery—and a deal was in the works. The story was that Strom Thurmond, approached by

Navy brass about some other defense project, had slyly told them he couldn't even start to think about other concerns until the *Hunley* was safe. The tale would grow to legendary proportions, just one more thing the old man had pulled off in his long tenure. Whether the story was true or not, a deal soon was reached. The U.S. government kept title to the *Hunley*, but the submarine would stay in South Carolina—in Charleston—forever. The *Hunley* Commission had power over how it was displayed, a concern for McConnell, who had seen political correctness transform the *Enola Gay* exhibit into a monument that vilified the use of the atomic bomb by the United States. He would not allow the *Hunley*'s crew to be portrayed as the bad guys.

Then, with a deal struck and an *X* on the map, the *Hunley* Commission joined with SCIAA, the National Park Service, and the Naval Historical Center to find out if the numbers they had would lead them to the lost fish-boat. At last.

ONE YEAR AFTER DISCOVERING THE *HUNLEY*'S GRAVE, Ralph Wilbanks returned to the site on *Diversity*. On board he carried a PVC pipe to mark the site where he claimed to have found the famous lost submarine. It was the first step in a new expedition to verify that what Cussler's team had found was, in fact, the *H. L. Hunley*.

Wilbanks found it easily, quickly, staked his plastic pipe in the sandy bottom, and sent out an army of divers from the National Park Service, the Naval Historical Center, and the South Carolina Institute of Archaeology and Anthropology. During magnetometer scans of the area a few days earlier, the oversized team of scientists and divers had struck something they thought was the *Hunley*. The problem was, it was more than 120 feet from the coordinates Cussler had turned over to the Navy. Before they even got started, they were stumped. They called Wilbanks back, and he soon realized the team was using a different global positioning system than he had. Once the two mapping systems were reconciled, the two sets of coordinates differed by 3 feet.

The early dives did not go well. On the first day of the expedition, no one could find Wilbanks's pipe. The water was especially murky off

South Carolina, where the ocean is clouded by decaying marsh grass and a rushing influx of freshwater from four rivers stirring up the silt on the bottom. On the second day the divers found the pipe—but couldn't see anything beyond it. Over the next week dozens of underwater archaeologists took turns splashing around in the Atlantic, blindly following ropes to the bottom and fighting off jellyfish. Even wearing ice-diving masks was not enough—jellyfish would wrap their tentacles around the divers' regulators, stinging their lips. It was an unpleasant working environment.

To satisfy themselves that the iron hulk buried in the sand was indeed the *Hunley*, the archaeologists needed to identify five distinguishing characteristics of the submarine as recounted in historical drawings and accounts. They didn't have much to work with, as many of those accounts were contradictory. But without five traits, they would not feel comfortable declaring the *Hunley* found. In science there is no room for mistakes. Smaller errors than misidentifying a major lost vessel had cost careers.

This team of explorers was as lucky as the last. The first excavation took the divers down on top of the submarine's front conning tower and snorkel box—exactly the spot on which Harry Pecorelli and Wes Hall had landed a year earlier. Soon divers began exposing more of the hulk. Using metal detectors, they figured out the orientation of the object hidden below the sand. Two teams went to work uncovering it— one at each end.

Among the divers feeling their way along the ocean floor was an underwater archaeologist named Bob Neyland. Neyland only recently had joined the Naval Historical Center staff and brought to the federal government an impressive résumé. A product of the Texas A&M Nautical Archaeology Program, he'd led expeditions around the world. Neyland was all business, and he was cautious. Like the best scientists, he didn't make statements he couldn't back up. At the time he found himself swimming blindly off Sullivan's Island, Neyland knew little about the *Hunley*. He'd been briefed on it when he took the job at the Naval Historical Center, and that was really his first extensive history lesson on the subject. It interested him, but no more than any other project. At the time it seemed to him just another dive.

What struck Neyland at first about the site was the blinding water. On most days the divers officially recorded visibility as zero or maybe a foot. Never in offshore diving had he experienced so little visibility. Once he even got turned around and went to the wrong end of a guideline, where he stayed for several minutes waiting on other divers to join him. It was just impossible to see. Several times Neyland ran his hands along the crusty iron hull the dive team was studying, but he never could actually see it. It just felt like iron to him. He couldn't tell what it was.

Once during the expedition Neyland dove on the wreck of the *Housatonic*, a dangerous place in the best conditions. Since it had been lowered beneath the seabed with dynamite several times, divers had to burrow 8 feet down in the sand before landing on the old sloop. There was always the fear that divers in that situation could dig themselves into a cave that would collapse on them. None of them—including Neyland—liked to think about that. They simply wanted to guard against it.

BY MAY 10, AFTER NEARLY THIRTY-TWO HOURS OF TIME on the bottom, the team had uncovered what they thought were four identifiable attributes of the *Hunley*: the forward hatch, the snorkel box, the cutwater mounted forward of the front conning tower, and the portside dive plane. To be sure, to officially announce to the world that the *Hunley* had been located, they needed one more feature: the aft hatch. But they would have to wait a week.

On May 11, 1996, unseasonably bad weather descended on the Atlantic Ocean off Sullivan's Island. The storms kept the divers out of the water—even off the boats—for five days. By the time they got back to the site of their alleged *Hunley*, the sand had shifted, and they had to start digging all over. Again, one team started at the forward end of the object, the other team at the after end.

At the end of the second day back, May 17, the after team uncovered the rear hatch of the *H. L. Hunley*. The scientists, harder than anyone on earth to convince of anything, said it was unquestionable. The grave of the *Hunley*, missing in action for 132 years now, had been found.

On Saturday, May 18, 1996, *The Post and Courier* announced the news under a screaming headline: IT's OFFICIAL!

Afterward Larry Murphy, one of the Park Service divers, joked, "Now we can quit calling it 'the object.' "

DIVERS SPENT THE NEXT TWO WEEKS MAPPING AND MEAsuring the submarine, locating various other surprises, including five rows of deadlights—or topside portholes—in the hull to let in light. Divers with sensitive cameras gave the modern world its first good look at the *Hunley*. A series of photographs portrayed fuzzy shapes that barely stood out in the murk. One looked like a garbage can with a rounded lid, a doughnut stuck to its side. That was the aft conning tower, with an encrusted porthole on its flank. Other photos showed the snorkel box, with nubs where long tubes used to be attached. In all, it was an eerie sight, reminiscent of the first images of the *Titanic*, found a decade earlier.

The divers were trying to dig out as many details as they could about the submarine but at the same time treat it gingerly. They were worried about damaging the potentially fragile time capsule. Save for one hole in the forward conning tower, where they discovered the Cussler note from the year before, the hull appeared to be intact. But then, they didn't risk uncovering too much of it. One dive team had found metal shards near the stern of the ship, so they quit digging for the propeller. Until the *Hunley* was ready to be raised, they wanted to leave the fragile machinery covered, insulated against corrosion. Divers looked for the spar, even scanned the seabed ahead of the sub's bow, but picked up no sign of the mysterious torpedo delivery system. It would remain a mystery. They uncovered only about half the submarine, enough to tell it was listing to starboard at a 45-degree angle. They found the expansion plate William Alexander had written about running the length of the hull about halfway down and keel ballast attached to the bottom. With a few strategic excavations, the divers verified that the *Hunley* was mostly intact. They were beginning to get the idea that the *Hunley* was a bit more complex piece of machinery than they had originally thought. They found a vertical seam, which seemed at odds with the old notions that this submarine was merely a converted boiler.

The 1996 expedition did solve one mystery: it put to rest questions about the *Hunley*'s dimensions. For a century everyone from Beauregard to Alexander had thrown out varying estimates of the fish-boat's length—everywhere from 20 to 40 feet—and at the time of the dive, no one had any idea who was right. After they cleared away the top layer of sediment, archaeologists measured the *Hunley*'s hull from the upper tip of the bow to the aftmost point on the upper hull and came up with a length of 39 feet, 5 inches. While the length was impressively on the high end of the scale, the submarine's other dimensions were horrifyingly small. At its widest point the cylindrical *Hunley* had a beam of only 42 inches—3½ feet. It was only 4 feet, 3 inches tall. The size of the hatches most clearly illustrated the size restriction to *Hunley* crew members—less than 2 feet long, only 1 foot, 3 inches wide. It was, even for nineteenth-century men, a tight squeeze. The crew sat in a space bookended by the conning towers, which were 16 feet apart. There was no room to spare in the fish-boat's cramped crew compartment. It was a small, uncomfortable place to die.

THE *HUNLEY*'S LOCATION WAS A CLOSELY GUARDED STATE secret. The dive team would anchor a decoy boat away from the site to distract any nosy boaters, and everyone involved still insisted the submarine rested in 18 feet of water to lead any would-be treasure hunter miles off course. They tried to put a plastic honeycomb webbing over the hull, but it kept floating off. Eventually the divers just hauled down sandbags to cover the submarine, then backfilled sand over the top like a dog hiding a bone.

The scientists reported the findings of the expeditions to the young *Hunley* Commission months later. The politicians and reenactors on that body listened as the archaeologists recommended the submarine be raised and moved to a safe location for excavation. But before anyone touches it, they warned, there should be a plan in place. Other wrecks hauled up from the deep have been left on the dock to rot, which they begin to do immediately.

The *Hunley*, they said, also should be guarded aggressively. Vandals and salvage experts would loot the site if they could find it. A camera from the Sullivan's Island Lighthouse, they said, could keep a lookout for pirates.

Whatever the commission decided to do with the *Hunley*, the scientists opined, they'd better do it fast. Just digging up enough of the submarine to verify its identity had let destructive oxygen in to attack the hull. Underwater the *Hunley* could keep its stability for some time—but not forever. By January of 2001, the archaeologists reasoned, the fish-boat would be far enough down the long road of deterioration that the damage might be irreparable.

The clock was ticking on the *Hunley*.

Chapter 9

THE BONEYARD

THE VOICE CALLED OUT TO RANDY BURBAGE. THERE was no escaping it. Inside his head it pleaded to him, "Don't leave me here. Don't leave me here."

The voice kept calling.

Burbage peered down into the grave, hidden for decades beneath a layer of twentieth-century concrete, and the sight brought a tear to his eye. Deep in the tan soil, the purple outline of a rotted coffin marked the remains of a long-forgotten Confederate sailor. The bones bore the marks of hacksaws, a sign that Burbage had finally completed a sixteen-year quest: he had found the lost Seaman's Burial Ground, and in it he had found the remains of the *Hunley*'s first crew.

The solemnity of the moment rushing through him, Charleston's best-known Civil War reenactor and promoter of southern heritage gathered the archaeologists and volunteers—many of them fellow reenactors—around the gravesite. Holding hands against a backdrop of Confederate flags, the group began to sing, in hushed tones, the first strains of the southern anthem "Dixie." In the concrete acoustics of the room where they had made their discovery, the song sounded as if it were being sung in a cathedral.

In June 1999, with state officials and leaders of the newly formed Friends of the *Hunley* deep into planning the recovery of the long-lost Confederate submarine, the only missing piece of the fish-boat's history was the final resting place of its first crew. The *Hunley* had gone down off the wharf at Fort Johnson in August 1863, just two weeks after it arrived in Charleston. In that accident five men drowned. History recorded them buried, but for a century, no one knew where. As Burbage led the group singing "Dixie," it marked the ending of a mystery that had lingered for years. These fiercely loyal southerners had unearthed the largest desecration of Confederate graves in South Carolina history. And what was worse, the deception and destruction had been carried out in the name of the South's other great love: college football.

For Burbage the quest had begun on a spring day in 1983. Dressed in the uniform of a Confederate soldier, he had a lot on his mind that breezy May morning. South Carolina's Confederate Memorial Day had been erased from the calendar, and a small platoon had followed him into Magnolia Cemetery that day, trying to bring it back. In the New South, it seemed to Burbage, not enough people cared about a war then 120 years behind them or the men it had claimed. Burbage, more than anything else, wanted to change that.

As he stood in the historic cemetery, he caught sight of an aged, nondescript marble pillar jutting out of a field of headstones. For reasons he couldn't really explain, Burbage began to walk toward it. The 5-foot-tall marker commanded his attention. It looked out of place, he thought, almost haphazardly orphaned in a line of geometrically aligned military tombstones. He walked up to the post, touched it with callused fingertips, and began tracing some of the thirty-six names etched into it. They were mostly Confederate sailors and marines who had died in various field hospitals set up in wartime Charleston.

"Bell, J., Georgia Naval Hospital; Carthageen, Lewis, Florida Naval Hospital; Caswell, J., North Carolina Naval Hospital"; and so on. Burbage studied the names and quickly came to an undeniable conclusion: none of the men on the tablet were buried anywhere within the square-mile confines of Magnolia Cemetery. Of that he was sure. Burbage had walked every inch of the walled graveyard; he knew where practically every individual Rebel soldier rested. It made no sense. So he decided to do some research.

STOCKY AND MUSTACHIOED, BURBAGE REPRESENTED THE heart and soul of Charleston's reenactment community. Almost every call to arms was coordinated through Burbage's kitchen telephone. He stood out as a leader among the troops. On the field he wore the tattered uniform of a captain in the Tenth South Carolina Infantry. Unlike the light gray wool worn by most officers in the Confederacy, Burbage's uniform was faded nearly black—"Richmond gray," he called it—a remnant of the only European materials left in the South near war's end. Every piece of his battle dress was dedicated to total period accuracy right down to weathered brass buttons, muddy leather shoes, and sweat-stretched kepi cap. Anything less would be an insult to the men Burbage honored with the most reverential respect.

Burbage had fallen in love with the southern history of the War Between the States as a child. When springtime allergies kept him inside, he spent hours poring through books that depicted men in romantic gray military garb, fighting for Southern independence in places with exotic names such as Chickamauga, Manassas, and Shiloh. As with many in his generation, the attachment to those few years of history stuck with him. After college he sleuthed through his family history and found a clue to why it meant so much to him. He was related to twenty members of a single, sixty-man cavalry unit from nearby Summerville, South Carolina.

Burbage's enthusiasm for honoring the fallen war dead was infectious, and by the time he discovered the missing graves, he had no shortage of friends to help him research the burial patterns of the Confederate military. The men spent weekends scouring potter's fields and vacant lots, wooded tracts and old battle sites—anywhere that might hide a lost or overgrown Confederate cemetery. Eventually Burbage and his troops found the first clues to solving the mystery not in the field but in a forest of paperwork. Cemetery records indicated that the stone marker had been moved to Magnolia around midcentury. Among the documents, Burbage was further intrigued by one passing reference to four unnamed "Men of the Torpedo Boat" interred with the marines and sailors commemorated by the marker. He vowed to find them, no matter how long it took.

THE CITADEL BULLDOGS HAVE BEEN PLAYING THEIR brand of smash-mouth football at Johnson Hagood Stadium since 1948. Dubbed the "Boneyard," the small, twenty-one-thousand-seat stadium named for a Confederate brigadier general is a short march away from the historic Charleston military college on the banks of the Ashley River. Thousands of fans gather on the stadium's asphalt parking lot on fall Saturdays to watch the corps of cadets march by before kickoff. When an opposing team is beaten, its name is painted on the west end-zone wall—another bone for the Citadel's mascot, Spike the Bulldog. After hours of research Randy Burbage came to the conclusion that, when cadets called the football stadium hallowed ground, they had no idea how right they were.

No one was sure whether the decision to build a football stadium on top of a Civil War graveyard was a bureaucratic mix-up or twentieth-century callousness. All that is certain is that in 1947 the Charleston City Council decided the cemetery was in the way of progress. Early designs for the Citadel stadium that didn't encroach on the cemetery were not working. Eventually it was decided to move the remains. What happened next remains a mystery. It might have been an innocent clerical error, a memo that gave approval for the "transfer of tombstones in the

sion members had been uneasy. There were rumors that already pirates planned to steal the *Hunley*'s hatch covers and rudder: they would easily bring $100,000 or more on the lucrative collectibles black market. It was a thought that made the men shudder. A camera mounted atop the Sullivan's Island Lighthouse kept surveillance on the water in the direction of the submarine, and divers had buried the *Hunley* after their last inspection of it. Still, it wasn't completely safe. The no-anchor protection zone around the wreckage only put an *X* on every nautical chart in the world. And all the *Hunley* Commission's talk of sensors on the submarine's hull was just that—talk. There was no cage built over it, either—another fib perpetuated by local officials. The Coast Guard monitored the *Hunley* camera, but there was no guarantee that rescue boats could make it to the site before some pirate plundered the defenseless submarine. For two years McConnell had dreaded the day someone might try to call his bluff because, in truth, the *Hunley* was vulnerable.

At the same time there was a growing anxiety over the salvage. Even though hard-hat divers had retrieved the *Hunley* from the bottom of Charleston Harbor twice, modern archaeologists did not have a great track record with submarines. Until then the most famous recovery had come in 1982, when a Royal Navy minesweeper 4 miles off the southern coast of England snagged something during a training cruise. It had caught a pickle-shaped, diesel-powered submarine that, in its day, was known as the *Holland 1*.

The Holland-class submarines were the evolutionary link between the *Hunley* and the U-boats that prowled the North Atlantic during World War I. The submarine's designer, John Philip Holland, was an Irishman who had immigrated to the United States in the 1870s, where he began his lifework—trying to build a working submarine. Initially his funding came from Irish-Americans who dreamed that submarines might one day be used to destroy the Royal Navy and allow Ireland to gain its independence. That idea soon faded.

As the nineteenth century passed, Holland found himself competing with Simon Lake for the honor of building the U.S. Navy's first official submarine. In 1900 Holland's design was adopted. Despite its skepticism, the Royal Navy didn't want to fall behind. It began building its own Holland fleet.

The submarines were military marvels. Sixty feet long, they carried nine crewmen, two torpedoes, and three white mice. The mice were important members of the crew. If gas fumes inside the submarine reached poisonous levels, the mice would die first—a warning to the humans to surface for fresh air.

No Holland submarine ever saw combat; as technology improved, the Hollands quickly became obsolete. In 1913 the *Holland 1* was being towed to the scrap yard when it sank in a heavy storm. For seventy years it was mostly forgotten. After it was found, scientists wasted no time getting a peek at the antique submarine. The same year it was discovered, they raised the *Holland 1*, using powerful balloons. Archaeologists were amazed at the condition of their catch: the frigid, 100-foot-deep waters had kept oxygen levels at a minimum. As one of her rescuers said, she looked perfect. That, unfortunately, would not last.

So it could be hauled into port more easily, the British submarine was cut into three pieces, in itself a sin against archaeology. On land the submarine was reassembled, given a freshwater bath, and had its barnacles scrubbed off. Soon workers slapped a coat of paint on it, and the *Holland 1* was put on display in the seaside town of Portsmouth. People were even allowed to walk around inside the hull. Out in the open it was exposed to the elements, and soon the salt air began to chew on it.

By the early 1990s cancerous rust had begun to eat the submarine from the inside out. Its hull was breaking down. That was because the *Holland 1* had not been preserved properly. The seawater that had penetrated deep into the boat's hull had formed crystals of decay, which were now gnawing their way out. The damage to the submarine had not been treated, just covered up.

Once the disease was discovered, British officials moved quickly to find a cure. A vault was built around the submarine, and it was flooded with a solution to treat the rust. It would cost millions of dollars just to save it.

But the salvage that caused the men who would raise the *Hunley* to shudder more than that of the *Holland* was the sad fate of the USS *Cairo*, the Civil War's hard-luck ironclad.

The *Cairo* was a flat, box-shaped armored gunboat that had been instrumental in the Union Navy's drive down the Mississippi River. The boat, for a while, seemed invincible to Rebel batteries as it steamed along the riverbanks. Its luck ran out in December 1862, when it hit a mine and was beached in the Yazoo River 10 miles north of Vicksburg. By the time the war ended, the ironclad had disappeared, swallowed by the river.

In the 1960s several expeditions were launched with the sole purpose of raising the *Cairo*. Earlier dives had proved that the wreck was a treasure trove of artifacts—swords, guns, even a riding saddle had been found. The preservation appeared, in the dark water, to be pristine. Tons of river mud had blanketed the boat, preserving it. It was a priceless find.

The state of Mississippi put thousands of dollars into the project, and eventually $300,000 was set aside for the recovery—a huge amount of money for an archaeology project in those days. Still, it was a gross underestimate.

The problems with the recovery were numerous: there wasn't enough money, engineering knowledge, or time. The nasty weather further speeded up the timetable for the lift. In October 1964, the salvage crew wrapped seven loops of 3-inch cable around the hull of the *Cairo* and decided it was time to yank the ship from the water. They were not prepared to lift a 175-foot-long, 512-ton Civil War gunboat.

When the *Cairo* pulled clean from the river, it lost buoyancy and became 500 tons of deadweight. The cables sliced through the keel with a terrifying ripping sound. "They acted like a hot knife through butter," said historian Edwin C. Bearss, who watched in horror as thousands of artifacts spilled out of the boat, into the Yazoo River.

That was not the end of the carnage. The recovery team decided to cut the *Cairo* into three pieces to try to save as much of the ship as possible. But the *Cairo*'s timbers were left to dry out under the hot Mississippi sun—a death warrant. The next year what was left of the boat was moved to the Gulf Coast, a new home port in which to rot under the constant sting of salty breezes. Congress eventually donated $5.9 million to a restoration project, but ultimately less than a third of the ship survived.

When the *Hunley* recovery team began looking seriously at salvaging the submarine, Bearss offered this advice: "There is no cheap way."

EVEN THOUGH IT HAD TAKEN MORE THAN A CENTURY TO find the *Hunley*, in some ways that was the easy part. Completing its journey home would prove to be a monumental task. The submarine lay in relatively shallow water only 4 miles offshore, but it might as well have been at the center of the earth. Recovering the submarine without damaging it would be extremely difficult; restoring it, extremely expensive. And the *Hunley* was strictly in the hands of governments, which have only as much money as taxes bring in. In the late 1990s the federal and state governments were bursting at the seams trying to juggle two impossible mandates: cut or hold the line on taxes while maintaining services that people expected, inflation be damned. It was an untenable situation but one that politicians had got themselves into, telling people whatever they wanted to hear—whatever it took to get elected. The political system had turned lawmakers into a nation of junkies—euphoric after the hit of reelection, paranoid when it came time to repay a group more unforgiving than loan sharks or pushers: voters. As a result, when education systems and public infrastructure collapsed behind smiling politicians, most discretionary money dried up—money that could have been used to salvage the *Hunley*.

Glenn McConnell knew the system all too well. He knew enough to squeeze some money out of the cracks, and South Carolina's Washington connections could get some out of the federal purse, but it would never add up to enough to bring the *Hunley* safely home. And the clock on the submarine was ticking more loudly in McConnell's head every day. They needed a way to raise private money, and government agencies such as the *Hunley* Commission could not just hold a bake sale or solicit donors. The *Hunley* needed its own charitable support organization. McConnell knew just how to set it up.

The Friends of the *Hunley* was established in 1997, the chief operational and fund-raising arm for the recovery, excavation, and conservation of the submarine. After McConnell passed the legislation setting up the body, he needed someone other than himself to run it. But he had no idea whom he would trust with his submarine.

It turned out to be retired Navy admiral William L. Schachte, Jr., one of the governor's appointments to the *Hunley* Commission, who gave McConnell an idea for the Friends chairmanship. Schachte had recently met and been impressed by a Charleston businessman who was new to the area. The man was juggling a handful of businesses—and doing quite well at it. The Cleveland, Ohio, son of a butcher was a self-made millionaire who had worked his way through college, paid his dues in big businesses, and then moved on to build an eye-bulging portfolio of his own companies. Among other things, he transported a huge percentage of the nation's imported luxury cars—Mercedes, Porsches, and BMWs—from the docks of Charleston to dealerships across the country. If anyone could run the salvage of the submarine, Schachte suggested, Warren Lasch could.

"He's the person," Schachte wrote, in a short note recommending Lasch to McConnell.

Lasch was a shrewd businessman and prided himself on being able to come at problems from all angles. He also knew how to lead, how to delegate responsibilities, and had little pity for anyone who did not keep a promise to him. He operated his businesses like a team, a page from the Vince Lombardi playbook. Still relatively young, Lasch and his wife, Donna, had moved to South Carolina not to retire but perhaps to slow down a bit. For Lasch that meant running only four companies. It was more than enough to keep him busy, but he agreed to hear out the *Hunley* Commission chairman when he came courting, even though he'd never heard of the submarine before Schachte mentioned it to him.

"What's the *Hunley*?" Lasch had asked Schachte innocently one day.

He didn't realize how soon he would become an expert at answering that question.

For his part McConnell was instantly impressed with Lasch. He, McConnell knew, was exactly what the *Hunley* needed. But no matter how much the senator pushed, the businessman would not budge. Lasch apologized. He was a busy man; he couldn't possibly manage any more than ten hours every other week.

"Warren," McConnell persuaded in his southern drawl, "that'll be more than enough time."

LASCH SOON WAS DEVOTING MORE TIME AND ENERGY TO bringing the *Hunley* home than he did to his other companies. In the months leading up to the launch of the recovery effort, he was putting in fifty hours a week on *Hunley* business alone. As options for the lift were explored, and plans for the submarine's excavation and restoration were finalized, the price tag on the *Hunley* kept growing. It was well on its way to $16 million. Lasch had good connections in the business world and soon started pulling in donors, companies that would give not only money but also equipment—the most state-of-the-art scientific tools in the world. As important, Lasch kept the Friends of the *Hunley*'s expenses down by handling most of its business through his private office. The charitable company never paid for a stamp or a ream of copier paper. In addition Lasch eventually put more than $1.5 million of his own cash into the project.

As the time to bring the submarine home grew near, the Friends of the *Hunley* needed one thing even more than money: they needed someone who could be trusted to deliver the fish-boat home undamaged. Lasch, a man never satisfied with second best, launched a search for just the right team.

IN A WAREHOUSE JUST OUTSIDE WASHINGTON, D.C., SITS a collection of unique equipment that its owners hate to use. When the call comes in to open the warehouse, it means only one thing: there has been an accident, and the remains of tragedy are in deep water.

For twenty years the U.S. Navy has called on the global firm of Oceaneering International to recover lost ships, planes, and boats from the bottom of the world's oceans. The private company's contract calls for its divers—and its equipment—to be ready to leave Andrews Air Force Base for any destination in the world in four hours or less. It is a clause Oceaneering has met more than a few times: when the space shuttle *Challenger* exploded; when TWA flight 800 erupted in a fireball off Long Island; when a CH-46 helicopter crashed off Wake Island in the Pacific. The helicopter recovery—that was one Oceaneering chiefs remembered. It set a world record for deepwater recovery: 17,250 feet.

From its beginnings as an oil field diving company in the Gulf of Mexico, Oceaneering had branched out. It retrieved boats for foreign countries, once solving a murder case in the process. The company developed remote-controlled vehicles to do work in places humans couldn't. Eventually the company began to recover historic artifacts on the side.

In 1999, just as Oceaneering officials were beginning to talk with the Friends of the *Hunley*, they were also deep in planning for a historic fishing trip. Late that year they plucked Gus Grissom's *Liberty Bell 7* off the floor of the Atlantic near the Bahamas. It was 3 miles down, sitting upright, as it had been for thirty-eight years. When Oceaneering engineers set the 9-foot-long spacecraft down on the deck of the ship, it was in nearly perfect condition. The recovery made international news headlines. The company's track record was more than impressive enough for the Friends. Oceaneering was hired to raise the *Hunley*.

Two men from Oceaneering would lead the *Hunley* recovery project: Steve Wright and Leonard Whitlock. Both knew their way around in the deep. Whitlock held the world's record for a deepwater dive, sort of. He and two other men had once lived for forty-two days in a Duke University pressure chamber that simulated life at 2,250 feet below sea level. Whitlock also was one of the first divers to explore the wreck of the Civil War ironclad the *Monitor*. After riding 230 feet to the bottom in a minisubmarine, Wright got out and swam around the famous wreck.

Wright, a burly bear of a guy who admitted a slight fear of sea snakes, had a magic touch for recovering wreckage. He'd once salvaged an early-twentieth-century biplane so gingerly that its aged pilot came back decades later and found his navigation pencil right where he'd left it. If anyone could find a way to raise the *Hunley*, Wright could.

The fact that the sub was in 30 feet of water certainly made things easier in one respect, but the shallow grave of the *Hunley* in no way solved all problems. Pulling the submarine out of the suction of the muck would require some heft, and some care. The problem was, no one knew how much the *Hunley* weighed or how fragile it was. Wright and Whitlock wanted to see for themselves. In the fall of 1999, Ocean-eering divers visited the *Hunley* to examine the strength of the iron plates. Earlier studies suggested that the hull was in remarkable shape, having lost only a slight hint of its thickness to corrosion. The *Hunley* had been, everyone agreed, remarkably preserved. But Wright and Whitlock knew that measurement wasn't everything. As Whitlock felt his way along in the near-zero visibility, he rubbed his hands along the hull, looking for seam lines. One theory held that the *Hunley* had sunk when its hull plates buckled from the shock waves of the torpedo exploding in the *Housatonic*'s side. But reading the *Hunley*'s history in the Braille of corrosion, the divers found a problem that was perhaps worse than split seam lines. One diver pushed his finger straight through a rivet hole. They soon found that several rivets had corroded away, vanished.

It wasn't entirely unexpected. In the nineteenth century the poorest-quality iron was often used for rivets. So even though the hull plates might be strong, the submarine could still crack open if the riv-ets couldn't hold those plates together. It was a worrisome problem. The Oceaneering team knew the story of the *Cairo* well. It was enough to make them shudder, picturing the *Hunley* breaking the surface of the Atlantic, splitting open as tons of sediment inside pushed its way out through small cracks in the hull. They could only imagine the consequences of spilling treasure of the Lost Cause into the dark seawater.

Wright and Whitlock had a new test. They had to come up with a safe way to lift a wreck they didn't know much about. They didn't know how much it weighed or how fragile it was. There would be some guesswork involved. But they knew one thing for sure: they had to get it right the first time. There would be only one chance to salvage the *Hunley*.

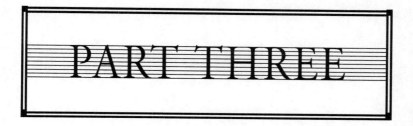

Chapter 10

RAISE THE *HUNLEY*!

S HE WAS RIGHT WHERE THEY HAD LEFT HER.
Listing to starboard, the *H. L. Hunley* sat silently on the ocean floor, its bow still stretching toward Sullivan's Island when divers began uncovering it—for the last time—in May of 2000. When the recovery crew began its work, there were high hopes of raising the tiny submarine and returning it to Charleston by the end of June. The team had a lot of work ahead of it. Just to reach the fish-boat, engineers and archaeologists had to dive 27 feet beneath the waves and then fight their way through 3 feet of silt, the current stirring the seabed into an angry storm of underwater earth tones, mixing the brown sand with the emerald Atlantic. On most days the dive teams were denied a clear view of the majestic submarine. But when the sunlight did penetrate through nearly 30 feet of seawater, when any of the divers caught a rare, fleeting glimpse of the *Hunley*, myths were shattered.

As they delicately vacuumed away tons of sand from around the submarine, inch by inch the hydrodynamic shape of the *Hunley* began to reveal itself. Its lines were so sleek, and its hull so smooth, that a few of the divers wondered if this wedge-shaped leviathan really was the long-lost Confederate war machine. This was not the clunky, boxy submarine depicted in the model on the lawn of the Charleston Museum. It was not a machine thrown together in desperation, and it bore little resemblance to an old steam boiler: its streamlined hull was shaped more like a marlin. This surprised Harry Pecorelli as much as anyone. Pecorelli, whom Clive Cussler had dubbed "the first man to touch the *Hunley* in the twentieth century," was the sole member of the NUMA discovery team who had signed on for the recovery and excavation. And even though he was one of the few divers who had seen it, he was still about to explode with excitement. Pecorelli was looking forward to a better peek at the submarine than he'd had five years earlier.

As the divers carefully dusted away the top layer of silt covering the *Hunley*, they could see what James McClintock had meant when, in a letter after the war, he described the fish-boat's "elliptical shape." Just forward of the front conning tower, the submarine narrowed sharply, its starboard and port flanks merging to form a pointed bow that, from the front, looked like the business edge of an ax. After taking his first good look at the *Hunley*, Pecorelli almost laughed underwater. When this thing comes up, he thought, it's going to make the model in front of the museum look as if it were made out of LEGOs.

"The first time we exposed the bow, it looked like something off of Captain Nemo and the *Nautilus*," Pecorelli would recall a year later.

On that day, as the divers stared wide-eyed at the *Hunley*'s knifing bow, they suddenly saw it—something they had never expected to find.

THE EXPEDITION TO RAISE THE *HUNLEY* HAD BEGUN A week earlier. Before they would begin to dig the submarine out of the ocean floor, scientists wanted to scour the seabed around it for other artifacts. They planned to vacuum and sift 20,000 square feet of sediment—an area roughly 40 feet wide and 130 feet long. Dr. Bob

Neyland, the Naval Historical Center diver who had been surprised by the black water during the 1996 dig, was leading the expedition, and he wanted to make sure they didn't miss anything or drop any heavy machinery on fragile artifacts. They would not leave any piece of the *Hunley* lying on the continental shelf.

During the first days of the dig, there was an unspoken understanding that what the divers were searching for, primarily, was the *Hunley*'s spar. The scientists felt that that simple but mysterious piece of equipment held several of the answers they were seeking. For more than a century, historians had argued over every little detail surrounding the spar, especially its trigger-activated torpedo. Gen. P.G.T. Beauregard, the commander of Charleston forces, had written only that he ordered the spar mounted to the submarine's bow because the towline delivery of torpedoes proved to be too dangerous: the line often got tangled in the boat's stern equipment. He never said what the spar was made of or where it was actually attached. Some believed it was a top-mounted, wooden pole, as depicted in the Conrad Wise Chapman painting. Even William Alexander, the submarine's builder, had written years later of a "yellow-pine boom" affixed to the bow. The allure of the lingering mystery was so great that an Internet forum was devoted to it, with engineers parsing historical documents looking for clues. Despite all that circumstantial evidence pointing to a bowspritlike spar, some people still believed the *Hunley*'s weapon was attached elsewhere. The engineers who built a model of the *Hunley* for a cable TV movie designed their submarine to carry a bottom-mounted iron spar, believing that made more sense. The Internet forum eventually concurred. Those engineers believed the spar was most likely an "iron pole, about twenty or twenty-five feet long, mounted at the bottom of the bow," that could be adjusted for angle, a necessity given the attitude needed to make a solid hit on the curved hull of a wooden ship.

But despite those opinions and the few scattered historical records, no one had found any evidence of a spar on the *Hunley* in any of the prior expeditions. And even though they had barely wiped the sand off the top of the hull, the scientists weren't optimistic. Few of them entertained any notion they would find it. Most likely, they supposed, the spar snapped off on contact with the *Housatonic*. Or if it were made of wood, it had rotted off decades earlier.

The spar was only one of a number of questions that nagged at the scientists. The *Hunley* was quickly teaching the underwater archaeologists that it would not give up its secrets easily. In the murky water, hidden behind a thin layer of concretelike marine growth, details of the boat's hull were few and far between. On all previous trips to the submarine, most of its hull had been left covered to keep out oxygen. Already a chemical virus was invading parts of the submarine that had been repeatedly exposed on previous digs. Water and oxygen were hacking off the iron's electron shield as if peeling back the skin of an onion. A thin layer of the iron hull had already started to weaken, effecting an elemental change. It was becoming iron oxide, commonly called rust. The recovery could not come too soon: the *Hunley* was slowly deteriorating right before the scientists' eyes.

Despite the recent onset of rust, the hull still was holding up quite strong. It had retained its shape even while sitting at a strenuous angle for 136 years. It was in good enough condition for scientists to quickly discern that the historical drawings—save for Chapman's once-ridiculed painting—were not quite right. Most surviving old sketches suggested a boxy, tossed-together old boiler with fins slapped on it. The scientists didn't completely understand how misinformed history had left them until they finally dug out the bow.

Just forward of the *Hunley*'s front conning tower, the hull begins to taper at a wickedly sharp angle, ending in a knifelike bow. When divers uncovered the sharp edge—and that's what it was, an edge—of the submarine's bow, they were astounded by the hydrodynamics. The *Hunley*'s bow was less than an inch wide, the better to cut through the sea, its hull expanding at a graceful angle to keep water flowing around it. And as the divers worked their way down into the seabed, they found that the profile of the bow curved inward from the top, like that of an ice-breaker ship ready to plow a course through the Arctic Sea. The smooth edge receded in a smooth swoop for nearly 2 feet, then swung back out in a pattern that would leave the bottom tip of the bow nearly even with the top. When the divers dug out the silt around it and ran their hands down that sleek bow, they felt a nub sticking out, bolted to the bottom of the hull. The nub, made of iron and as big around as a beer can, didn't seem to end. It disappeared into the sand, as if leading the way toward Sullivan's Island.

It was the spar.

The discovery of the *Hunley*'s spar came little more than a week into the expedition. Later, after it was hoisted from the ocean floor, scientists quickly began to put the pieces together. The spar was iron and hollow, attached to a solid, Y-shaped yoke 2 feet long mounted at the bow's bottom. That yoke appears in the Chapman painting, but for years people had dismissed it as a shadow. Scientists figured that the wooden bowsprit at the top of the bow in the painting, long mistaken for the spar, most likely held line that lowered and raised the heavy iron shaft. But those discoveries would come only months later. Because when the spar was first discovered, it caused more problems than it solved. It was in the way.

OCEANEERING INTERNATIONAL HAD BEEN WORKING WITH Neyland on a recovery plan for months. Neyland, who had been drafted to lead the project by Warren Lasch and Glenn McConnell, wanted Leonard Whitlock and the Oceaneering team to come up with a way to raise the *Hunley* without shifting its position. He wanted the submarine to break the surface with the same list to starboard that it held on the ocean floor. If the submarine were righted, it could potentially jumble the artifacts inside—an archaeologist's worst nightmare. In an excavation the placement of artifacts speaks volumes, often more so than the actual objects. The location of everything inside the *Hunley* would tell the story of the submarine's final moments. But Oceaneering engineers did not need to be reminded of that. Whitlock's company had lifted bigger things in deeper water, always with the intent of recovering clues. Whitlock knew it could be done, but he also knew that they could not take for granted the shallow water and the relatively small size of the submarine.

Lasch, the chairman of Friends of the *Hunley* and the coach of the project, would not let this discussion of how to raise the submarine be a private one. When Oceaneering delivered its plan, Lasch and McConnell, the *Hunley* Commission chairman, invited scientists and archaeologists from around the world to critique it. It would ensure that they had missed nothing and that the plan was as good as it could be. It also would keep them from second-guessing themselves through the entire recovery. As it turned out, they need not have worried. The plan Oceaneering devised drew unanimous praise. It was a complex, multistep operation to gingerly lift the submarine from the seabed and put it on a transport barge without shifting its position one inch. It was a state-of-the-art plan, but it was most impressive because it was also amazingly simple.

In *RAISE THE TITANIC!* CLIVE CUSSLER'S HERO, DIRK PITT, salvages the grand old ocean liner by pumping tons of compressed air into its hull until it floats to the surface, leaping out of the waves like a modern submarine blowing its ballast tanks. Perhaps inspired by the work of the submarine's discoverer, some suggested using balloons to lift the *Hunley*. It was just one of the more, well, inventive ideas that others offered the scientists. As soon as the fish-boat was found, plans for its recovery seemed to drop from the sky; everybody had an idea. One plan called for scooping up the *Hunley* and the sand around it in a giant, steel-toothed crane; another suggested building a wall around the submarine, pumping the area dry, and excavating it there. But Whitlock's—Oceaneering's—plan was the best, most simple idea there was. And it offered the one thing the scientists wanted most of all: it would raise the *Hunley* still listing to starboard.

Oceaneering would sink two huge suction piles into the sand, one about 12 feet off the bow, the other the same distance from the stern. The 18-foot-wide pilings were hollow, and as they were lowered into the seabed, a pump would suck the sand and seawater out of the top of them, driving their bottom edges more than 12 feet below the ocean floor. It made for a sturdy platform.

When the piles were in place, a truss would be set over the submarine, its ends resting on the pilings. The steel cage, 55 feet long and 10 feet wide, would frame the work area and form the top part of a lift cradle. After the truss was in place, divers would bolt foot-wide straps to one side of the truss, burrow under the submarine, and attach the straps to the other side. By stringing one strap at a time, they would never leave the *Hunley* unsupported: there would always be either strap or sand beneath every inch of its keel.

The most inventive part of the recovery plan may have been the straps themselves. Each one was fitted with a bag that had a tiny, closable opening on its top. Into those bags, divers would shoot a space-age polyurethane foam called Froth-Pak. Developed by Flexible Products Company, a subsidiary of Dow Chemical Company, the heavily pressurized gunk was used to insulate refrigerator cars, pad materials that were shipped overseas—it had even filled in cracks in buildings. The foam was shot out of a canister like shaving cream, hardening as solid as concrete in forty seconds. Using Froth-Pak in those bags, Oceaneering engineers figured, would cushion the *Hunley* like a piece of stereo equipment in molded Styrofoam. Oceaneering divers had already tested the goo in Louisiana—it would harden underwater.

Divers would hang a strap, add the Froth-Pak, and move on to the next one in a continuous pattern. Each of the thirty-three straps needed to completely cradle the *Hunley* would take about five hours to attach by the most conservative estimates. The Oceaneering divers would work in two twelve-hour shifts to keep the project moving. The longer the submarine was exposed, the greater the danger of irreversible damage. When the *Hunley* was completely strapped in, it would be lifted—truss and all—by an oceangoing crane and set on a transport barge for the ride home. It was a perfect plan. But then archaeologists found the spar.

THEY DISCOVERED 17 FEET OF SPAR EXTENDING FROM THE *Hunley*'s bow. Just figuring that out proved to be a nearly impossible task: crews had to dig a trench 4 feet down, with it collapsing behind them as quickly as they could uncover another foot of the iron pole. It was obvious there had been more of the spar at one point, but it was gone. Perhaps it had broken off in the *Housatonic*, the scientists thought.

As good as Oceaneering's plan was, it had not taken into account the possibility that the spar was still attached to the submarine. To keep the two pilings close enough together for the lift truss to sit on would have meant dropping the bow piling directly on top of the spar. Even the tank at the conservation lab, 55 feet long, could not house 40 feet of *Hunley* and 17 more of spar. On May 25 Neyland dived on the wreck for a closer look at the spar attachment, but he could not see in the coal-black water that day. Later, a week after they found the spar, another diver felt a bolt sticking 3 inches out of the hull. It took several more days just to determine that there was only one bolt, with a hexagonal nut, holding the spar's yoke on the bow. That, at least, was good news.

For a week scientists had been struggling with a dilemma: should they cut the spar off? They were in a tough spot. Their stomachs were tied up in knots. They knew how cutting the *Hunley* would sit with some people. Besides public relations considerations, it violated their principles, too—it was destroying an artifact. However, they feared it might be the only way to recover the submarine. Their goal was to retrieve the *Hunley* as intact as they could—but first and foremost, just to retrieve it.

ULTIMATELY IT WAS SUCH A SIMPLE IDEA THAT SOME SCIentists felt a little silly afterward. Paul Mardikian, the Frenchman who served as lead conservator on the project, was readying the lab for the *Hunley*'s arrival when he learned that the spar had been found. Mardikian, a veteran scientist who had restored artifacts recovered from the *Titanic*, nonchalantly told the divers to "just unbolt it." He explained that since it had been buried for so long, the bolt was likely in excellent shape. It may not even be rusted, Mardikian said. The disbelieving divers said they would give it a try.

Digging through their toolboxes on board the *Marks Tide*, the recovery team's boat, the engineers could find nothing to help. They needed a six-point, 2-inch wrench, something not especially easy to find at the turn of the new century. One archaeologist strolled the aisles of a local hardware store looking for a fit, and a welder on the *Marks Tide* tried to make one—but it didn't fit snugly enough. The archaeologists were afraid of stripping the nut. Soon they were asking around to all their contacts. An answer came from a nearby source, a worker at Charleston International Ports—also on the Navy base, also operated by Warren Lasch. The rough old socket looked as if it were made to fit the *Hunley*. The recovery team borrowed it with a promise to dry it off when they were done.

On a Sunday morning, June 4, divers did exactly what Mardikian told them they could do: they unbolted the *Hunley*'s spar. Neyland was astonished; the nut had spun off on its threads. The spar nut was the first piece of the submarine actually recovered, but the celebration was short-lived. Although the unbolting was a neat trick, the spar problems weren't over. The square-headed bolt would not back out of the hole through the yoke and hull. They tried using a 12-pound hammer and a brass punch, but still it would not budge. Neyland suspected that perhaps the bolt had bent on impact with the *Housatonic*—a modern reminder of the historic battle the submarine had fought a century before. The bolt ultimately had to be cut.

A day later the spar was removed from the bow of the *Hunley*. Oceaneering engineers built a lift truss for the spar that looked like a steel construction beam and raised the whole thing with a winch off the dive boat *Marks Tide*. After a three-hour trip, the spar became the first piece of the fish-boat returned to dry land. A huge crowd had gathered in the warehouse where the sub would be housed, eager for their first glimpse of a piece of the *Hunley*. The slightly warped pipe was encrusted with oyster shells and clay the hue of Confederate gray. Glenn McConnell was beaming with a look of pride and satisfaction probably close to what the submarine's builders had worn during its first test runs.

"It sends chills up you to touch part of the *Hunley*," he said to a room of enthralled scientists and reporters. "It's phenomenal we found it, much less to get it back in this shape. This is a historic moment. It's been 136 years since this touched South Carolina soil."

Maria Jacobsen, the scientist who would lead the excavation of the submarine's interior, said the luck of geography had saved the spar. If it had been top-mounted, it would have broken off under its own weight. Being on the bottom of the submarine had preserved it much better: it had rested on the ocean floor and was covered by sediment quickly. As it was, the 17-foot spar had corroded to the point that it was essentially in two pieces—13 feet that had been attached to the submarine and another 4 feet found lying ahead of it. And when, weeks later, Mardikian studied the crusty pipe more closely, he found that it did indeed suffer from impact damage. Impact with the *Housatonic*. The spar had a bend—it was warped a few degrees to the right. Studying an X ray of the spar on his computer in the *Hunley* lab, Mardikian said history was recorded in the angles.

"We've got the memory of the battle in the spar," he said.

OVER THE NEXT MONTH ARCHAEOLOGISTS BATTLING SEA-sickness and jellyfish would find nearly every piece of the *Hunley* within a few feet of the wreck site. The rear cutwater, a triangular piece of metal used to keep water out of the aft hatch, was found lying in the silt beside the submarine. The two snorkel tubes used to draw air into the submerged *Hunley* were also found alongside the hull. A rod that may have been part of the steering mechanism was recovered and hauled to the conservation lab. As the pieces started to add up, scientists grew more impressed by the craftsmanship that had gone into the sub's construction. Pecorelli studied the forward hatch, admiring how tightly it was made to seal. This, he thought, was not something quickly hammered out with an anvil. It was cast with great care. The people who did this, Pecorelli could tell, knew what they were doing. As they uncovered more of the *Hunley*, the archaeologists—just like the men who built it—thought the fish-boat was beautiful.

"These guys were artisans, and the *Hunley* was their canvas," Pecorelli remarked.

And then one day, as divers were putting on the final lift straps, they found one piece of the *Hunley* they had given up on: the rudder. Curiously it was beneath the submarine. That the rudder had come to rest under the sub might be the result of the currents' reshuffling the bottom, scientists believed, or it could have implications in the submarine's sinking. If the *Hunley's* rudder had come loose or broken off after the attack on the *Housatonic*, it likely would have been enough to put the fish-boat on a course to the bottom. It was perplexing. For every answer the team found, it seemed another mystery came with it.

As the discoveries racked up, scientists realized they had on their hands a nearly complete submarine. They had not found the spool that held the spar torpedo's mine trigger line, which was depicted in the Chapman painting, but they had everything else that they knew had existed. The *Hunley* was not a fragment of a find, scattered across the ocean floor like most shipwrecks. The world's first attack submarine was intact with most of its accessories included. That, the scientists realized, made the project all the more important. Little detective work would be needed to decipher how the sub worked: this was as accurate a picture as anyone could get of nineteenth-century engineering. Jacobsen said that it was like finding an early Wright brothers airplane. And with the weight of added importance on their shoulders, the scientists grew uneasy. This was quickly turning into one of the biggest maritime discoveries of all time, ranking right up there with the *Monitor*. Perhaps even more important.

The discovery of various pieces of the submarine stirred rumors of black-market treasure hunters looking to make a mint selling pieces of the *Hunley*. For more than a century, the submarine's protection had been its anonymity. Once the sub was found, its location proved to be a weakness. It was just too close to shore, almost within reach of anybody with a boat. Since 1995 the Coast Guard had kept watch on a no-anchor zone, with both traditional patrols and a camera on the Sullivan's Island Lighthouse. In all those years, though, only one boat had hesitated over the site too long—a government boat piloted by the National Oceanic and Atmospheric Administration that had errantly anchored nearby to collect ground samples off the seafloor. Still, the men who would raise the *Hunley* found little comfort in that statistic. They knew all too well that there were many poachers out there who would do almost anything for a piece of the Civil War treasure.

THE PRESSURES ON THE *HUNLEY* PROJECT TEAM WENT FAR beyond archaeological ramifications. With the ever-intensifying gaze of public interest in—and scrutiny of—the *Hunley* recovery, this was not some clinical science project. On many levels the return of the Confederate submarine was driven by pure emotion. Thousands of southerners viewed the submarine almost as a Holy Grail—a time capsule to the Lost Cause arriving just as fast-food restaurants and condominiums were overrunning hallowed battlegrounds across the country. The *Hunley* stirred precious memories for the people who, by the end of the twentieth century, had raised reverence and respect for the Civil War—and the men who had fought and died in it—almost to the level of a religion. Since the *Hunley* was discovered in 1995, Confederate battle flags and Civil War reenactors had been under attack by the forces of political correctness. They were charged with being insensitive at best, racists at worst. These people felt they were misunderstood. Honoring their history, their heritage, in no way dishonored anyone else's, they argued. The *Hunley*, and the widespread interest in it, seemed to validate the heroism and ingenuity they cherished. In some ways the submarine was their salvation.

Those emotions collided head-on with the political landscape of 2000. That year the National Association for the Advancement of Colored People had declared a boycott on South Carolina for flying the Confederate battle flag above its Statehouse dome, a position the flag had occupied since 1962. Politicians argued over the meaning of the flag: some said it was hoisted to celebrate the war's centennial, while others claimed it was a gesture made in defiance of the civil rights movement. The controversy threatened to pull the *Hunley* into the fray. Already several potential corporate sponsors had politely declined to donate money to Friends of the *Hunley*, worried that they might get caught up in the bad publicity of the NAACP boycott. Although the poisonous political atmosphere was having an effect, Lasch and his public relations team steered the submarine through the turbulent waters of 2000 without great problems and were able to land a handful of good corporate partners. By the time the state moved its Confederate flag from the Statehouse dome to a nearby monument on July 1, the Friends of the *Hunley* were receiving almost exclusively positive publicity for their cause. No one had a bad word to say about the project. It appeared that not even politics could keep the *Hunley* from coming home.

ON BOARD THE *MARKS TIDE*, THE 180-FOOT SALVAGE BOAT the team was using as its base, the churning seas had kept veteran archaeologists vomiting over the rail into July. The ship had been at four-point anchor over the *Hunley* since May 13, and a team had been on board the cramped quarters ever since, rotating in and out in twelve-hour shifts. A transport boat would deliver one crew and pick up another. It was an exhausting forty-five-minute water-taxi ride. Most of the excavation work would be managed from the *Marks Tide*. In late July, however, the day the suction pilings were delivered to the site, a barge crane was towed out to attempt a test lift. The Friends of the *Hunley* had been ecstatic to be offered use of a barge crane from Detyens Shipyards, a local company, but when they got it on the water, their enthusiasm waned considerably. Abnormally high, 5-foot seas rocked the barge mercilessly, making it a shaky work platform. The nervous *Hunley* team could not trust it. They quickly returned the floating crane and began looking for a stationary crane to do the job.

They found what they wanted in the *Karlissa B*, a six-legged monster owned by Titan Maritime Industries. The barge could be there in a matter of weeks, plant its pilings in the ocean floor, and stand sturdy, but there was governmental red tape holding it back. To protect the jobs of American salvage workers, federal maritime laws prohibit foreign-flagged ships from doing salvage work in U.S. waters if an

American salvage company is available to do the same work. The *KB*, owned by an American firm, flew the flag of Belize. An East Coast company that heard about the job filed a complaint to block Titan from taking the job. By the time the matter was cleared up by U.S. Customs agents' declaring this a case of "marine peril," valuable weeks had been lost. By then the summer had stretched well into hurricane season.

THE STRAPPING BENEATH THE SUBMARINE'S HULL WAS moving along more quickly than expected. Divers were finding they could string a strap in two or three hours if the conditions cooperated—nearly twice as fast as they had anticipated. Since there was no visibility anyway, they worked in shifts around the clock. Slowly the submarine became supported more by the lifting truss than the seabed.

After the *Karlissa B* arrived, all operations moved over to it and its stationary work environment. It was like having a hotel on the water: there was no more pitch of the sea to contend with. There were two distinct tribes on board the *Karlissa*—the scientists/archaeologists and the Oceaneering divers. Whereas the scientists were perpetually tense, the Oceaneering crews remained calm and relaxed. They grilled hamburgers on deck and fished for sharks while the archaeologists fretted about the approaching lift date. Steve Wright, Oceaneering's on-site manager, exuded confidence. Lifting the *Hunley*, he said, would be like picking up a piece of pipe. No problem. Still, the scientists worried.

One day Wright decided to break the monotony with a little fun at the scientists' expense. He heated the tip of his knife with a torch and etched a simple message on a piece of driftwood he'd found. Later he had one of his divers working the vacuum line below release the stick of wood into the suction. The wood shot through the hose and dumped into a sluice box on the *Karlissa B*, where archaeologists were sifting for artifacts that might have fallen out of—or off of—the *Hunley*. When the inscribed chunk of driftwood landed on the screen to the sluice box, it nearly sent the archaeologists into a frenzy. Etched into the side of the wood was a simple plea: "Help." Archaeologists fired off a handful of photographs of the mysterious message before the Oceaneering divers, unable to stand it any longer, doubled over with laughter.

BY THE BEGINNING OF AUGUST 2000, HOWEVER, THE TEN-sion on board the *Karlissa B* was almost unbearable for everyone. Every day they waited to raise the *Hunley* increased their chances of having to deal with an Atlantic hurricane. Originally they had planned to have the submarine recovered long before the season kicked into full swing, but the crane barge fiasco had put them behind. While there was no storm on the radar yet, they knew it was only a matter of time. It was a threat to which Charleston was hypersensitive. Slightly more than a decade earlier, the monster Hurricane Hugo had descended on the Holy City with all the wrath of a category 4 storm. Mansions on the Battery were filled with 6 feet of seawater, yachts littered the streets, and the drawbridge to Sullivan's Island was left mangled, its deck pointed skyward. It was a storm from which the city still had not fully recovered. Every summer since 1989 had been tense, with people wait-ing for another tempest to strike. Although Charleston had not suf-fered a direct hit since, the past few years all manner of hell had descended on the rest of the coast. Over the course of the four previous seasons, a slew of storms had pounded Wilmington, North Carolina, 150 miles to the north, one right after another—two within a couple of months. It was not a matter of "if" a hurricane would cross the *Hunley*'s grave; it was a question of "when."

So it was with one eye on the weather forecasts that McConnell and Lasch pushed the "Go" button at the beginning of August. It ap-peared the last strap would be in place under the submarine by the fifth of the month. They set the lift day for August 8, giving them a little leeway. It made them nervous, publicly committing to a date, but na-tional and international news outlets wanted a time to show up with-out having to wait, so they would not have to waste time or money paying for hotels in the pricey tourist town. The *Hunley*'s return trip was set: the men charged with its delivery just hoped it would be ready.

As it turned out, the last of the strapping was finished easily. By August 6, 2000, water was flowing freely under the hull of the *Hunley* for the first time in more than 136 years. It was completely suspended in the lift straps, held in place by the concrete-hard foam pillows, the whole lift hammock swaying gently in the underwater current. Divers patrolled the submarine constantly, keeping an eye on their captive beastie. They had found a total of three breaches in the sub's hull, all of which were by then patched. There was the hole in the forward conning tower, discovered by Cussler's team when they found the sub in 1995; there was a bowling-ball-sized gash low on the starboard side, just forward of the dive plane; and there was a large tear—about 18 inches tall and more than 2 feet long—on the starboard stern. They used a piece of sheet metal to patch the largest hole and sprayed some of the strap goo into the conning tower hole. There would be nothing dropping out of the *Hunley* as it was raised from the seafloor.

With all but last-minute checks done, there was a calm before the lift. On that Sunday Ralph Wilbanks, the surveyor who had led Clive Cussler's expedition to find the submarine, made a trip to the site and dived on the *Hunley* in its lift truss. Looking like an aquarium decoration in a hard copper helmet, Wilbanks walked the length of the submarine. Alone in the deep, he thought about Angus Smith and David Broadfoot—the divers who, wearing the same type of equipment he had on, had lifted the *Hunley* after its two previous accidents. Those men did twice in 1863 what was now taking a huge team and millions of dollars to repeat. Wilbanks took his slow lap around the old submarine, gazing at its newly exposed hull, and said it was in Smith and Broadfoot's honor.

It was still dark on the morning of August 8, 2000, when the boats carrying the final recovery crew shift arrived at the *Karlissa B*. As they approached, they could see a blue light on its deck, twinkling toward Breach Inlet. The light was a replica of the *Hunley*'s final signal to the troops on Sullivan's Island. From shore the light shone eerily across the water, a marker of history about to be made. Many of the people in the crew had suffered through a short and sleepless night in anticipation of a solemn and, they hoped, celebratory day. One member of the team said the mood was akin to Cape Canaveral before a launch. Others thought about it more practically. A successful lift meant they would not have to sleep out on the cold Atlantic another night.

As the black night faded to a gray morning, the air held a muggy chill and an occasional raindrop fell on the water, pitching 4-foot swells at the base of the *Karlissa B.* A dive crew vacuumed beneath the *Hunley* once more. If the bottom silted up to the keel of the *Hunley* or the straps, there could be suction when the crane pulled on it, and that would slow the lift and put more pressure on the submarine's fragile hull. On the surface there were more dangers to the fish-boat. The recovery barge, where the *Hunley* would be placed for its ride to the conservation lab, was bobbing like a fishing-line float just in front of the *Karlissa B.* To shield it from the chop of the sea, another barge was anchored behind the *KB.* It helped a little.

By dawn there was an artificial reef to help—a fleet of civilian craft and tour boats gathered in tight formation around the barge, each filled with people craning for a better look at the spot where the *Hunley* would break the surface for the first time since February 17, 1864. The wait would last for hours, the tension as thick as the humid sea air. By the time Jenkins Montgomery, the local man who operated the *KB*'s crane, pulled the lever that reeled in the crane's steel line, many people felt the burn of nausea, but it wasn't from the rock of the ocean. It was the fear that something could go wrong, that the *Hunley* was not yet safe.

WHEN THE CONFEDERATE SUBMARINE *H. L. HUNLEY* BROKE the surface at 8:39 A.M. on August 8, 2000, it resembled a dolphin in a rescue sling. As it hovered for a moment, on display over its former resting place, horns shrieked and ripped through the air, cameras flashed like lightning strikes, and people screamed and cheered and cried at the antique submarine swaying before them, seawater cascading off of it. Sunlight shined on the *Hunley*'s hull for the first time in more than a century; it was as sleek as a fish and the color of the sand that had hidden it since 1864. It looked as solid as the day it was built. The men who had raised it could not believe what swung before them.

"We did it!" Warren Lasch screamed as he hugged a mesmerized Glenn McConnell.

For McConnell it was a moment too special for words. He had fought to recover the submarine since the week after its discovery. He'd changed state laws, cajoled federal officials, and spent countless hours of his own time in pursuit of the *Hunley*. He had considered learning to dive just to get an early peek but had spent much of the spring bedridden, a serious infection coursing through his body. At one point he'd said a sad prayer: "Don't let me go and leave all this on Warren. And don't let me go before I see it."

And now there it was. The *Hunley*. He couldn't express how he felt.

"Oh, my gosh," he almost whispered.

McConnell marveled at how sleek the submarine was. He tried to imagine her in 1863, loaded with a crew. *The crew.* It hit him then that he was looking at a tomb for men whose names he'd memorized long ago.

"Those fellas will not spend another night in the Atlantic Ocean," McConnell said, his voice cracking with emotion.

The senator stood hypnotized as the *Hunley* was lowered gently onto the transport barge, where he would finally get to touch it. McConnell stared at the submarine, carefully studying every feature.

"Look at that fin. Look at that incredible fin."

Lasch, who only four years earlier had not even heard of the *Hunley*, now stood choking back tears. Together Lasch and McConnell—the two men most responsible for the submarine's safe recovery—stood silent for a moment, gazing at their Holy Grail.

As the *Hunley* hung there in space, live cameras broadcast the image around the world, a triumphant shot of the submarine returned from the deep. But the sub was not safe yet. The transport barge rolled lazily in the swells, making a soft landing for the fish-boat and its lift truss uncertain. If all four legs of the truss did not set down at once, scientists were afraid that it might put enough stress on the *Hunley's* hull to crack it. Jenkins Montgomery had a twenty-eight-second window when the barge was mostly level between swells. He would not get a second chance. Playing his crane controls like a fine instrument, he delivered the fish-boat with a four-point landing, and men immediately ran to all four legs and began welding them to the barge. Finally, they had the *Hunley.* As the sub was secured, Montgomery climbed down from his perch, boarded a small launch, and took a victory lap around his catch. Like everyone else in the world, he wanted a closer look.

LESS THAN 100 YARDS AWAY ON THE WATER, CLIVE CUSSLer had been entertaining on a boat loaded with journalists. He spent the morning numb with anticipation, politely answering endless questions from reporters. Watching the submarine raised from the ocean, the realization of a longtime dream behind him, the novelist was euphoric. In tribute to the submarine that his team had found, Cussler stepped to the rail of the boat and, just before jumping into the Atlantic, told the gape-jawed reporters, "Well, I have to go now."

Cameras turned to film the sixty-nine-year-old writer's dive into the choppy ocean water, reporters watching in amazement. He not only gave good quote, he provided great video. Cussler had his exit planned, however, and soon Wilbanks motored by with *Diversity* and plucked His Authorship out of the drink. Cussler had written his own departure from the *Hunley* recovery.

Like Cussler, the archaeologists and engineers assembled on the transport barge were as giddy as little kids. Paul Mardikian, the French conservator, said, "If I don't cry today, it's incredible." Harry Pecorelli jumped into McConnell's arms. He said he was ready to open the submarine and begin the excavation right away.

"It's going to be one of the biggest attractions we'll ever have," he said. "You can't build one of these, you can't float a bond to get one."

Originally the scientists had planned to cover the *Hunley* with wet burlap blankets for its ride into port, just to keep it from drying out.

But that, they decided, would cause a riot. People had to *see* the *Hunley*. So instead of blankets, lawn sprinklers hanging from the lift truss kept a continuous spray of cool water on the hull. And what a hull it was, the archaeologists decided as they walked circles around the truss, leaning in occasionally to touch their catch, to more closely admire its design. It was their first unobstructed view, blocked only by three months' worth of barnacle growth.

Nearly two hours after breaking the surface, the sub and its lifting truss were secure enough on the transport barge to get under way. Then, with an armada of boats in the procession, the *Hunley* set course for Charleston, after more than a century on eternal patrol.

The *Hunley* paraded through the harbor, past Fort Sumter where the war began, past the Charleston Battery, where women cried on the night of the war's opening bombardment. A jubilant crowd of more than 20,000 lined the beaches, parks, and marinas that surround the harbor to get a glimpse of the lost submarine's voyage home. On Sullivan's Island, from which the *Hunley* sailed on its last mission, people ran along the beach, trying to keep up, trying to see it a little bit better. Trying to stay close to it as long as they could.

On the deck of the USS *Yorktown*, a World War II–era aircraft carrier retired and on permanent display in Charleston Harbor, a regiment of Confederate reenactors fired a twenty-one-gun salute as the *Hunley* came into view. Women portraying grieving widows in black dresses and veils threw flowers into the harbor. And across the deck of the old carrier, a lamp with a glowing blue light answered the *Hunley*'s sign for mission accomplished, a signal sent from another time. Airplanes buzzed overhead, and national news programs carried live images of the *Hunley*'s parade of boats up the Cooper River. Traffic on the roads and bridges stopped; people got out of their cars and saluted. It was an emotional welcome to the twenty-first century. The thousands of people who crowded Charleston's waterfront had skipped work, driven hundreds of miles, and planned their vacations around this moment.

Because it's not every day you see a legend.

As the barge made its way up the Cooper River, dozens of boats puttered up for a closer look, girls in bikinis decorating their bows like tanned hood ornaments. Steve Wright could not believe the carnival scene, could not believe this many people had come out to watch this crusty old sub barge pass. Nearby, a worn-out Bob Neyland lounged in a lawn chair on the deck beside the submarine, a huge load lifted from his shoulders, while Pecorelli gazed out over the Harbor, a grin stretched wide across his face. It was a moving moment.

"She's coming home," he said. "A little bit late, but she's coming home."

Just before it reached the Navy base, at a bend in the river, the *Hunley* sailed past a clump of live oaks on the west bank that marked Magnolia Cemetery, the final resting place of Horace Lawson Hunley and the first two crews that died aboard the submarine.

When the sub sailed by on its transport barge, it was the closest Horace Hunley had been to his creation since it killed him.

THE THREE-HOUR, 15-MILE TRIP TO PIER JULIET ON THE old Charleston Naval Base ended just before two P.M. that day as the barge docked within sight of the *Hunley* lab, recently named the Warren Lasch Conservation Center. When the *Hunley* reached the dock, it had a two-hour wait outside while welders cut off the ends of the lift truss, which, with the legs used for the pilings at sea, was too long to fit in the railroad-car-sized tank. With sparks flying off the ends of the truss, a steady stream of VIPs trickled out onto the pier for a close look at the encrusted catch. The *Hunley* hung stoically in its cradle, just off the dock, as the tugboat that had helped guide the barge to the dock was moored alongside, a Confederate naval jack flying above its pilothouse.

Among the people granted a closer look, Randy Burbage stood quietly on the dock, gazing at history. He had carried a lump in his throat since watching the *Hunley* break the water from the VIP boat, and on the dock tears welled up in his eyes. The Sons of Confederate

Veterans camp commander and *Hunley* Commission member—the man who had led the expedition to rebury the submarine's first crew—was already contemplating his final duty.

"I'm looking forward to getting these men an honorable, proper burial," he said. "We'll reunite them with the other two crews."

WHEN THE TRUSS HAD BEEN TRIMMED, A ROLLING SHIP-yard crane plucked the submarine from the barge, and as it rolled silently along its track, a Confederate color guard guided it to the lab. The men, in period uniform, carried four flags: the United States flag, the South Carolina flag, the Second National Flag of the Confederacy, and the Charleston Naval Squadron flag. Jim Tapley led the men of the color guard—none of whom could keep their eyes dry as they gazed at the tomb reverentially. Tapley said it was the greatest day of his life.

"I've been on this Earth for sixty-two years, and I can't remember anything better than this," he said. "I know a thousand men who would trade places with me right now."

It took another hour to inch the *Hunley* into its cold-water storage tank, the shipyard crane moving it to the door and two 20-ton cranes mounted on a rolling track in the lab's ceiling taking it from there. Hundreds of people with passes to get in the lab watched as the submarine crept toward its new home, engineers carefully lining up the truss to fit in the tank. As it was being lowered, Lasch spotted someone on the mezzanine deck at the rim of the tank and motioned for him to get off. Engineers thought he was telling them to drop the sub, and they lowered it more quickly. When it landed, Leonard Whitlock looked at the scientists as if to say, "My job's over. It's yours now."

A LITTLE WHILE LATER, FOLLOWING A THUNDEROUS ROUND of applause when the submarine was safe in its tank, McConnell led a quiet ceremony laying the *Hunley* to rest. His remarks were punctuated with a short benediction, and he told his team that there was one thing he knew from the bottom of his heart. "If these men could stand here today, they would tell you thank you for bringing them home."

As the crowds wandered off and the day lingered into evening, Lasch, Neyland, and *Hunley* Commission attorney John Hazzard puffed on celebratory cigars in the lab while others peered over the tank's rim for a better look at the legendary submarine. The official ceremony had ended solemnly, one reenactor playing "Taps" on an old bugle, tears once again welling up in the eyes of others standing rigidly at attention. On support beams near the tank, a simple plaque with a cross on it listed the names of the men entombed inside the submarine, men who had made history and vanished.

After more than 136 years on eternal patrol, their journey was over.

Chapter 11

GOLDFINGER

T HERE WAS THE SLIGHT SOUND OF METAL AWAKENING, A CRACK like old bones unexpectedly called into service, and then the rust-colored plate peeled back silently, easily. As the iron was moved away from the hull, where it had been attached for more than a century, it revealed a thick, gray mud filling the submarine. For the first time since February 17, 1864, human eyes peered inside the *H. L. Hunley.*

It was one day before the 137th anniversary of the sinking—February 16, 2001—when light flooded the submarine's crew compartment for the first time since the nineteenth century. The 3-foot-wide plate of ⅜-inch iron had come off without a snag, much to the delight of the archaeologists, who had waited six long months to enter the mysterious fish-boat. As they gazed at the pallid, gooey muck—a sign of good preservation, they noted with some satisfaction—they felt drunk with anticipation. Now they could dig into the past. They could sift for artifacts. They could touch the controls that operated the submarine. Finally they were within arm's reach of the *Hunley*'s crew.

In that mud lay the remains of Lt. George E. Dixon, his crew, and the answers to dozens of century-old questions. They would find out how the submarine operated, how it was built, perhaps even how it sank. Now, with the hull breached, this team of scientists brought in from across the globe was ready to decipher that story. It was time to see what treasures lay inside the *Hunley*.

IN THE SIX MONTHS FOLLOWING THE RECOVERY OF THE *H. L. Hunley*, the fish-boat had stewed stoically in its green storage tank at the Warren Lasch Conservation Center, still suspended in its lift truss, slumped over to one side, beckoning to the archaeologists who would unlock its secrets. With the submarine tucked safely away in a high-tech, high-security laboratory on the old Charleston Navy Base, the men charged with the care of the *Hunley* were able to breathe a little easier. But with the submarine so close, the mysteries nagged at them mercilessly, like an itch they couldn't reach.

Bob Neyland, the project manager, insisted his team would not rush into anything: they would not open the sub until they were sure they had found the best—that is, the least intrusive—way to do it. So with *Hunley* Commission chairman Glenn McConnell chomping at the bit, studying any theory of the submarine's demise consistent with the condition of its hull, Neyland's team fell into the routine of normal archaeological procedures. They spent the fall of 2000 studying their catch, mapping, measuring, and charting every feature of its encrusted hull. The early details, tedious to an anxious media and public, nonetheless had to be recorded. To get into the submarine, the scientists would have to destroy much of the growth on its hull, forever erasing any information that might be stored in the earliest layers of coral.

But then, getting inside the submarine was one of the things the archaeologists were trying to figure out. Paul Mardikian, the senior conservator on the project, had said matter-of-factly that he could have the submarine's hatches open within an hour or so, for what good it would have done. Barely 15 inches wide, the hatches were so small that scientists had never considered excavating the interior of the submarine through them—even if they could have. Just as quickly they ruled out cutting through the *Hunley*'s hull to gain entrance. Not only would it have been destructive, contrary to the mission of archaeology, but it would also have been a public relations disaster. It was the same situation they had faced when the spar was found. McConnell and Warren Lasch, the Friends of the *Hunley* chairman, repeatedly joked that if something happened to the submarine, it would be a race to the ticket counter to get out of town. The *Hunley* was a sacred artifact—cutting it would have been a desecration.

In the winter of 2000–2001, the scientists were at a decided disadvantage. There were no surviving plans or schematics of the submarine; they literally did not know what they were getting into. And despite the laboratory's high-tech gadgetry, they hadn't even had a peek inside. After weeks of debate over whether it might hurt any remaining traces of DNA, scientists had agreed to X-ray the submarine. But hindered by the water and silt trapped inside the iron hull, the lab's portable X-ray machine was as blind as Superman behind lead. Even when gamma rays or microscopic cameras were used, the thick sediment denied them the faintest glimpse. All of it conspired to make reverse-engineering the nineteenth-century technology nearly impossible.

Months after the submarine was delivered to the lab, they had no idea what might be behind the hull plates—but they had, at least, figured out that there were indeed plates. On one of the underwater surveys before the submarine was recovered, divers had spotted a vertical seam in the hull but didn't know if it was an errant crack or a solitary line. They were initially skeptical because historical accounts said the *Hunley* was made of an old steam boiler, but boilers didn't have a lot of seams and plates. After mapping the hull in the controlled environment of the lab, they had discovered that each of the tapering ends of the submarine seemed to be made of single, solid pieces, but the central compartment was built out of eight semicircular plates on top, eight more on bottom, connected on either flank to expansion strakes that ran nearly the entire length of the hull. (William Alexander had mentioned the strakes in his postwar writing, explaining that they were added to make the interior big enough for the men to fit.)

The forward conning tower was mounted atop the first of the eight plates, the after tower on the eighth. The scientists believed that getting inside might be as simple as popping some rivets. There were risks. They could punch out the rivets and the plates still might not move because of machinery mounted to the underside, but it was their best chance. With a few plates out of the way, they would have an almost luxurious amount of space in which to conduct their excavation. The plates were each about 33 inches wide, as big as most doorways: they would be able to reach every corner of the submarine's interior. Tentatively they decided to remove the third plate, just behind the snorkel box; the fifth plate, which was in the middle; and the seventh plate, just forward of the aft tower.

They would drill out the rivets, even though they worried about the effect the vibration might have on the *Hunley*'s hull. Remote sensors on the lift truss would alert them if added stress was put on other areas of the hull, but by then it might be too late. Still, there wasn't any choice. They started with the middle plate, Harry Pecorelli and other archaeologists taking turns with an industrial drill, and over several days routed out the ninety-four rivets holding it in place. They had chipped off only enough concretion to see the rivet heads—Mardikian insistent they leave the natural shell of concretion on for as long as possible to aid the preservation. After a few days of work, they found that the plate—though sturdy—was coming loose with some help from the vibration of the drill. When they removed the last rivet, they pried the plate back enough to get lifting straps around it. A 20-ton crane mounted in the lab's ceiling lifted the 250-pound plate easily. Soon reporters were studying the uniform rivet holes along the plate's border. Set on its end, it looked like a stray piece of film negative, in both shape and color. Despite the orange glow of oxidation, the iron was as good as new. Mardikian made a show of mock-polishing it and posing alongside it like a happy fisherman.

"The old lady gave up some of her secrets today." He beamed.

OVER THE NEXT TWO WEEKS, THE ARCHAEOLOGISTS RE-
moved two more hull plates, each in a little worse shape than the last.
However, none of them showed any signs of a hull breach resulting
from the *Housatonic*'s explosion—one theory of the submarine's sinking
that scientists were exploring. The *Hunley* was holding steady all the
while it was being disassembled. It was a sturdier boat than they had
imagined. As each plate was removed, workers put hard plastic sheeting
around the mud to keep it from falling into the tank, but that didn't
seem to be a problem. The sediment had the appearance and consis-
tency of raw cookie dough. It showed no sign of giving way to gravity.

About that, chief archaeologist Maria Jacobsen was as optimistic as
her scientific mind would allow. If the interior were completely filled
with that sort of muck, she knew that meant very little artifact-eating,
clue-destroying oxygen had remained inside. It would greatly improve
their chances of recovering both personal belongings and human remains. But with the submarine opened, those decaying processes
would start all over. The excavation would be a race against nature.
Not only did the scientists have to find the artifacts; they had to map
their position and study their context before removing them from the
submarine. To slow the process of almost imperceptible deterioration,
the water filling the *Hunley*'s tank was chilled to nearly freezing tem-
peratures. When the tank had to be drained during the day for the excavation, the water was kept as high as possible on the hull, the
archaeologists standing on scaffolding built around the submarine
while lawn sprinklers kept the upper parts of the hull wet.

NEYLAND WOULD DIRECT THE WORK BUT LEAVE MUCH OF
the digging to Jacobsen, a Texas A&M colleague with whom
he'd worked a number of times. Jacobsen, a Danish nautical archaeologist, carried impressive credentials to the job. She had surveyed
seventeenth-century shipwrecks and even excavated the world's oldest
shipwreck, discovered in Uluburun, Turkey. In two dozen digs around

the world since the early 1980s, Jacobsen had earned an odd nickname: "Goldfinger." She always seemed to find the precious metal on every expedition she worked, beginning at an ancient gravesite in Israel—one of her first. The nickname was promising to McConnell and Lasch. They took it as a sign she was meant to uncover Dixon's gold coin good-luck piece, the *Hunley*'s most fabled artifact. The coin was considered the ultimate find on this, the ultimate dig. But Jacobsen, logical above all else, did not allow herself to think about it very much. Even if the story of the coin were true, she felt it would be nearly impossible to find it. A lot of things could happen to such a small object in more than a century at sea. To recover something that significant would just be pure luck. And although Jacobsen didn't really factor luck into her work, she did have her own good-luck piece—a hat she had worn to projects on three continents. Under the fluorescent lights of the conservation center, she wouldn't need the hat, but she brought it anyway and kept it hanging from the end of an overhead camera 12 feet above the *Hunley* tank. This dig, though seemingly charmed, could still use all the help it could get.

THE EXCAVATION OF THE *H. L. HUNLEY* WOULD BE PERHAPS the first archaeological dig watched live around the world. The Friends of the *Hunley* set up lab cams that its members could watch on the Internet. The three cameras showed the work from different angles, each picture changing every few seconds. At first, however, there wasn't much to see—coal slag, pieces of driftwood, and oyster shells carried out of the tank in plastic buckets by the archaeologists, who wore matching blue jumpsuits with a diagram of the *Hunley* stitched on the back. At first they also wore disposable masks. Neyland had said they worried that festering nineteenth-century illnesses might still survive inside the submarine, and besides, the smell of the wet muck wasn't that great.

Their first find was the propeller shaft, which they had reached while digging in the stern hole. Below the shaft they found iron ballast bars that looked exactly as they appeared in a James McClintock sketch of "the vessel that sank the *Housatonic*" made after the war. But that was all they had. Shortly after the work began, the scientists deduced that at some point water had flowed freely through the submarine—probably entering through the gash in the stern and going out of the grapefruit-sized hole in the forward conning tower, in the process dragging in all manner of ocean debris. They'd even found a cow's rib bone. It was enough to erase any optimism the team initially had. Water running through the submarine could have flushed out valuable clues and artifacts. The archaeologists began to worry. They had nothing in hand that appeared to be an actual artifact from the *Hunley*. Maybe it had all been washed out, forever lost at sea.

The gashes in the submarine's hull were worrisome. There was little explanation for them, but scientists supposed anchors could be blamed for all three. Certainly that was the leading suspect for the pie-sized hole in the *Hunley*'s starboard flank near the dive fin. And the punch to the conning tower was the result of either the sharp point of an anchor catching it or a bullet from a *Housatonic* sailor's gun shattering the brittle cast-iron tower. The stern gash, large enough for scientists to stick their heads inside, also could have been made by an internal expansion of methane gases produced by the decaying bodies of the crew. Whatever caused the hull breaches, however, was not as important as what effect they had had on the interior. If water had flushed out the *Hunley*'s artifacts, it could be a very unrevealing dig.

Still, there was hope. They knew the water hadn't always been inside the submarine. Archaeologists found a few small, pencil-sized stalactites suspended from the ceiling. Although the scientists were hypersensitive to quick conclusions, the stalactites left little doubt about one thing: the *Hunley*'s interior had remained at least partially dry for years after it disappeared. That was a scenario few people had considered, and the archaeologists knew it could have serious implications for solving the submarine's mystery. It would turn out to be one of the most telling clues found during the excavation.

After two weeks of digging through junk—pieces of seashell and coal—they hit smooth, flat, finished wood. Initially they tried to tell themselves it was a shelf, but soon the archaeologists realized they had uncovered the crew's bench. It was mounted at a slightly sloping angle and was about 15 feet long. The angle of the bench would have prevented the crewmen from hitting their knees on the propeller crank and, Jacobsen noted, kept the men hunched over, moving the center of gravity to the middle of the hull. That might help explain how the *Hunley* had kept an even keel with the crew sitting alongside the port side. For the time being it was all they had, because as they dug deeper into the fish-boat's belly, they were finding very little.

WHEN THE DISCOVERIES FINALLY STARTED TO COME, IT was as if someone had turned on a faucet. There was a continuous stream of artifacts, traces of the *Hunley*'s final crew that began to show up in the muck in the days after the bench was found. First there were buttons, the most durable pieces of clothing. Soon there were four pipes, a couple of pocketknives, several canteens, and even a wallet. And then there was the bottle. It was small, made of glass, and only about 6 inches tall. It was twelve-sided and still corked. "That's 1864 air in there," a fascinated McConnell noted.

The strange little bottle was filled with something, but no one wanted to open it to find out what. It was most likely sediment, but mixed in with that mud might be traces of whatever was originally corked inside. The speculation concocted a number of tales, the wildest being that it was poison—a remainder of some sort of suicide pact among the crew. Neyland said it could have just been "bottled courage"—whiskey. They decided to test it. Most likely, they said, it was some sort of elixir, probably just a medicine for seasickness. It seemed that everything pulled from the submarine would come with its mysteries, spawning its own set of far-fetched notions. While their test of the contents was inconclusive, it turned out the bottle was made for medicine, according to researchers at a state museum in Columbia.

The first of several buttons that were found, while hardly exciting, spoke volumes about the crew. They were a ragtag bunch, wearing whatever they could find: there were no uniforms for the crew of this submarine. The first cast buttons found were from the coat of an artilleryman. The two small, probably brass, buttons sported an ornate *A* on their face. On the back of each button, orbiting eyes still strong enough to hold them on a shirt, was the company name "Halfman & Taylor." Halfman & Taylor was a Montgomery, Alabama, business that distributed military wares made in Great Britain during the war. Mostly the company's stock was swords and other gear, but it also imported buttons. The *A* stood for "artillery." That seemed to suggest that the buttons came from the coat of Cpl. C. F. Carlson, the last man to join the *Hunley*'s crew. Carlson had replaced William Alexander on the crew when Alexander was called back to Mobile in early February 1864. Dixon filled out his crew complement with Carlson, the only member of the crew known to have come from an artillery unit. The buttons were found on the bench in the middle of the submarine, the darkest and tightest position on the submarine's propeller crankshaft. It was just where a rookie would have been made to sit.

Some of the other buttons were more interesting and more telling. Archaeologists found three large black rubber buttons farther aft, each stamped "Goodyear" on the back and with the insignia of the United States Navy on the front—a fouled anchor surrounded by the initials "U.S.N." The buttons, scientists guessed, may have come from a Navy overcoat, the kind a sailor wears on a ship at sea. It appeared that Carlson was not the only crewman still wearing clothes from his last assignment. James Wicks, the old salt of the crew, most likely carried those buttons on board. Wicks, a Southerner and father of four, had been in the U.S. Navy when the war broke out. He stayed at his station even though his sympathies lay elsewhere. He had jumped ship during a battle at Hampton Roads and later joined the Confederate Navy. Aside from Dixon, Wicks was the best-documented member of the *Hunley* crew: scientists were almost sure he was one of the men on board. Since he was the only one they knew for certain had been in the U.S. Navy, it stood to reason that those large rubber buttons belonged to Wicks. Slowly the pieces of the puzzle were beginning to emerge, but scientists had a long way to go before they would all fit together.

In the next few weeks, new finds turned up almost daily. At the end of the crew bench, archaeologists soon uncovered the controls to the aft ballast tank, deformed by concretion. The handle for the aft pump, which Alexander had disassembled in the dark once to save the crew, was a long, wooden stick, easily within reach of the last seat on the bench. In fact, the protruding edge of the bench had been cut off, notched to save the first officer's knuckles when he pumped the tank empty. Despite these finds, as they neared the halfway point in their dig, the scientists had yet to recover any major artifacts. And they still had not found the handles the crew used to crank the propeller. The archaeologists had expected they would be mounted high, down the middle of the interior—where old drawings placed them. But nothing was exactly as they had expected, none of the interior sketches exactly right.

It was killing Glenn McConnell to miss the dig. By the time the excavation started turning up artifacts, the state senator was deep into the 2001 legislative session in Columbia. He could do little more than watch the excavation on the Internet cameras. On most days McConnell had to rise from his desk in the Senate chamber and brief the other lawmakers on the latest from the *Hunley* lab. Interest in the submarine was spreading throughout the state, seemingly without end. McConnell, chairman of the Senate Judiciary Committee, kept people lined up out the door of his office on important state business. Often he was showing some constituents—or tourists—photos of the *Hunley*. It was hard for him to think about anything else. During his daily briefings to the Senate in early March, he made the same promise every day: "We are only days away from a rendezvous with the crew."

He could feel it.

One day in late March, Maria Jacobsen actually climbed into the submarine, becoming the first person to fully enter the *Hunley*'s crew compartment since Dixon and his men. Lying flat on her belly, she was going to start digging forward at a point just underneath the snorkel box. Neyland was anxious to see if they could excavate the forward part of the crew compartment without removing a fourth hull plate. The *Hunley* had shown no signs of additional hull stress with three plates off, but Neyland didn't want to further disassemble the submarine if he could avoid it. Jacobsen was sent in for two reasons: she was the chief archaeologist, and she was small.

Archaeologists are accustomed to such inconveniences, of crawling into places no one else would even think to go, to dig in muck that most people would take great pains to avoid. They work in the most uncomfortable of situations: excavations usually take place in deserts, fields, swamps, even underwater. The *Hunley* project was the envy of the scientific community in several ways, not the least of which was the relative comfort in which the team got to work. Still, crawling inside the Confederate submarine was no picnic. Once Jacobsen got inside the cramped, 42-inch-wide compartment—which was still mostly packed with muddy sediment—she felt closed in and had trouble breathing. The air was stale and filled with the sulfur smell of rotting marine life. It nearly choked her: she had to come up for a fresh breath often. Eventually the team had to pump fresh air into the submarine to allow Jacobsen to work. If she had had the time to think about it, Jacobsen would have realized that not having enough air to breathe was a common sensation inside this submarine. She was crawling into a space that few people had ever come out of alive.

It was while she was still struggling with the discomfort of working inside the *Hunley* that Maria Jacobsen had her rendezvous. She was digging beneath the snorkel box, no more than a foot or so down into the sediment. It was too high in the muck to find any artifacts, she thought, much less human remains. But as she delicately scooped away tiny bits of the gray mud, she came across something strange. Carefully she concentrated her digging on a single spot, and as she scraped away a century of ooze, it became more clear that what she had found was a human rib cage.

Jacobsen was stunned. Since she had not expected to find a crewman so early, she had not emotionally prepared herself to look upon the bones of a sailor who died a horrible death in this dangerous nineteenth-century experiment. She just wasn't ready to face a member of the *Hunley*'s final crew yet, but there he was. And he was so *young*.

The submariner couldn't have been more than nineteen or twenty. He was slightly built, just a kid, really—but he had suffered a man's death. He died in a pitch-black iron tube 5 fathoms down, and until Maria Jacobsen found him 137 years after that maritime disaster, no one had known for sure what happened to him. He was stretched out flat in the sediment as if he were moving toward the forward hatch. It appeared his body was propped up on something wooden, perhaps a stool. He was just below the snorkel box, one of the more photographed features of the *Hunley*. He'd held that death pose for more than a century.

Over the next few weeks, the archaeologists found the remains of what they believed to be six other members of the *Hunley*'s crew. For a short stretch it seemed they found a new man every day. Experts were brought in from around the country to study the remains more closely, including Dr. Doug Owsley, the head of physical anthropology at the Smithsonian Institution, and Dr. J. C. Upshaw Downs, the chief medical examiner for the state of Alabama and a former Charlestonian. Alabama officials wanted to keep close ties to the submarine built in their state and gladly donated Downs's time to the project. Working alongside the *Hunley* team scientists, Owsley and Downs painted a sad portrait of a determined, overworked—and young—crew. The bodies showed the stress of hard labor aboard the cramped submarine. These men had herniated disks, abscessed teeth, and likely suffered from malnutrition. They were small, but then they had to be to get inside the *Hunley*. It was ironic in a way, but the remains were in such good condition that the archaeologists had trouble identifying some of them. Inside the *Hunley* they found some of the smallest, most fragile bones in a human body—bones that rarely turn up in archaeological digs. Jacobsen and Neyland, particularly, were astounded. The state of preservation inside the submarine was far beyond what they had imagined, far better than they had even hoped for.

The discovery of the crew put to rest a fear that McConnell and some members of the Sons of Confederate Veterans had that the men were not on board. In the vacuum of information about what really happened to the *Hunley*, theories had sprung almost without limit. One of those theories was that the crew might have got out. If the submarine had suffered a hull breach, there might have been time to open a hatch before it sank. Even if the *Hunley* did go down with water pouring into the crew compartment, when it was halfway full, the pressure inside would have been equalized with the water pressure outside, allowing them to open the hatches. There had even been that one account of a man who might have been Dixon spotted in a Charleston pub. Until the crew was found, McConnell knew there was no real guarantee they were on board. But he'd had a feeling.

A MONTH AFTER THE FIRST REMAINS WERE FOUND, ARchaeologists discovered the first skull. Due to the weight of a human head, and because nothing holds it on but muscle, it is one of the first things to fall off a decomposing body. Unless a body is found lying flat, there is little chance the head will be found in its original position. That was the case on board the *Hunley*. Most of the remains they found were slumped over, partially still in skeletal form and partially jumbled. The skulls were found lying low in the cabin, near the floor, where they would have fallen, and all of them were in pristine condition. After the first remains were found, the discovery of the skulls was no huge surprise—but the tissue was.

Since the project began, Jacobsen and Mardikian had prepared the media and the public for the likelihood of finding human flesh or brain matter on board. Remains aboard a seventeenth-century shipwreck discovered off the coast of Texas a few years earlier had contained brain tissue, so it was possible there would still be more than just bones aboard the *Hunley*. They had already found what they believed were a few stray strands of human hair. Still Jacobsen had been worried. During the recovery efforts, divers had found a crab living in the hole in the front conning tower. The divers dubbed him "Horace," but Maria Jacobsen called him trouble, theorizing that if crabs got inside the submarine shortly after it sank, there might be nothing left of the crewmen. It was simply the way of nature.

But as clues reminded them almost daily, the submarine may have remained airtight for some time after it sank. The bones of the crewmen were found at their duty stations: there was only minor mingling of the remains, as best scientists could tell. It suggested a quick, perhaps even peaceful, end for the crew. It also hinted that there was little or no water in the submarine, which would have caused the bodies to float to one spot, leaving a single, huge pile of bones. The crabs hadn't been a problem, either.

THE FIRST FLOOR OF THE WARREN LASCH CONSERVATION Center resembled an emergency room—sterile white, packed with stainless steel examination tables, high-powered X-ray machines, microscopes, and refrigerated chambers. In the lab the scientists would study every artifact, every piece of evidence they recovered from the *Hunley*'s interior. Mardikian, the French conservator, had a room for freezing the water out of artifacts and a humidor for preserving them after he had restored them. The facility had been finished just weeks before the *Hunley* was raised and brought ashore, and already it had an international reputation: a cannon hoisted from the deck of the Confederate blockade-runner CSS *Alabama*, sunk off the coast of France near the end of the Civil War, had been hauled to the lab for restoration. Despite all the gadgetry, the one feature of the lab that seemed to capture everyone's attention was a huge, walk-in freezer. Inside the vault, which looked like a grocery store meat locker, were three metal shelves holding nine autopsy trays. They almost suggested the myths of secret government bases holding the remains of aliens from the Roswell UFO crash. In that climate-controlled closet, the men of the *Hunley* would await their burial.

As sophisticated as the Lasch Conservation Center was, it was not set up for the detailed study of human tissue. Quietly, before they publicly announced their discovery, scientists took some of the skulls to the Medical University of South Carolina in downtown Charleston to do CT scans—three-dimensional, diagnostic X rays—to better show them exactly what was inside the skulls. Initially the scans only confirmed that they had intact brains from the crew. Further tests on the remains would eventually take more than a year to complete. Aside from normal autopsy procedures, scientists planned to attempt computer-generated facial reconstructions of the sailors, as Lasch and McConnell said, to "put a face on the crew." The brain tissue would likely reveal more about the crew but would complicate the process and delay the burial for more than a year, much to the chagrin of anxious reenactors.

By early May 2001 archaeologists had recovered what they believed to be the remains of seven or eight members of the fish-boat's final crew. As they carefully extracted the bones from the sediment, they turned off laboratory cameras, as Lasch said, "out of respect." They would allow no photos of the bones. The remains made for tedious work: each bone had to be photographed, assigned an artifact number, and mapped to show where it was found. If they had nine crewmen on board, that would mean there were more than eighteen hundred bones to account for. But as the excavation drifted into its final weeks, the archaeologists began to wonder if there were nine men board: they still had only seven skulls. And they had yet to find the *Hunley's* captain, Lt. George E. Dixon.

THE INTERIOR OF THE *HUNLEY* WAS REVEALING ITSELF TO be as different from historical renderings as the exterior. It had been assumed that Dixon steered his boat nearly blind, but archaeologists found there were two square viewing ports on the forward conning tower—one on each side of the cutwater. Additionally they discovered a small glass port in the forward hatch that would have let in light and let the captain know when it was above water and safe to open. It was becoming clear the submarine was not as primitive as they had thought. Most accounts said the *Hunley* was built of an old boiler, but inside they found ribs between the rivet joints making a skeleton for the submarine. It didn't appear to be a boiler; it seemed to have been designed to be just what it was: a diving boat.

As surprising as these newly discovered features were, the archaeologists were more perplexed by what they weren't finding. They had expected to find the hand cranks for the propeller shaft weeks before they actually uncovered the first handle. They had based all assumptions on William Alexander's sketches, which had been fairly accurate on content, if not proportions. When they were finally found, the cranks were lower than scientists expected and were offset to the starboard side of the interior. Alexander had drawn them right down the middle, which led scientists to believe the boxy handles were part of the actual propeller shaft. But the cranks, mounted with brackets at high and low angles on the starboard wall, could not be directly attached to the shaft if they were offset—the propeller was centered on the stern. Neyland surmised there must be a reduction gear connecting the cranks to the shaft. Of course, no gears show up in the old drawings. The alternating angles of the cranks were an ingenious feat of engineering. Not only would it prevent the men from having to work together; it would ensure there was always some torque on the drive shaft.

Alexander had been relatively accurate forty years after the fact, but he left out some details and was even wrong about a few others. The steering was one of the worst examples. Alexander had shown a steering wheel attached to the rudder by cables or rods mounted along the interior ceiling, giving the captain the ability to steer from his position under the forward conning tower. In fact, the scientists' faith in Alexander had been a minor hindrance to getting inside the submarine. They feared that the steering rods or cables and their mounting brackets might stop them from lifting hull plates. But no brackets were there. Scientists began to suspect that the steering rods (or cables) ran beneath the bench, out of the way of the crew.

Also, James McClintock, Alexander, and just about every other historical source had said there were eight positions on the crank to turn the propeller, but as the excavation moved forward in the compartment, the hand cranks suddenly stopped at seven. The scientists were shocked. If Dixon piloted and controlled the diving fins while seven men cranked, what did the other crewman do? Perhaps there were only eight members of the submarine's crew, which would have meant that most historical accounts were wrong. Almost everyone associated with the project, and anyone who wrote a reminiscence of the fish-boat, claimed the *Hunley's* crew complement was nine. But they all said there were eight positions on the crank as well. It seemed that even with the *Hunley* in the same room, it stubbornly refused to reveal too much of its mysterious past.

ALL ALONG, THE ARCHAEOLOGISTS HAD BELIEVED THAT the first crewman found was held up by a stool of some sort that had become wedged on top of the axle for the diving planes. But as the excavation moved forward, they realized the young man who had died against the ceiling of the *Hunley's* hull was lying atop a large wooden bellows. Alexander and others had written dismissively of the fish-boat's air and snorkel system: most said it never worked or was never used. Alexander wrote that Dixon surfaced every twenty minutes and refreshed the air supply by opening both hatches—the insinuation being that the two small snorkel pipes did little or no good. But as more mud was removed from the interior and the bellows was uncovered, it soon became obvious that the bellows attached to the underside of the snorkel stuffing box and had hoses coming out of its bottom. One hose, the scientists speculated, could have run underneath the bench, like modern air-conditioning, circulating air throughout the claustrophobic cabin. Could one crewman have been solely responsible for the air bellows, or did the man at the first crank position occasionally slide down the bench and give the bellows a few pumps? Perhaps Dixon even did it himself. The young man found lying atop the bellows might have died pumping it in a futile attempt to draw in air. The bellows was a perplexing find. How did a major part of the *Hunley's* operation escape notice or slip the minds of nearly everyone who survived to give an account of the submarine? It was baffling—almost to the point of making some people wonder if the bellows hadn't been a last-minute addition.

The submarine's other features were found to be as described by Alexander and others, in varying degrees of accuracy. The scientists had found piping in the aftmost areas of the crew cabin and a handle that operated the aft ballast tank pump. The seacock, the valve that would allow water into the ballast tank, was found but was so heavily crusted over with growth that the archaeologists couldn't tell if it was set in the open or closed position. Farther forward, the archaeologists found a handle they believed operated the bow ballast tank pump. It stretched all the way back to the position of the crewman they believed had worked the bellows, the handle crossing over the top of the axle connecting the dive planes. The lever for the fins, which worked against water pressure like airplane wings against the wind, was offset to the port side and had a counterweight to help the captain move the dive planes against the enormous pressure of the water.

Every little feature the archaeologists uncovered brought a new surprise but also a better understanding of exactly how this submarine—primitive, yet advanced for its day—actually worked. The scientists had so constantly commented on the remarkable technical savvy of the men who built this nineteenth-century war machine that it was almost a cliché, but then it was true: the *Hunley* was far more advanced than anyone had ever realized.

Then, just as it seemed there were no more surprises left, they found something inside the *Hunley* that should not have been there at all.

IT WAS COPPER, ABOUT THE SIZE OF A HALF DOLLAR, AND stuck to the back of the first officer's skull. On one side was a relief profile of George Washington, just like a modern quarter, and on the other side was a name: Ezra Chamberlin.

The medallion was the sort of thing a young soldier in the Civil War bought with his own money to help identify his body in case he were killed: it would be a half century before the advent of official dog tags. These medallions were made by private merchants and sometimes even sold on the sidelines of battlefields. It was stamped with enough information to cause the biggest uproar of the *Hunley*'s excavation so far. Ezra Chamberlin had entered service early in the war—September 6, 1861—as a private in Company K of the Seventh Regiment of Connecticut Volunteers. The scientists were speechless. Could it be true—a Connecticut Yankee on a Confederate sub?

The discovery of the Union soldier's identification tag set off a furious round of speculation and conspiracy theories. Some said this soldier from the North had defected and joined the *Hunley* crew. Others believed the man on board the submarine must have known this soldier and was carrying his identification to return to the man's family later. Perhaps Chamberlin was a prisoner of war forced to work aboard the fish-boat. Or the crewman who seemed to wear the medallion around his neck might have killed the soldier in battle. The most likely scenario, historians believed, was that the *Hunley* crewman had simply picked this shiny medallion up as a souvenir. Perhaps he couldn't even read what it said.

In the days following the discovery, researchers plunged into historical documents at the request of *Hunley* Commission members. They soon picked up the tracks of Ezra Chamberlin, and they seemed to stop at the entrance to Charleston Harbor on Morris Island—a month before the *Hunley* arrived on the East Coast. Chamberlin's was a sad story, one all too common in the War Between the States.

He had enlisted when the Civil War was barely five months old and was assigned to the newly formed Connecticut Volunteers. With his company Chamberlin made his way south, stopping in Washington on his way to Port Royal, South Carolina—a Union stronghold near Hilton Head, where Rear Adm. John A. Dahlgren commanded the South Atlantic Blockading Squadron.

In June 1863 Chamberlin and Company K moved north 70 miles to invade Morris Island, a strategic spit of sand guarding the southern entrance to Charleston Harbor. On July 10 Union troops began a bombardment on the Rebels' Fort Wagner there, and the next morning Company K charged. Some of the young Union soldiers made it all the way to the earthen battery, and two even made it over the wall, bayoneting two Confederate gunners to death. But with no support behind the company, the men were soon massacred.

One historian researching Chamberlin found an account of the young man's demise there on Morris Island. After the war a survivor from the company recalled Chamberlin's rallying the troops during the battle, yelling "Close up! Close up!" But they didn't, and Chamberlin fell dead—one of 340 Union casualties that day. (Later the Union tried again with the Fifty-fourth Massachusetts Regiment of free blacks, events chronicled in the movie *Glory*.)

In spite of that evidence, some people refused to give up on the notion that Chamberlin was a member of the *Hunley*'s final crew. Perhaps it was because so little was known about the men aboard the submarine that anything seemed better than not knowing. They just wanted to believe. And so McConnell and others kept looking for information. They had enough morsels to keep the ghost of an idea alive.

War records indicate there was also an *Ezera* Chamberlin in the same company as Ezra: perhaps that old account had got the two confused. While there was a headstone for Ezra Chamberlin in his hometown of Killingly, it was most likely just a memorial marker. Even if he had died on Morris Island, his body probably would not have been carried back to Connecticut for burial. Most chillingly, Chamberlin's mother was denied a military pension after the war: somebody said there was no proof Ezra was dead. He was officially listed as missing in action.

As May dragged on, Bob Neyland decided a fourth hull plate had to be removed. Time was running short. The crews were working twelve-hour days six days a week to finish before some had to leave for summer commitments, but the excavation still wasn't going fast enough. They had reached a point at which only a couple of people could work at once in the tight spot where they were concentrating their efforts. Progress had slowed to a crawl. There were concerns about removing yet another plate. The one that the archaeologists needed to remove had the snorkel box mounted to it; the other three plates had been bare save for deadlights. They didn't want to hurt the snorkel stuffing box as they lifted the plate. But they had little choice: the bellows, concreted to the diving fins, was in the way, and there was no way around it.

By this time, however, they were old pros at handling the hull. In a matter of days, the fourth plate was off, stewing in a bath of cold water alongside other pieces of the disassembled *Hunley*, the snorkel box having suffered no damage in the removal. When that plate was removed, the archaeologists pushed ahead with one final goal—to find Dixon.

IF THE SCIENTISTS SUSPECTED THERE WAS ANY CREDIbility to H. Pacha's 1885 tale of meeting someone—possibly Dixon— the night after the *Housatonic* sank, they showed no sign of it. They were certain that they were close—that the legendary commander of the *Hunley* was just below the forward conning tower. If he wasn't there, if there was not another body on board the *Hunley*, history would have to be rewritten. But they were confident. They were sure they would have him in a matter of days.

As the archaeologists moved forward, beneath the submarine's forward conning tower, they tried the portable X ray once more— anything to give them a clue about what they were about to encounter. There were vague notions of something of indeterminate shape and size before them, but they couldn't tell what it might be. Finally on one piece of film they recorded a haunting image harkening back to February 17, 1864. It was a lamp.

Legend had it that Dixon had popped out of the forward hatch sometime after detonating the torpedo in the side of the *Housatonic* and signaled the Confederate troops on Sullivan's Island with a blue phosphorus lamp. The signal was sighted by sailors clinging to the

Union ship's wreckage and by Rebel sentries on shore. It was the last confirmed sighting of the *Hunley* for more than a century. And there, cocooned in a concretelike shell, was a crusty lump that probably was the famous blue light.

LESS THAN AN ARM'S LENGTH AWAY FROM THE LIGHT, ON May 17, 2001, archaeologists touched Lt. George E. Dixon. The remains of the young submarine commander fit historical descriptions of him perfectly. He was tall, in his mid-twenties, in good health. His teeth were well kept save for a single cavity he had had filled with a piece of gold. Even his coat was of the finest material, several grades above that of the rest of the crew. X rays suggested that the captain still carried a pocket watch and even binoculars. His remains were far from the rest of the crew, beneath the forward tower, where he would have looked out, got his bearings, signaled shore. There was no doubt this was the man in charge of the submarine. Just as his crew, he had died at his station, slumped forward—but why he died remained a mystery. Dixon's skull showed no sign of damage, a serious blow to theories that he might have been shot during the attack on the *Housatonic*. Whatever Dixon's fate, he had met it with his crew.

AS MUCH AS THE DISCOVERY OF DIXON WAS A RELIEF TO the scientists, it raised as many questions as it answered. Initially the inventory of bones had looked larger than it actually was. The archaeologists now suspected that, even with the captain found, they could account for only eight men. History, it seemed, might soon have to be rewritten. They had seven hand cranks and eight skulls, and they had gone nearly from one end of the submarine to the other; only a short wall of muck remained in front of both the fore and aft bulkheads. Maybe there never were nine men on board. It wasn't impossible: the scientists had certainly found that historical accounts had numerous flaws. But the strange thing was, nearly everyone had agreed on the crew complement. In an odd way, though, it almost fit. When the *Hunley* sank for the second time—with Horace Hunley himself on board—only eight men had died. General Beauregard himself had said it was only because Dixon was out of town that there weren't nine men on board. But Alexander, who was closer to the story and likely remembered it better, claimed Dixon was in Mobile with him at the time. Perhaps only eight died on board during that sinking because that's all the men that were ever on board. Even the first accident was suspect: the captain got out through the forward hatch, and Charles Hasker had been trapped trying to escape. Was there really time for two others to squeeze out through the tiny after hatch? The scientists would not know for some time, as they were about to shut down their excavation until well into the fall. They had to study hundreds of bones to see exactly what they had in the lab, and even then they couldn't be sure until they had completely emptied the submarine. And that would take months, if not longer, to explore every inch of the *Hunley*. The fish-boat refused to let go of some secrets.

The questions about exact numbers mattered little to most people. With Dixon found, reenactors began to plan for the funeral of the last *Hunley* crew. They would be interred with the other two crews at Magnolia Cemetery, beneath the comforting shade of a live oak tree that had seen the war. Finally the men would be given the respectful, military service they were due. It was a thought that pleased McConnell.

"We have it in our grasp to bring all three crews back together," he said.

IF THAT HAD BEEN ALL, IT WOULD HAVE BEEN ENOUGH. The initial excavation of the *H. L. Hunley* had resulted in the recovery of the torpedo boat's heroic captain and crew and had answered century-old questions about how the first attack submarine operated. Millions of people had watched the excavation daily over the Internet, and the Friends of the *Hunley* office was besieged with requests for interviews, for photographs, for anything. The *Hunley* had reentered the public consciousness and didn't appear to be going away anytime soon. Anticipation was high for summer tours that would give visitors to the lab a chance to actually look inside the mysterious fish-boat. First, however, scientists had one final surprise awaiting them.

IT WAS AROUND 9:30 ON THE EVENING OF MAY 23 THAT the second-shift excavation team was working in the *Hunley* lab. With the discovery of Dixon, the excavation was for all intents over, but there was some cleaning to be finished before the tank could be filled with water. Maria Jacobsen was working methodically to remove Dixon's remains, one of the last chores. The mud that held Dixon's bones and clothing was too thick, she decided; they would have to do a block lift.

A block lift is how archaeologists remove the most fragile material from a dig site. Rather than try to pull textiles out of the thick muck, which could tear the fabric, they slide a support underneath an area and lift everything at once—mud, bones, clothes, and all. In the laboratory water could be poured gently on the material until the mud was washed out. It was a procedure the *Hunley* team had been through a dozen times already: most of the crew's clothing was too fragile to handle.

The plan was to slide a thin piece of metal, about the size of a baking sheet, beneath Dixon's torso, removing part of his uniform and some of his bones. Before they did that, Jacobsen would feel around to make sure the thin metal sheet didn't slice through anything but mud. Public television cameras that had been privately recording the entire excavation for the *Hunley* Commission files captured the scene. Jacobsen ran her arm gently underneath Dixon, slowly, feeling for obstructions near his left pelvis. And then she stopped, a blank look on her face.

"I think I've got it," she said to one of the other scientists.

"What?"

"I'll bet you $100 this is it," she said. The expression on her face could have been apprehension or amazement. As she withdrew her arm from the mud, Jacobsen's dainty hand was a mass of black muck, and she asked for some water to be poured on it. As the mud washed away, the camera recorded the suggestion of a glint, and Goldfinger's hands began to tremble. Later Jacobsen would say that she might never experience another moment like it in her life. She was holding the most brilliant piece of gold she'd ever seen. It was round—and warped.

IN HER HAND MARIA JACOBSEN HELD GEORGE E. DIXON'S famous good-luck piece, a $20 gold coin. It had been a gift from his Mobile sweetheart, Queenie Bennett, and he'd carried it off to war in 1862. At the battle of Shiloh, it had taken a bullet meant for his leg. It had saved his life. According to legend, Dixon carried the coin with him everywhere after that, but until that moment it had been just that—a legend. Jacobsen had not thought they would find it, and then, suddenly, she had it. She had magically pulled it from the muck. Once again, Goldfinger had earned her nickname.

The coin represented so many things. It removed any doubt that George Dixon was indeed the man sitting before her. It confirmed the romantic story of the sub commander's heroic service in the war and, by association, the story of the *Hunley*. Sometimes, it proved, legends are true.

The coin had been the most sought-after artifact in *Hunley* lore, and now this team—these archaeologists—had recovered it. It was beautiful. Dated 1860, the U.S. coin carried the dent of a bullet in the hair bun at the base of Lady Liberty's head. It was thick, had substantial heft, which is probably how it had saved Dixon's life. Its ridged edges were worn smooth in places, and parts of its surface appeared to be almost buffed. *Where he'd rubbed it.*

As Jacobsen held the coin in her still-trembling hands, the other people in the room stood in awe looking at what may be the greatest Civil War artifact ever recovered. The coin would be taken away to a hidden location by armed guards, fears of theft were so great. But for a moment Jacobsen just held it there, feeling it, feeling what he felt, taking it all in. As she rubbed it, the scientist in her examined the artifact, memorizing every dent in the coin. Then she turned it over, and on the back there was an ornate inscription, unrecorded by history.

Shiloh
April 6th 1862
My life Preserver
G.E.D.

George E. Dixon, war hero, lost love of Queenie Bennett, and commander of the *H. L. Hunley*, sent his greetings from the grave.

Chapter 12

WANT OF AIR

SULLIVAN'S ISLAND, FEBRUARY 17, 1864:
The order to load up the fish-boat came just after 6:30, a calm ges-
ture from a tall, fair-haired man silhouetted against a silvery twilight sky.
The man, whose name was George Dixon, studied the water swirl-
ing around the dock as it gained momentum, a running ebb tide marching
around the end of the island and out to sea. He would let the tide carry
them out, too, anything to ease the burden on his poor, overworked crew.
He stood alone looking beyond the water where his submarine was moored,
across a vast wasteland of golden marsh grass to the west, which, set against
the gray sky, seemed to glow. If the man appeared preoccupied, his men did
not disturb him. On this night he had much on his mind.

WHEN THE ORDER WAS GIVEN, HIS CREW HAD MOST LIKELY BEEN
savoring a few last puffs of sweet tobacco before extinguishing their pipes
forever. Milling about, talking to Battery Marshall sentries, these men

hardly projected the classic image of sailors: they were skinny, gaunt, and stood slightly slumped, partially out of habit but also from the constant ache of back pain. Their clothes were cobbled together from various sources, previous assignments—one even wore the uniform of the enemy. But their appearance mattered little; their duty was, in fact, to not be seen. As the first of them entered the submarine, others would have passed down supplies, canteens, medicine. They left nothing on shore for fear that it might disappear—one man even brought his hat. They stored their belongings beneath a wooden bench, the only place inside the boat where these things would not be in the way. As they squeezed through the impossibly tiny hatches, they concentrated on keeping the boat steady.

Most likely none of them thought to take a final look at the island or the stars just beginning to appear in the sky.

As he watched his men—boys, really, save for their courage— climb into the submarine, the man reached into his left pants pocket for reassurance. He fondled the coin resting there, his left thumb fumbling until it found the indentation where it rested comfortably—where the bullet had struck nearly two years earlier. He'd had the coin engraved afterward in Mobile, commemorating the time and place it had saved his life. He'd had the jeweler add the inscription in a spot where they buffed off the words United States—*an unspoken, defiantly patriotic, statement—and in the time since, he'd nearly rubbed the rest of the coin smooth. The phrase "My life Preserver" ornately added above his initials had been a sentimental afterthought. If he was conscious of its possible second meaning, he said nothing of it.*

As the last of his crew climbed into the fish-boat, perhaps George Dixon rubbed the coin one last time. It was difficult to reach it, deep in his pants pocket, when he was inside the smothering confines of the submarine, so he may have allowed his thumb to find the comfortable spot once more before he got on board. For luck.

Dixon climbed into the submarine, wiggling his body sideways through the hatchway to his station. A single candle was already lit, casting a pale light down the rounded ceiling of the interior. Once in, he called down the shaft to the first officer and gave the order to close the after hatch. A brace screwed in place kept the aft hatch secure; a rubber gasket around its lip guarded against even a trickle of water. Dixon would fasten the forward hatch, rigged differently, in a way that allowed his head to remain in the conning tower. It gave him a little more room to stretch out his 6-foot frame. Square glass viewing ports in the tower on either side of the cutwater allowed him to see directly forward, while rounded ports on the side of the tower enhanced his field of vision to port and starboard. A glass deadlight in the 150-pound hatch let in precious light and told him when it was safe to open the hatch. Most anyone who inspected the arrangement would have been horrified by the limited view, but Dixon had grown accustomed to it. Confederate soldiers quickly grew accustomed to discomfort.

With the submarine sealed, the troops on shore unfastened the mooring lines and pushed the fish-boat away from the dock, the heavily ballasted submarine jerking slightly and then righting itself from the shove-off. With an order to begin cranking, the H. L. Hunley was under way.

AS DIXON NAVIGATED THROUGH THE INLET, THE NOISE OF THE machinery behind him was a monotonous, dull roar. Seven men turned cranks mounted in front of them, the handles powering a reduction gear that spun the propeller shaft and ultimately the three twisted blades of the screw. The handles were mounted at alternating angles so the men were not forced to crank in concert. Still, the crew seemed to move with a purposeful sense of rhythm. They went about their work without complaint and with little talk. Conversation burned up precious air. Despite the occasional pumping of the air bellows by the young man sitting at the first cranking station behind Dixon, there was never an excess of sweet oxygen inside the submarine.

The light inside the submarine grew dim as it went farther back, and to Dixon, the first officer's station near the stern was but a small light at the end of a long tunnel. Between the noise of the cranking and the sloshing of seawater against the hull, it was hard to hear. To speak to the first officer, he had to raise his voice, his commands often echoing off the iron bulkheads. He had to give few orders, however. These men knew what to do.

The last suggestion of light fading out of the evening, Dixon set his course for where he suspected the Union ship—he most likely did not know its name—would anchor for the night. Later he could steer toward the small lights that would sometimes appear on its deck. Inside, the candle flickered constantly, throwing dancing shadows on the wall. Aggravated by the movement of the men, the flame flirted with going out. Dixon may have checked the compass, making use of the light while he had it. Course set, there was little for him to do but anticipate the ride and later the attack.

THE WATER WAS REMARKABLY FLAT, A NEARLY IMPERCEPTIBLE MIST OVER the top of it, and the fish-boat sliced through it almost effortlessly. They were running 3 knots more or less, Dixon figured, normal for the boat. At that speed it was plodding progress toward the blockade 4 miles out. But then it was hard to measure how quickly they were closing in on their target. With the submarine cruising just on the surface, water occasionally washing over the top of the hull, for most of the trip they were too low for Dixon to make out the Union ships out there. But he knew where they were going. Using the lever in front of him to move the rudder, he steered toward Rattlesnake Shoal, where the unlucky ship lay at anchor.

IT WAS DARK WHEN DIXON ORDERED THE MEN TO STOP CRANKING, to let the fish-boat drift a moment while he checked their position. The calm seas on this evening made it relatively safe to open a hatch, a luxury he didn't always have. As he pushed open the heavy lid, cool air would have drifted inside the submarine slowly, raising chill bumps on the men, who had worked themselves into a lather of clammy sweat. As they waited on their captain's report, they would have been content to enjoy whatever hint of fresh air they could suck down. Perhaps as they rested, the men allowed their minds to wander, to think about the money they would make as a reward if they succeeded this night. If they broke the blockade, they would be heroes. It was a thought that kept them turning the lifeless cranks in front of them.

The ship was closer now, maybe less than a mile away. The huge sloop looked imposing from this short distance, its sleek lines silhouetted by a waning Carolina moon, its bare masts stretching upward, disappearing in the night. It had taken just over an hour to get this close, which was good. In another thirty minutes, they would ram their torpedo home and find out, finally, if this scheme would work. There was no turning back now.

In his small station it was nearly impossible for Dixon to move without brushing against the long handle that controlled the diving planes. The handle did not move easily; he had had it weighted with a counterbalance to help him adjust the fins against the water pressure. Still, he avoided touching it. He would use the submarine's remarkable powers sparingly. Beauregard had ordered him not to dive at all. He would obey that command—for now.

As they drew nearer to his prey, Dixon could not have helped but feel anxious. He was going into combat, and he was certainly an experienced enough soldier to know that every battle could be his last. If he felt any fear, he did not show it. He was comfortable in the water—he'd grown up working on steamboats—and this submarine had put him closer to the water than almost anyone in history. Or perhaps he felt little fear because it did not feel real, this battle playing out before him through a tiny glass viewing port. This was a world apart from Shiloh.

The memory of the Tennessee battle was a splinter in his mind. You always remember days when you are shot. He could not forget the blinding smoke on the battlefield the day his "life preserver" had done just that. The pain of the coin slammed against his thigh by a Yankee bullet was the only thing that had rivaled the feeling of helplessness that must have coursed through him as he heard the screams of teenage boys—boys who would never grow to manhood, who would never enjoy the company of a lady. Who would never know love. He did not like to think about that often. Perhaps it reminded him of Queenie.

Queenie, his teenage sweetheart, had given him the strength to go on after Shiloh. If things went right on this night, perhaps he would see her soon. Perhaps they could be married. Perhaps Dixon had time to think of all this. Whatever thoughts were in his mind evaporated as the Hunley *closed on the Union sloop, as the sound of bells ringing and men shouting became clearer.*

It took a moment to figure out what the tinny, plinking sounds were. Rain? Hail? No, gunfire. Perhaps Dixon recognized it first. At just over 100 yards out, they had been spotted. The element of surprise, the Hunley's single advantage, was gone. There was no choice. Dixon had his crew cranking at full speed as he aimed for the huge ship's starboard flank. It took only a few moments to close the remaining distance.

At 25 yards out, scarcely two submarine lengths, perhaps Dixon even felt confidence as surely as he felt the weight of the coin against his thigh. He knew the fish-boat better than anyone, knew it was working perfectly—had checked out the spar rigging only hours earlier on shore, now 4 miles astern. This would work—he knew it would.

The hailstorm of bullets never stopped, was still raining down when the thud of impact brought the submarine to a dead stop and jostled the men in their seats, causing each one to slide down the bench and slam into the man to his left. As soon as the men righted themselves, Dixon ordered a full reverse, the lanyard that would trigger the torpedo slowly spinning out its line as they went. The men changed their motion and turned the handles in the opposite direction as they had on the way out. The Hunley lumbered from its change in momentum. Dixon could only guess as to whether the bomb had stuck to the ship. He strained his eyes trying to peer through the forward viewing port, constantly flinching as the bullets struck close by on the hull. He did not realize it, but the fish-boat had rammed the USS sloop of war Housatonic so hard that the iron spar had bent.

As the submarine began to pick up speed as it backed away, Dixon's heart would have been pounding hard against his chest. They were doing it. He looked out the starboard conning tower port to see if the trigger rope was reeling out, and then he saw the monstrous ship lurch to port.

THE EXPLOSION CAME AS A SURPRISE: THEY WERE NOT FAR ENOUGH away when the torpedo trigger line went taut and the ship exploded, part of its hull simply vanishing in an instant. Dixon would have watched the mighty ship heave and begin to sink. The crew of the fish-boat would have heard the blast, perhaps even felt the concussion of it. No one will ever *know for sure how loud or how shocking it was to the crew in the iron sub-marine, but in and of itself it was not a crippling blow. The* Hunley *con-tinued to move away.*

AFTER A HALF HOUR, MAYBE LONGER, DIXON FELT IT WAS SAFE *enough to open the forward hatch again. The tide would be turning soon, and then they could crank for home. They had considered playing pos-sum by resting on the seabed until it turned, but their main concern was simply to get out of the way. Once Dixon squeezed his torso through the hatch, he scanned the horizon for a hint of land. From the vantage of sea level, he might have had to rely on a compass reading or blind luck. When he determined which direction to send his signal, he reached for the lamp.*

Dixon had told the troops at Battery Marshall he would shine the blue phosphorus light when he was ready for them to build a signal fire to steer home by. Once the lamp was lit, he would display it as long as he felt safe doing so, or at least until he was comfortable that someone on shore had taken notice of it. The light was spotted, not only by Confederates on shore but also by a lone sailor clinging to the foremast rigging of the dying battle-ship less than a mile away.

After Dixon extinguished his light, he took in his last fresh breath and closed the hatch, perhaps not even noticing the even larger ship, which was called the Canandaigua, *coming from astern, closing in fast on the fish-boat's position.*

SOMETIME LATER IT ENDED PEACEFULLY. FIRST THE CANDLE WENT *out, the flame shrinking into its wick until there wasn't even a notion of precious light inside the cramped interior. The men were blind; they could not see one another or their own hands as they blew into their fists to keep warm. Cold condensation formed on the iron walls, and the only sound was that of underwater currents outside, surging menacingly around the hull. Inside, it was dry, quiet. If words were spoken, they are lost forever. There was no scramble to the hatches, because there was either no hope of escape or no awareness of danger. There was no panic, only a want of air in the smothering darkness. And then it was over.*

M ORE THAN A CENTURY AFTER THE DISAPPEARANCE OF the *H. L. Hunley*, and more than a year after its recovery from the ocean floor, its sinking continues to baffle scientists. In the short time since the submarine was returned to its home port, archaeologists have uncovered countless secrets about its construction and operation, about its crew and its years of hibernation beneath the Atlantic. But they still aren't sure they are any closer to answering the biggest mystery of all: what happened in those final moments, in the last minutes of February 17, 1864, aboard the Confederate torpedo boat? If there is a smoking gun, which is looking more and more unlikely, it is hidden deep in the unexplored corners of the fish-boat or in some combination of facts already collected in archaeologists' notebooks, waiting to be analyzed.

Of course, there are theories—there have always been theories. In more than a century since the *Hunley* was lost at sea, men concocted dozens of supposed endings for the world's first attack submarine. The first stories, proved untrue simply by virtue of where the *Hunley* was found, claimed it was sucked into the hole it made in the side of the *Housatonic*. Later people supposed it was buried under the Charleston Harbor rock jetties (in some ways that is not completely inaccurate, as the jetties rerouted sand patterns, which helped hide it).

Later suspicions held that because the *Hunley* was between 50 and 80 feet away from the *Housatonic* at the time of the explosion, its hull buckled from the concussion of the blast. That was a possibility that remained viable until the submarine was recovered. While scientists aren't completely ruling that out—they rarely dismiss anything until there is absolutely no question—it is unlikely. If the submarine had cracked from the pressure of the explosion, it most likely would have sunk immediately, inland of the *Housatonic*, and Dixon would not have had time to signal with the blue lamp, which witnesses say he did. The best proof against this theory is that archaeologists have found no indication of hull breaches or plate buckling. The *Hunley* remains a sturdy, if antiquated, war machine.

Soon after the discovery of the *Hunley* by the NUMA team in 1995, the hole in the forward conning tower—made famous in grainy pictures taken by Clive Cussler's team—suggested a new ending. The single-bullet theory contends that small-arms fire from the sailors on board the *Housatonic* shattered the cast-iron conning tower, allowing enough water into the submarine to sink it. In the years between the discovery and recovery of the *Hunley*, the most popular speculation ran along these lines. The submarine, it was well documented, needed little additional weight to send it plunging into the depths: after all, its first sinking off Fort Johnson was attributed to the lazy wake of a passing Confederate ship.

The single-bullet scenario is a bleak picture of the crew's final minutes—the fish-boat losing buoyancy slowly as the crew tried desperately to either dump the water in the ballast tanks and pump it out or plug the hole in the tower and limp home. It would have been a horrifying ending.

By inference the single-bullet theory also assumes that Dixon was shot, either wounded or killed, in the attack. Because his head would have been in the conning tower guiding the *Hunley* to its target, any shot that hit the tower would almost certainly have struck at least a glancing blow to Dixon. It only makes the story that much more reasonable. Had Dixon been shot, the submarine would have spiraled out of control, the interior being too cramped for any other crew member to crawl forward, move him out of the way, and take control.

Again, there are facts that seem to rule out this scenario. Although Union sailors fired countless shots at the *Hunley*, in later interviews they didn't seem to believe they had done any damage. The submarine backed away from its prey smoothly and made its blue lamp signal—something it could not have done with a dead or injured Dixon. The most persuasive argument against the theory is Dixon himself. Archaeologists said the best evidence of a single bullet sinking the *Hunley* might be Dixon's skull. If it showed signs of a bullet wound, it would go a long way toward legitimizing that hypothesis. But when Dixon was found, his skull showed no obvious signs of trauma.

One of the most intriguing finds of the excavation introduced a more likely scenario. Early in the investigation of the *Hunley's* interior, archaeologists found small, pencil-sized stalactites hanging from the ceiling. Stalactites—basically calcium icicles—are formed from mineral deposits in dripping water. That water could have been condensation, or it could have been the slow trickle of a pinhead leak in the seal of one of the deadlights or hull plates. However they were formed, the more important fact is this: they do not form underwater. The presence of stalactites in the crew compartment suggests that the interior of the *Hunley* was dry for years after it sank. Later there clearly were hull breaches of undetermined origin—a gash in the stern, a pie-sized punch to the starboard hull, and the conning tower hole. Because of the presence of stalactites, it is quite possible that those holes were not contemporary to the sinking but, in fact, weren't made until many years after the fish-boat vanished.

If the submarine's central compartment did not flood, the men of the *Hunley* may simply have died of anoxia, a lack of oxygen to the brain. It would have been a quiet, quick end. Inside the pitch-dark interior of the submarine—the candle would have run out of air before the crew—the men would simply have passed out from a lack of air and then suffocated. It would have been almost like going to sleep.

Anoxia is a leading suspect for the *Hunley* crew's cause of death. Besides the stalactites, the position of the crew's remains supports this theory. For the most part the skeletons were found at their duty stations, partially articulated—that is, in skeletal form. Had the interior been filled with water immediately, the bodies would have floated to the same, highest spot in the submarine, resulting in a single, massive pile of bones in one part of the crew compartment as the remains settled. Archaeologists feared that would be the case before going into the submarine and were amazed to find the skeletons still at their battle stations.

If the crew did indeed succumb to anoxia, it only begs the question: why? The men of the *H. L. Hunley*'s final crew were intimately acquainted with their vessel. They had proved only a month earlier that they could lift their boat from a sandy bottom working blind. If they had gone down to the bottom, less than 30 feet below, why could they not get back up? Some historical records suggest Dixon steered by the tides almost religiously. Instead of fighting the tide, he might have waited for it to turn. The incoming tide would have started just a couple of hours after the attack on the *Housatonic*. Perhaps the crew simply submerged to avoid the traffic of blockade ships coming to the *Housatonic*'s rescue and lost track of time beneath the surface. It would have been dark and quiet, the men exhausted. Their mission accomplished, they may have felt a weight lifted and relaxed. It is a chilling thought: they got too comfortable.

There are other scenarios. Perhaps the *Hunley* took on enough water to rob it of positive buoyancy, sending them to the bottom. Even if they plugged a leak, there might not have been a way, underwater, to expel the added weight. They would have known they were stuck on the bottom, waiting for the end in a dark tomb, much as Horace Lawson Hunley himself had died, his head in the forward conning tower, water up to his neck.

For years some historians believed that the *Hunley* may have been involved in a collision with another boat, and that was the cause of its sinking. The *Housatonic* sailor who saw the blue light on the water reported that it was just ahead of the *Canandaigua*, the flagship of the Charleston blockading fleet on its way to rescue the *Housatonic*'s survivors. Even if the two boats had collided, the crew of the *Canandaigua* might not have felt the tiny fish-boat bouncing off their ship's massive hull. That theory was largely dismissed after the *Hunley* was raised and scientists found no obvious signs of a crash—no dents in the submarine's hull.

There was this curious thought, however. Shea McLean, one of the archaeologists on the project, noticed a series of strange gashes in the submarine's propeller shroud—or what's left of it. The port side of the shroud—which was designed to keep ropes, anchor chains, and seaweed from getting fouled in the propeller—is completely missing. On the starboard side there is a series of triangular gashes—cuts, really—on the back. Perhaps, McLean and a number of other people believe, those could be the marks of the *Canandaigua*'s propeller. Dixon may have spotted the huge ship on the water while signaling to the troops on shore but didn't have enough time to get his little boat out of the way. If the *Canandaigua*'s screw clipped the submarine's stern, it would explain the gashes in the shroud, and it might also have severed the *Hunley*'s rudder. During the recovery the submarine's rudder was found beneath the hull, an odd place for it, but not so odd if it was dangling from a controlling rod or cable when the *Hunley* crashed into the seabed. If the rudder had rotted off, it most likely would have been found behind the submarine, right where it fell. A severed rudder would have led to a terrifying end. Without the ability to steer, the *Hunley* would have been almost helpless. It would have been drifting in whatever direction the tide saw fit to take it, until it sank. Dixon may even have ordered them down to keep them from being pulled out to sea by the ebb tide.

SCIENTISTS MAY NEVER KNOW WHAT HAPPENED TO THE *Hunley*. They continue to analyze data from their initial excavation and a follow-up dig in the fall of 2001, when they confirmed that the *Hunley* carried a crew of only eight and discovered that Dixon steered using a lever much like a joystick, a kind of upright tiller. A Marine Forensic Panel, a standing committee of the Society of Naval Architects and Marine Engineers, is studying the puzzle. It will investigate the submarine's end as if it were a modern-day accident. It hopes to re-create the sinking, and do a blast analysis and metallurgical study of the submarine to gain a better understanding of what, if anything, might have happened to the *Hunley* after the attack on the *Housatonic*.

Luckily there is a lot to study. The *Hunley* was recovered more intact than probably any other wartime shipwreck in history. It has provided a wealth of information about itself and the times in which it was born. Scientists also say that it sank in an ideal location for preservation. If it had come to rest on the ocean floor farther out to sea, where there is less sediment, it might have foundered and remained uncovered, exposing it to repeated snags by anchors or less than noble treasure hunters. Closer to shore it could have been buried so deeply after the construction of the Charleston Harbor jetties that it might never have been found. As it was, the *Hunley* went down in the perfect location to be preserved pristinely.

Still, it stubbornly clings to its greatest secret, even as it sits stewing in a chemical bath in a North Charleston laboratory. Perhaps the *Hunley* deserves to cling to that one final secret. It was the beginning of stealth technology on the water, a ship shrouded in secrecy so long that an entire mythology has been created around it. It has given up so many answers, maybe it deserves to hold that one thing back, to cling to a bit of mystery about the final haunting minutes of its last night, when it forever etched its name in history.

EPILOGUE

In 1872 **James McClintock** secretly met with officers of the British Royal Navy outside of Halifax, Nova Scotia. Disillusioned and feeling unappreciated in his own country, McClintock suggested he would like to become a British subject and offered to build a submarine for the Royal Navy. Long after he was forced to walk away from his *Hunley* in Charleston in 1863, McClintock believed he had perfected a motor that would sufficiently power a submarine. But the English weren't interested. In his lifetime James McClintock was never credited as the designer of the world's first successful attack submarine. He never received the praise he was due for his contributions in the development of submarine technology. He died in 1879 at the age of fifty, when a new submarine mine he was testing in Boston Harbor exploded. It was the one time in his life when McClintock was not cautious enough.

The effects of the American Civil War haunted **Robert Ruffin Barrow** for the rest of his life. The brother-in-law of Horace Lawson Hunley watched his wife, **Volumnia**, mourn her last surviving blood relative until she developed an ulcerated stomach and died in 1868. Barrow broke down following the death of his dear wife, which came on the heels of physical and financial ruin after the war caused by the loss of business and the slaves that ran his eighteen plantations. Around New Orleans people for years spoke in hushed tones about "poor Barrow" until he died in 1875.

When **William Alexander** passed away in May of 1914, the *Mobile Register* hailed him in its obituary headline as the BUILDER OF FIRST SUBMARINE. Alexander left behind a large family and a town full of admirers who remembered him as a pleasant man, a volunteer in his church, and "an inventor of some note." In his later years Alexander enjoyed some celebrity due to his connection with the *Hunley*. He used the notoriety to honor the memory of the crew that vanished on a voyage that, but for fate, would have killed him, too. If Alexander had not survived to write the most complete firsthand history of the *Hunley*, the fish-boat might have faded from memory and never been found. In some ways Alexander did the next best thing to saving his crewmates— he immortalized them. With full veteran honors Alexander was buried in a Mobile cemetery that bears the same name as one in Charleston that serves as the final resting place for all other *Hunley* crew members—Magnolia.

Seven years after the *Hunley* sank, **Queenie Bennett** married and started a family. She moved to Mississippi, where she lived a happy life and spoke rarely—if ever—of her first love. Years after her death Bennett's grandchildren found an old photograph hidden in one of her scrapbooks. The fair-haired young man, whom no one in the family recognized, seemed to match historical descriptions of a brave young Confederate lieutenant named **George E. Dixon**. To this day, no one can identify the person in the photograph.

B. A. "Gus" Whitney died shortly after the Confederate Army seized the *Hunley* in August 1863. The cause of death was casually attributed to "exposure" but may have been pneumonia contracted in the cold, damp confines of the secret weapon of which he was part owner. For years his friends considered him another casualty of the fish-boat.

Gen. **Pierre Gustave Toutant Beauregard** never regained the fame and status he had achieved as a Confederate war hero. During Reconstruction Beauregard drifted through a number of jobs—railroad president, adjutant general for the state of Louisiana, commissioner of public works for New Orleans. His stint as supervisor of the questionable Louisiana lottery cost him his reputation. He wrote books and gave speeches about his efforts in the war—including his association with the strange torpedo boats in Charleston Harbor—until his death in New Orleans on February 20, 1893.

Rear Adm. **John A. Dahlgren**, inventor of a smoothbore cannon and the commander of the Union Navy's South Atlantic Blockading Squadron, who warned his fleet of the coming torpedo boat, returned to a desk job with the U.S. Navy after the Civil War. When he died five years later, in 1870, he was still commander of the Washington Navy Yard.

Throughout his long career, **Jules Verne** was praised for predicting the future—the automobile, flight, the Aqua-Lung . . . and the submarine. It was a plaudit Verne dismissed, repeatedly noting that most of the things he wrote about had already been invented in some early stage when he turned them into something fantastic—as the case had been with the *Hunley*. When he died in 1905 at the age of seventy-seven, the prolific French author and father of science fiction was returning to one of his favorite frontiers. His last book was titled *The Invasion of the Sea*.

Charles Hasker, the only man who "went to the bottom with the 'Fish-Boat' and came up to tell the tale," moved to Richmond, Virginia, after the war. Following the death of his first wife, Hasker married again and went into business in the onetime capital of the Confederacy. He enjoyed telling the story of his wild, harrowing ride on the *Hunley* all his life. He died in July 1898, shortly after taking a ride on Simon Lake's new submarine, the *Argonaut*. He was sixty-seven.

In December 1863, occupying Union forces in New Orleans found near the New Basin Canal a "Rebel Submarine Ram" believed by some to be the **Pioneer**, McClintock and Hunley's first torpedo boat. A sketch of the 35-foot, hand-cranked submarine was forwarded to the assistant secretary of the Navy just weeks before the battle of the *Hunley* and *Housatonic*. In 1868 a New Orleans newspaper reported that a submarine boat found in a canal outside of town was to be auctioned off that day. The only submarine officially registered as a Confederate privateer during the war was sold for scrap metal. It brought $43 and was never seen again.

For decades treasure hunters, wreck divers, and archaeologists have searched the murky waters of Mobile Bay off Fort Morgan for McClintock and Hunley's mysterious second submarine, the **American Diver**. It has never been found.

The first submarine that **Simon Lake** built was only 36 feet long—4 feet shorter than the *Hunley*. In 1898 his *Argonaut* made a 300-mile trip from Norfolk, Virginia, to New York City powered by its own, gasoline-powered engines. The New Jersey native and Father of the Modern Submarine, who took early tips from the construction of the Confederate fish-boat, built well over one hundred submersibles in his long career. Among his other innovative contributions to the field, he is credited with inventing the periscope. He died in 1945.

Rear Adm. **Robert Bentham Simons**, USN (Ret.), died in Charleston in July of 1971 at the age of eighty-three. A decorated war hero and historian who witnessed history on December 7, 1941, at Pearl Harbor, Simons wanted his entire life to find the *Hunley*. In 1957, when the Navy delayed a search for the submarine that Simons had instigated, he lost all hope of ever seeing the missing Confederate torpedo boat.

Clive Cussler—author, sea hunter, and leader of the expedition that found the *H. L. Hunley*—is still looking for the *Bonhomme Richard*, the only other ship he swore he would find before he died. The car aficionado continues to write his best-selling novels featuring NUMA underwater archaeologist Dirk Pitt. His NUMA team recently found the legendary ghost ship *Mary Celeste* off Haiti.

Ralph Wilbanks, **Wes Hall**, and **Harry Pecorelli**, who together found the lost submarine in May 1995, formed a four-man pact with Cussler to commemorate their place in history. The last man surviving wins the right to drink a bottle of French cognac with a handblown glass replica of the *Hunley*.

In 1997 the *Hunley* Commission ruled that **Lee Spence** could not have found the *Hunley* in 1970. State archaeologists said that the low amount of marine growth on the *Hunley*'s hull suggests it was never uncovered until the NUMA team found it in 1995. Spence continues to press his case from his own office less than 2 miles from the Warren Lasch Conservation Center. He has yet to visit the submarine in its new home.

After his fallout with Clive Cussler, **Mark Newell** left SCIAA and would never again be associated with the *Hunley*.

The *Hunley* **Commission** and **Friends of the *Hunley*** in 2001 received the Civil War Preservation Trust's Preservation Award for exemplary dedication to the cause of preservation. Scientists, historians, and archaeologists around the world are unanimous in their praise of the *Hunley* project. Many say it has set a new benchmark for maritime archaeology.

In May 2001 Friends of the *Hunley* chairman **Warren Lasch** was awarded an honorary doctorate in business administration from the Citadel, both for his private enterprise and for his management of the recovery of the lost Confederate submarine.

Glenn McConnell went on to become president pro tem of the South Carolina State Senate. He is one of the state's leading champions of southern heritage issues and remains the only chairman the *Hunley* Commission has ever had.

The search for the final resting place of **Ezra Chamberlin** continues.

Marine archaeologists **Bob Neyland** and **Maria Jacobsen** are studying evidence recovered from the *H. L. Hunley* in their continuing quest to discover what happened in the submarine's final minutes. The research could take years.

Paul Mardikian was working on a conservation project in France in 1995 when he heard that the *Hunley* had been found and thought how he would like to be involved in *that* project. Now he spends his days at the Warren Lasch Conservation Center lab, where he is in the process of restoring the *Hunley* and all the artifacts that have been found inside it. He insists that one day soon the submarine will be nearly as good as new.

In 1999, one year before the *Hunley* was raised, its recovery team and a crew of National Park Service divers visited the wreckage of the **USS Housatonic**. The most in-depth study ever of the sloop's wreckage determined that on February 17, 1864, the *H. L. Hunley* rammed its spiked, 90-pound keg of explosives into the Union ship's most vulnerable spot—near the rear powder magazine, just below the main fighting deck, where much of the 7,000 pounds of gunpowder on board was likely stored. It was, scientists said, a direct hit.

On August 12, 2000—four days after the *Hunley* was plucked from the bottom of the Atlantic Ocean—the Russian submarine *Kursk* suffered a terrible explosion in its bow, causing it to sink to the bottom of the frigid Barents Sea. All 118 crewmen were lost, including several who spent their last tortured hours alone in the dark writing farewell notes to their families. The loss of the *Kursk* became the latest entry on a long list of submarines to go on eternal patrol, a list that began with the *Hunley*.

On February 17, 2001—"the 137th anniversary of their sacrifice"— more than three hundred people gathered on Sullivan's Island for a memorial to the men of the *H. L. Hunley* and USS *Housatonic*. The church service was followed by a short march that ended at Breach Inlet at the exact hour the submarine would have departed. At the water's edge black and white reenactors fired a twenty-one-gun salute after women in nineteenth-century mourning dresses threw roses into the sea. The ceremony was led by **Randy Burbage** and ended with the crowd softly singing "Dixie."

In 1962 the United States Navy named one of its five nuclear submarine tenders after **Horace Lawson Hunley**. A plaque on the ship's quarterdeck praised him as the "Pioneer of Submarine Warfare." It was an honor of the highest order: all the tenders in the series were named after luminaries in the field of submarine development. Finally, almost a century after his death, Hunley had achieved a goal he secretly harbored as a young lawyer in antebellum New Orleans.

He was a Great Man.

NOTES

Reconstructing the story of the *H. L. Hunley* was a daunting task. The short life of the fish-boat is almost as much a mystery as its disappearance. There was little Confederate paperwork in those days, especially for a project considered a state secret. Most mentions of the submarine in the official war records are vague. The original plans for the sub, of course, have been lost forever. And the men who designed, built, and piloted the *Hunley* left behind little evidence that they had been involved in the birth of stealth technology. In all, the story of the submarine is hidden in a few surviving orders and notes and a handful of eyewitness accounts that remain filed in libraries and archives around the country.

To tell the story as accurately as is possible more than a century after the fact, we started from scratch, photocopying as much primary material as we could, transcribing the rest. We studied dozens of short notes and telegrams; the few surviving letters of Horace Hunley, James McClintock, George Dixon, and William Alexander; along with newspaper and magazine reminiscences. We found as many contradictory facts as we did supporting ones. After gathering, examining, and comparing all the information we could find, we determined what we believed to be the most logical facts, the details that rang true, and culled those that seemed unbelievable even by the logic-defying standards of the *Hunley*. Much of it was purely common sense. For instance, some accounts suggested the submarine sank as many as six times in Mobile Bay and Charleston Harbor. That just could not have happened. The two documented accidents prior to the *Hunley*'s February 17, 1864, disappearance resulted in huge undertakings. After each sinking it took more than a month to lift and refurbish the submarine. There simply wasn't time in its eight-month tour of duty for it to have suffered that many accidents. The submarine shipped out for Charleston within a month of the time it was hauled out of the Seaman's Bethel in downtown Mobile. Less than two weeks after it arrived, the *Hunley* sank off Fort Johnson, and it was late September or early October before it sailed again. When it went down with Horace Hunley on board on October 15, 1863, it was not raised until early November and was still being repaired in early December, when Conrad Wise Chapman captured its sleek lines in his elegant painting.

In deciphering contemporary accounts, we gave more weight to some than others. James McClintock and William Alexander provide what we feel are the best historical accounts simply because they were closest to the submarine. Alexander, in particular, had an eye toward history in everything he did. We got chills gazing at the actual handwriting of Alexander in one letter, when he wrote that he recounts the stories for "future historians." For others, such as Gen. P.G.T. Beauregard, the *Hunley* was but one of a thousand things going on at the time: details tended to be fuzzier in the accounts of outsiders. When accounts differed, we most often trusted the words of someone who had had hands-on experience with the submarine.

The mystery of George Dixon's role in the second crew is the best example of conflicting histories. Beauregard wrote that Dixon was a member of the second crew who just happened to be out of the city when the submarine sank with Hunley at the controls. Alexander claims Dixon was in Mobile, however, having been denied a seat on that crew. We accepted Alexander's version of the story, given his close relationship with Dixon and the fact that he should have known if his friend was in Mobile with him when they heard the news about the accident. Friends of the *Hunley* historian Mark Ragan, however, has uncovered documents that suggest Dixon was indeed in Charleston at the time of the second sinking and perhaps even traveling with a secret agent of the Confederacy. It is an intriguing story if true. But Dixon's own letter to his regiment commander suggests he arrived in early November, as other accounts say. Alexander dismisses the mysterious "Dillingham" as a man who accompanied him and Dixon to South Carolina to crew the fish-boat but was not brave enough to dive in it. Many people close to the project like to speculate on Dixon's close ties to clandestine operations for the Confederacy (as if the *Hunley* weren't enough). It could be true, but we did not find enough evidence to convince us to make it a part of our narrative. The story is written in such a way as to leave any role Dixon may have played in the second crew ambiguous simply because we don't know for sure and suspect we never will.

Much of the material used in writing this book was found in the remarkable Eustace Williams Collection in the Local History and Genealogy department of the Mobile Public Library. Williams was perhaps the first *Hunley* historian (after William Alexander) and spent his long life tirelessly compiling records on the fish-boat. The California resident was born a mere eight years after Appomattox—according to his own writings—and died only in the mid-1960s. He provided the *Hunley* papers that sailed beneath the North Pole on the *Nautilus* and left scores of notebooks of information in libraries across the country. His six-volume set of photocopies, transcriptions, and interpretive notes in Mobile is a researcher's dream. After William Alexander, Eustace Williams did more than anyone to keep the memory of the lost submarine alive.

All quotes in Part I of this book were taken from the surviving documents, and nearly all thoughts attributed to the many characters in the story are gleaned from the same letters and notes, except in the instances in which it was so obvious what a person would have been thinking that we could safely infer. We have added nothing to the *Hunley*'s story.

For Part II we were fortunate to be able to interview everyone who had a major hand in the search for the *H. L. Hunley*. All were helpful and gracious with their time. Clive Cussler—a man busy with his own books—was a saint about calling back, no matter how many times we had to track down His Authorship at one of his homes out west. Mark Newell was kind enough to consent to a few telephone interviews. Lee Spence gave us several hours of his time one afternoon, nearly all of which he spent trying to convince us—as he has everyone else for thirty years—that he found the *Hunley* first. When we asked biographical questions, he said he would share no more information unless we conceded that he found the submarine first. Ultimately our time with Spence came down to a single statement. He said, "You're chicken if you don't say I found the *Hunley* first." We could only promise him that we would never say he did *not* find it. Spence's claim is a mystery that will likely never be resolved completely.

Chapters 8 and beyond represent the time when we first became involved with this project. Schuyler had come to *The Post and Courier* in 1987 and shortly after learned of the *Hunley* as one of Charleston's local legends. When Cussler announced his discovery in 1995, Schuyler jumped at the chance to cover the story. He's been following it ever since.

Brian stumbled onto the story a year later. A Nashville-based political reporter at the time, he was vacationing in Charleston in May of 1996, when, on the way to the beach, he picked up that morning's edition of *The Post and Courier*. The headline screamed IT'S OFFICIAL and told of the Park Service divers' identifying Cussler's find as the *Hunley*. He carried the article back to Tennessee, and when he began looking for a life beyond political reporting a year later, his wife, Beth, reminded him of the *Hunley* and Charleston.

As a result of this tag-team approach to coverage, most of the information in the later chapters is from our own reporting—about four hundred newspaper articles between 1999 and 2001. While we have sourced everything else, we do not cite our own stories: it would be far too tedious. Suffice it to say, anything from Chapter 9 forward, we witnessed firsthand. We watched as the *Hunley*'s first crew was uncovered at the Citadel. As plans were cemented for the recovery, we were in daily contact with members of the team. On August 8, 2000, Schuyler watched the recovery from the *Karlissa B* and sailed into Charleston aboard the *Hunley* recovery barge. Brian saw it pass from Sullivan's Island and the USS *Yorktown* and later stood on the docks with Randy Burbage, watching as the submarine was moved into its holding tank at the Warren Lasch Conservation Center. Throughout the excavation one of us—if not both—was at the lab nearly every day. If we couldn't be there for some reason, at the very least we spoke by telephone with project manager Bob Neyland. We were closer to the project than any other journalists.

Warren Lasch and Glenn McConnell granted us special access throughout: we were allowed to peer inside the submarine, to see what the men of the *Hunley* saw, and later to hold Dixon's warped gold coin in our own hands. McConnell calls it being "*Hunley*tized." We can vouch for the magical attraction of the coin. Brian held the gold coin for forty-five minutes before he could tear himself away—it had that powerful a hold.

Ultimately we believe this is a remarkable story that transcends the politics and controversy of the Civil War; it is a story of outstanding ingenuity and engineering marvel, of bravery and courage in the face of overpowering danger. It is an all-too-human story, a tale of ordinary men doing extraordinary things in extraordinary times. The *Hunley* might have stayed lost forever; it was just luck that it crashed into the ocean floor where it did. Now that it has been found, perhaps it will educate generations of people, as a very real and important piece of history that shows, ultimately, what men can do when they set their minds to it. We feel lucky to have witnessed some of this amazing submarine's history.

A portion of our royalties will be donated to the Friends of the *Hunley* (www.hunley.org) to aid in the preservation of the submarine.

PROLOGUE: AUGUST 8, 2000

1–2 Aboard the crane barge: The account of Jenkins Montgomery's hours aboard the *Karlissa B* on August 8, 2000, is taken from an interview with Montgomery in January 2001.

3 In 1971 the U.S. Navy: Press materials on the christening of the submarine tender USS *Dixon (AS 37)* filed in the archives of the state of Alabama.

3 It was December 1860: Walter Edgar, *South Carolina: A History* (Columbia: University of South Carolina Press, 1998), 351–52.

3 "If South Carolina refuses . . .": Will G. Albergotti III, *Abigail's Story: Tides at the Doorstep. The MacKays, LaRoches, Jenkinses, and Chisholms of Low Country, South Carolina, 1671–1897* (Spartanburg, S.C.: Reprint Company, 1999), 145–46.

CHAPTER 1: PIONEERS

13 She was sleek: James R. McClintock, letter to Matthew Maury, 1868, copy in the Eustace Williams Collection, Mobile Public Library.

13 In trial runs: James E. Kloeppel, *Danger beneath the Waves* (Orangeburg, S.C.: Sandlapper Publishing, 1992), 7.

13 There were a few: The maladies of the *Pioneer* are chronicled briefly in William Morrison Robinson's *The Confederate Privateers* (Columbia: University of South Carolina Press, 1990, 165–72) and in Eustace Williams's "The Dawn of Modern Warfare," a research paper the longtime *Hunley* historian included in the huge set of papers he donated to the Mobile Public Library. The *Pioneer's* flaws are not surprising, as all of the McClintock-Hunley submarines had similar problems.

14 Slowly *Pioneer* sank: William Alexander, "The Heroes of the *Hunley,*" *Munsey's Magazine,* August 1903, 746.

14 It proved they could: McClintock, letter to Maury, 1868.

15 Bringing down the *New Ironsides*: E. Milby Burton, *The Siege*

of Charleston, 1861–1865 (Columbia: University of South Carolina Press, 1971), 216.

16 He was an attorney: Ruth H. Duncan, *The Captain and Submarine CSS "H. L. Hunley"* (Memphis: S. C. Toof & Company, 1965), 53–54.

17 Heavily involved in: Horace Lawson Hunley, Memorandum Book, record group 140, folder 12, Louisiana Historical Society.

17 In a tiny ledger: Ibid.

18 One notation: Ibid.

18 He was born: Duncan, *Captain and Submarine,* 16.

18 Just a few years after: Ibid., 20.

18 A few hard years: Ibid., 20.

18 As soon as he was: Ibid., 53.

18 The gambling man: Hunley, Memorandum Book.

19 In June that year: Duncan, *Captain and Submarine,* 59.

20 Just thirty-two when: Mrs. Edwin J. Palmer, "Horace Lawson Hunley," *United Daughters of the Confederacy Magazine,* May 1962, 14.

20 A stray letter: Mark K. Ragan, *The "Hunley": Submarines, Sacrifice, and Success in the Civil War* (Charleston: Narwhal Press, 1995), 15.

20 The word was: This refers to the submarine found in 1879 on the banks of Lake Pontchartrain—once believed to be *Pioneer*—that is now owned by the Louisiana State Museum. Although the sub's origin remains a mystery, most researchers believe it was built by Southerners before the fall of New Orleans.

21 It was 34 feet long: *Official Records of the Union and Confederate Navies in the War of the Rebellion (ORN),* series 2, vol. 1 (Washington, D.C.: Government Printing Office, 1921), 399–400.

22 The early tests: McClintock, letter to Maury, 1868.

23 They applied for: *ORN,* series 2, vol. 1, 399–400.

23 In the chaos: Alexander, "Heroes," 746. Most historical accounts say that Horace Hunley and James McClintock sank the *Pioneer* in the New Basin Canal just outside the city as Farragut was approaching. Later, in December 1863, occupying Union forces reported finding a strange torpedo near the New Basin. They sketched it

and sent word of it to Washington, where it arrived just weeks before the *Hunley* sank the *Housatonic*.

24 To stay in deep water: Interview with Chuck Torrey, historian, City of Mobile Museum.

24 As a result of all that: Ibid.

24 As soon as the crew arrived: William Alexander, "The True Story of the Confederate Submarine Boats," *New Orleans Picayune*, June 29, 1902.

26 The sandy-haired soldier: Erwin Craighead, *From Mobile's Past: Sketches of Memorable People and Events* (Mobile: Powers Printing Company, 1925).

26 The work began: Alexander, "True Story."

26 McClintock busied himself: McClintock, letter to Maury, 1868.

26 He tinkered with it: Ibid.

26 The time for experimentation: Ibid.

27 A bullet meant for: John Kent Folmar, ed., *From That Terrible Field: Civil War Letters of James M. Williams, Twenty-first Alabama Infantry Volunteers* (Tuscaloosa: University of Alabama Press, 1981), 53.

27 The iron hull played: Alexander, "True Story."

28 Where they practiced: *The War of the Rebellion: A Compilation of the Official Records of the Union and Confederate Armies (OR)*, series 1, vol. 26 (part 2) (Washington, D.C.: Government Printing Office, 1901), 180.

28 The first true mission: *ORN*, series 1, vol. 19, 628.

28 Hunley was absent: Duncan, *Captain and Submarine*, 63. Various sources show that Hunley could barely keep still and moved from one town to the other—usually where there was some action—until he arrived in Charleston in the late summer of 1863. No one has yet been able to explain what he was doing on these jaunts.

28 The plan was to tow: Alexander, "True Story."

29 On the day the *Diver*: Horace Hunley, letter to Gen. [P.]G.T. Beauregard, September 19, 1863, copy in the Eustace Williams Collection, Mobile Public Library.

30 One minute the *American Diver*: Alexander, "True Story."

30 The order had come: *OR,* series 1, vol. 28 (part 2), 265.

31 Maury felt he wouldn't: Maj. Gen. Dabney Herndon Maury, Southern Historical Society Papers, vol. 4 (1894), 81.

31 "It is much needed": *OR,* series 1, vol. 28 (part 2), 265.

31 Hunley quickly sold two-thirds: Kloeppel, *Danger beneath the Waves,* 23.

33 The inventors had returned: Alexander, "Heroes," 746.

33 Determined to move quickly: McClintock, letter to Maury, 1868.

33 A pine bowsprit: Harry Pillans, letter to the editor, *Montgomery Advertiser,* November 8, 1924. Pillans mentions the pine spar, which may be what is depicted in the Conrad Wise Chapman painting of the *Hunley,* Museum of the Confederacy, Richmond.

34 On a test run: Maury, Southern Historical Society Papers, 81.

34 Scaffolding was built: D. Morris, "The Rebels and the Pig-boat," *Argosy,* October 1954, 81.

CHAPTER 2: MELANCHOLY OCCURRENCES

35 When Gus Whitney: *The War of the Rebellion: A Compilation of the Official Records of the Union and Confederate Armies (OR),* series 1, vol. 28 (part 2) (Washington, D.C.: Government Printing Office, 1901), 285.

35 Brig. Gen. Thomas Jordan promised: Ibid.

36 Holding the 3,500 miles: Craig L. Symonds, ed., *Charleston Blockade: The Journals of John B. Marchand, U.S. Navy, 1861–1862* (Newport: Naval War College Press, 1976), xi.

36 "I have been . . .": Horace Hunley, letter to James R. McClintock, August 15, 1863, copy in the Eustace Williams Collection, Mobile Public Library.

37 Hunley had great confidence: Ibid.

37 ". . . under its present management": *OR,* series 1, vol. 28 (part 1), 670.

38 "He is timid": Ibid.

39 He seized the submarine: In his postwar writing Beauregard never admits he did this. However, a letter from Maj. John F. O'Brien (*OR,* series 1, vol. 28 [part 2], 376) makes mention of the military's

taking possession of the submarine boat. Also, a letter found by James Kloeppel (Kloeppel, *Danger beneath the Waves* [Orangeburg, S.C.: Sandlapper Publishing, 1992], 38) states that the boat was "seized." That letter suggests the *Hunley* sank the very day it was commandeered, a stunning—and telling—fact if true.

39 When he arrived in Charleston: Gen. [P.]G.T. Beauregard, "Torpedo Service in the Harbor and Water Defences of Charleston," Southern Historical Society Papers, vol. 5, no. 4 (April 1878), 146.

41 Lt. John Payne: Ibid., 153.

41 The eager Virginian recruited: Beauregard wrote in the Southern Historical Society Papers that Payne assembled his crew from the Confederate Navy, and the brief mention of the fish-boat's first sinking in the August 31, 1863, edition of the *Charleston Daily Courier* lists the casualties as sailors from the *Chicora* and *Palmetto State*.

42 During the war: *Official Records of the Union and Confederate Navies in the War of the Rebellion (ORN)*, series 1, vol. 15 (Washington, D.C.: Government Printing Office, 1921), 229.

42 On the night of October 5: Beauregard, "Torpedo Service," 151–52.

43 McClintock had always warned: James R. McClintock, letter to Matthew Maury, 1868, copy in the Eustace Williams Collection, Mobile Public Library.

43–44 Lt. Charles Hasker sat: W. B. Fort, "First Submarine in the Confederate Navy," *Confederate Veteran* 26, no. 10 (October 1918), 459.

44 With all his men: Ibid.

44 Charles Hasker, a native: Ibid.

44 He lunged at the water: Ibid.

45 Payne escaped without: C. L. Stanton, "Submarines and Torpedo Boats," *Confederate Veteran* 22 (1914), 398.

45 Payne told friends: Dr. Berry Bowman, "The *Hunley*: Ill-Fated Confederate Submarine," *Civil War History,* September 1959, 318.

46 "I was the only man . . .": Fort, "First Submarine," 459.

47 *"Sir—I am part owner . . .":* Horace Hunley, letter to Gen. [P.]G.T. Beauregard, September 19, 1863, copy in the Eustace Williams Collection, Mobile Public Library.

47 Within a week: Special requisition to the Confederate government signed by Hunley, copy in the Eustace Williams Collection, Mobile Public Library.

47 At the shop a handful: William Alexander, "The True Story of the Confederate Submarine Boats," *New Orleans Picayune*, June 29, 1902.

48 On the day the crew: Ibid.

48 In a letter written: Robert Barrow, letter to Horace Hunley, September 1863, Tulane Special Collections, Barrow Family Papers, Tulane University.

48 "This is the place . . .": Ibid.

48 October 15, 1863: This account comes from several sources. Charles Stanton, who witnessed the sinking from the deck of the *Indian Chief*, wrote a chilling account in *Confederate Veteran* magazine (vol. 22 [1914], 398); Beauregard wrote about it in the Southern Historical Society Papers; and Alexander offered his secondhand recollections as well ("True Story"). This passage was based on facts from all three accounts, with Stanton providing the best details.

49 They turned the T-bolts: Alexander, "True Story."

50 The submarine's bow: Ibid.

50 But Park and Hunley: Ibid.

50 "Madam, It becomes . . .": Gardner Smith, letter to Volumnia Hunley, November 29, 1863, Tulane Special Collections, Barrow Family Papers, Tulane University.

51 "It is more dangerous . . .": Mark K. Ragan, *The "Hunley": Submarines, Sacrifice, and Success in the Civil War* (Charleston: Narwhal Press, 1995), 82.

52 Soon they left: William Alexander, "The Heroes of the *Hunley*," *Munsey's Magazine*, August 1903, 748.

52 Angus Smith: *ORN,* series 1, vol. 15, 693.

52 A northeast wind: Smith, letter to Volumnia Hunley, November 29, 1863.

52 It was Saturday: Ibid.

52 Inside, the men lay: Beauregard, "Torpedo Service," 153.

52 "It was indescribably ghastly": Ibid.

53 His chief of staff: Francis D. Lee, letter to Gen. [P.]G.T. Beauregard, May 15, 1876, copy in the Eustace Williams Collection, Mobile Public Library.

53 Beauregard knew that Dixon: Beauregard, "Torpedo Service," 153.

53 It would work: Alexander, "True Story."

53 Hunley absentmindedly forgot: Ibid.

53 Beauregard had just recovered: William C. Davis, *Jefferson Davis: The Man and His Hour* (New York: HarperCollins, 1991), 523.

54 And then the president: Ibid.

54 If Dixon would fit: Lee, letter to Beauregard, May 15, 1876.

54 Lee objected at first: Ibid.

54 It took lime: A requisition to the Confederate government signed by Lt. George E. Dixon indicates that on November 17, 1863, he asked for "5 scrubbing brushes, 1 bbl lime, 1 box of soap, 21 pounds." Copy in the Eustace Williams Collection, Mobile Public Library.

54 The submarine was perched: William Alexander, letter to J. G. Holmes, September 7, 1898, Augustine Smythe Papers, South Carolina Historical Society, Charleston.

54 At first Beauregard refused: Alexander, "Heroes," 748.

54 They started on the *Indian Chief*: Ibid.

55 In the end: These are the names most commonly associated with the final crew, and aside from Dixon and Wicks, there is little solid proof that they are correct. The names show up on a monument in White Point Gardens on the Battery in downtown Charleston and in several historical accounts. In his 1898 letter to J. G. Holmes, Alexander wrote that "I am familiar with Dixon, Ridgeway, Miller, Becker, Wicks, Collins and, I think Simpkins, but Beck and Carlson I can't place (wonder if Beck could mean Becker)?" Four years after that, when he published his history of the submarine in the *New Orleans Picayune*—after consulting his letters from Dixon—he recalled that a man from a German artillery (Carlson) was his replacement on the final crew.

55 James A. Wicks: Documentation provided by Hope Barker, wife of Wicks's descendant.

55 As they were working: Alexander, letter to Holmes, September 7, 1898.

56 The next Sunday: Ibid.

CHAPTER 3: UNDER A CAROLINA MOON

58 The moon hung . . . ; It was piercing cold: *Charleston Daily Courier,* February 18, 1864.

58 When his latest leave: Mark K. Ragan, *The "Hunley": Submarines, Sacrifice, and Success in the Civil War* (Charleston: Narwhal Press, 1995), 124.

59 One night the *Hunley's* floating mine: This account is from the journal of J. H. Tomb, first assistant engineer on one of the Confederate torpedo boats called Davids. Tomb wrote that the David towed the *Hunley* out of Charleston Harbor "three or four times" but that he refused to give Dixon a lift after that because on "the last night the David towed him down the harbor his torpedo got fouled of us and came near blowing both boats before we got it clear." From a copy of Tomb's journal, Hunley Papers, Tulane University Library.

59 they stayed together: The routine of the *Hunley's* final crew has been recounted expertly by William Alexander in two places: his June 29, 1902, account in the *New Orleans Picayune* ("The True Story of the Confederate Submarine Boats") and, more briefly but with some significantly different details, in his September 7, 1898, letter to J. G. Holmes, on file in the Augustine Smythe Papers, South Carolina Historical Society, Charleston. This account is culled from those Alexander writings.

60 One afternoon in January: Alexander, "True Story."

61 They would rather drown quickly: Ibid.

61 Beauregard had ordered Alexander: Ibid. The order was actually delivered by Beauregard's chief of staff, General Jordan.

61 the two men would lie on the beach: Ibid.

62 He wrote letters: Ibid.

62 Dixon's regiment stormed: John Kent Folmar, ed., *From That Terrible Field: Civil War Letters of James M. Williams, Twenty-first Alabama Infantry Volunteers* (Tuscaloosa: University of Alabama Press, 1981), 53.

63 But he longed for Mobile: George E. Dixon, letter to Capt. John F. Cothran, commanding Cedar Point, Company A, Twenty-first Alabama Regiment, February 5, 1864, copy in the Eustace Williams Collection, Mobile Public Library.

63 "I am fastened to Charleston . . .": Ibid.

64 "I am heartily tired of this place": Ibid.

64 Dixon had made final adjustments: D. W. McLaurin, "South Carolina Confederate Twins," *Confederate Veteran,* vol. 33 (1925), p. 328.

65 Among the crew: Alexander, "True Story." Actually Alexander says only that his replacement is from a German artillery company, which is what Carlson's previous assignment had been. Also, Carlson was not among those listed as crewmen when Alexander was still acting as first officer.

65 Dixon would flash: The "signal agreed upon" is mentioned in Lt. Col. Dantzler's report to Beauregard on February 19, 1864 (*Official Records of the Union and Confederate Navies in the War of the Rebellion [ORN]*, series 1, vol. 15 [Washington, D.C.: Government Printing Office, 1921], 335). In the U.S. Navy inquiry into the *Housatonic's* sinking, crewman Robert Flemming reported seeing a "blue light" on the water. In *Reminiscences of Charleston* (Charleston: Joseph Walker, 1866), J. N. Cardozo said that Dixon told Dantzler, "if it comes off safe," he would show two blue lights.

65 The Union Navy knew: *ORN,* series 1, vol. 15, 227–33.

67 A year earlier Dahlgren: Ivan Musicant, *Divided Waters: The Naval History of the Civil War* (New York: HarperCollins, 1995), 373.

68 Lincoln was brooding: Ibid., 383.

68 "He let off a joke": Ibid.

68 "I have reliable information . . .": *ORN,* series 1, vol. 15, 226.

69 "It is also advisable . . .": Ibid., 227.

70 The *Housatonic* had arrived: The description and history of the USS *Housatonic* come from the Naval Historical Center's *Dictionary of American Naval Fighting Ships,* available on-line at www.history.navy.mil.

70–74 That night the *Housatonic*'s watch: The account of the attack on the *Housatonic* comes from the Proceedings of the Naval Court of Inquiry, February 26, 1864, conducted on board the USS *Wabash.* More than twenty members of the *Housatonic*'s crew testified, leaving a wealth of color and vivid details of the attack. Without it we would never have known what happened. Also of use in this section were two letters that John Crosby, an officer on the blockade ship, wrote to his wife in the days following the attack.

74 On Sullivan's Island: Accounts of D. W. McLaurin suggest that no one at Battery Marshall saw any sign of the *Housatonic*'s sinking, and official reports to Beauregard over the next two days indicate that no one had any idea there had been any change in the blockade.

75 the young soldier watched: McLaurin, "South Carolina Confederate Twins," 328.

Chapter 4: Eternal Patrol

77 A rare dusting of snow: *Charleston Daily Courier,* February 19, 1864.

78 The commander at Battery Marshall: *Official Records of the Union and Confederate Navies in the War of the Rebellion (ORN),* series 1, vol. 15 (Washington, D.C.: Government Printing Office, 1921), 335.

78 "I have the honor . . .": Ibid.

78 "Unless she has gone . . .": Gen. R. Ripley, letter to Gen. P.G.T. Beauregard, February 19, 1864, copy in the Eustace Williams Collection, Mobile Public Library.

79 "As soon as its fate . . .": *ORN,* series 1, vol. 15, 336.

79 The six Yankees on board: News of the capture of a "federal picket boat" ran as brief notices in the *Mobile Register* on February 27, 1864, and the *Daily Picayune* in New Orleans on March 10, 1864.

79 "A gunboat sunken . . .": *ORN,* series 1, vol. 15, 336.

79 "There is little hope . . .": Ibid.

80 Dahlgren feared that the worst: *ORN,* series 1, vol. 15, 329–30.

80 "The success of this undertaking . . .": Ibid., 330.

81 A few miles off Charleston: Ibid., 328. J. F. Green, captain of the *Canandaigua*, notes in a report to Dahlgren that he had most of the crew of the *Housatonic*—which his crew rescued—on board his ship but had transferred fifty-seven members of the crew to the *Wabash* because of overcrowding.

81 John Crosby: John K. Crosby, letter to Irene Crosby, February 18, 1864, copy of letter in private collection. (Donor wishes to remain anonymous.) This account is taken from two letters Crosby wrote to his wife while a passenger aboard the *Canandaigua* in the days following the sinking of the *Housatonic*. They provide better insight into what was going through his mind than what he revealed during the inquiry, when he only answered questions asked.

81 "I cannot describe . . .": Ibid.

82–84 The trial was held: Proceedings of the Naval Court of Inquiry, February 26, 1864, transcript in the Eustace Williams Collection, Mobile Public Library.

84 News of the *Housatonic*'s sinking: In the *Mobile Register*, February 27, 1864, and the *New Orleans Picayune*, March 10, 1864.

84–85 Volumnia Washington Hunley Barrow: Ruth H. Duncan, *The Captain and Submarine CSS "H. L. Hunley"* (Memphis: S. C. Toof & Company, 1965), 51.

86 Queenie Bennett first realized: Bennett's biographical information comes from her descendants.

86 William Alexander did not hear: William Alexander, "The True Story of the Confederate Submarine Boats," *New Orleans Picayune*, June 29, 1902.

86 "No news of the torpedo boat": Ibid.

86 Finally he concluded: Ibid.

87 *"We can't get at the truth . . .":* Letter from Susan Middleton of Charleston, March 4, 1864, copy in the Hunley Papers, Charleston Museum.

88 Hunley's death had left him: Henry J. Leovy, letter to Gen. [P.]G.T. Beauregard, March 5, 1864, copy in the Eustace Williams Collection, Mobile Public Library.

88 "It is therefore feared . . .": *ORN,* series 1, vol. 15, 337. The letter was actually sent by one of Beauregard's underlings and not the general himself.

88 the general ordered new flags: E. Milby Burton, *The Siege of Charleston, 1861–1865* (Columbia: University of South Carolina Press, 1971), 318.

90 In 1865 Sand told Verne: Herbert R. Lottman, *Jules Verne: An Exploratory Biography* (New York: St. Martin's Press, 1997), 113.

90 "The Blockade Runners": Ibid., 107.

91 "Death on the Bottom . . ."; "Within her are the bones . . .": *Charleston Daily Courier,* October 11, 1870, in a story attributed only to a Houston newspaper.

91 Churchill's report: Lt. W. L. Churchill, U.S. Navy, "Report to Rear Admiral J. A. Dahlgren on Condition of USS *Housatonic,*" November 27, 1864, copy in the Eustace Williams Collection, Mobile Public Library.

92 "The cabin is completely demolished . . .": Ibid.

93 Benjamin Maillefert won the bid: Burton, *Siege of Charleston,* 238.

93 "the torpedo-boat . . . could not be found": Ibid.

93 For years Southerners: Shortly after the *Hunley* disappeared, Capt. M. M. Gray, in charge of torpedoes for the Confederates, theorized that the fish-boat had been sucked into the hole it made in the *Housatonic* with its torpedo (*ORN,* series 1, vol. 15, 338). That theory was widely repeated for decades. William Alexander for the longest time believed that the submarine had been swept out to sea (Alexander, "True Story"), and later the Army Corps of Engineers reported that perhaps a 1909 contractor removing the wreck of the *Housatonic* mistook the *Hunley* for a ship's boiler and blew it up (Burton, *Siege of Charleston,* 239). The story of the mysterious divers who claimed to have turned the sub's propeller and seen the "bleached bones of her crew" (*Charleston Daily Courier,* October 11, 1870) was repeated for nearly a century. One nineteenth-century Boston newspaper article, quoted in a 1961 book by Virgil Carrington Jones, claimed that Ben-

jamin Maillefert, the 1872 salvage contractor, had recovered the *Hunley*, which he found fouled in the rudder chains of the *Housatonic* (*State and Columbia Record*, November 19, 1961).

94 "I went to work . . .": Alfred Roman, *The Military Operations of General Beauregard*, vol. 2 (New York: Harper and Brothers, 1884), 528. This 1876 letter from Smith may represent the last confirmed sighting of the *Hunley* until it was unearthed in 1995 by the NUMA team. It was overlooked for years.

94 In the late 1870s: This story has become legend over time, but few details are known. Accounts of the offer are limited to a single letter written by James Gadsden Holmes to Joseph Daniels, secretary of the navy, on April 27, 1915 (copy in the *Hunley* Commission files). In the letter Holmes says that Angus Smith's son told him that his father and an old diving partner, presumably Broadfoot, searched 5 acres of the sea bottom after P. T. Barnum offered his reward. Given that Smith did not mention any search beyond his 1872 expedition in the letter to Beauregard, it seems safe to assume that Barnum made his offer after 1876. That would have been more than a dozen years after the *Hunley* sank, more than enough time for Atlantic sands to have buried it. Smith may have stumbled over the submarine when it was sitting on the bottom, but it's highly unlikely that, with 1870s diving technology, he would have been able to excavate the ocean floor.

94 In 1843 Barnum's uncle: Neil Harris, *Humbug: The Art of P. T. Barnum* (Boston: Little, Brown, 1973), 65–66.

95 Smith and his old diving partner: Holmes, letter to Daniels, April 27, 1915.

96 *In 1879 government engineers:* Burton, *Siege of Charleston*, 238.

97 *By the time the jetties:* The effects of the jetties on the ocean floor are obvious to anyone who wades into the surf off Sullivan's Island or has had a boat accidentally beached there. The jetties stopped the flow of sand, causing it to build up unnaturally north of the harbor mouth. In "USGS Assists in Recovery of the Civil War Submarine *H. L. Hunley*," an article in the September 2000 issue of *Sound Waves*, a newsletter for the U.S. Geological Survey, Center for Coastal

Geology, Mark Hansen explains the likely scenario probably better than anyone has before. This paragraph paraphrases some of Hansen's theories.

CHAPTER 5: THE MYTHS OF DIXIELAND

98–100 George Dixon was alive: H. Pacha, "The Torpedo Scare," *Blackwood's Magazine,* June 1885, 745–46.

100 In 1899 a former Confederate Navy lieutenant: *Charleston News and Courier,* May 10, 1899.

100 In a lecture: Col. Charles H. Olmstead, "Reminiscences of Service in Charleston Harbor in 1863," Southern Historical Society Papers, vol. 11 (1883), 168.

100–101 the fish-boat sank an astonishing six times: This comes from various accounts of the *Hunley,* many of which were published in *Confederate Veteran* magazine. That periodical reprinted letters from any veteran who wished to write, and the *Hunley* was a fairly common topic in its pages.

101 Bearded and gray-headed: Erwin Craighead, *From Mobile's Past: Sketches of Memorable People and Events* (Mobile: Powers Printing Company, 1925).

103–105 They had cut an iron boiler in two: The section is culled entirely from Alexander's *New Orleans Picayune* article ("The True Story of the Confederate Submarine Boats," June 29, 1902), the only firsthand account of the building of the *Hunley.* Also used are some details from his September 7, 1898, letter to J. G. Holmes (Augustine Smythe Papers, South Carolina Historical Society, Charleston) and "Heroes of the *Hunley,*" the August 1903 *Munsey's Magazine* article.

105 In front of the Iberville Historic Society: William Alexander, speech to the Iberville Historic Society, December 15, 1903, transcript in the Eustace Williams Collection, Mobile Public Library.

106 "What mingled reminiscences . . .": Alexander, "True Story."

106 In a brief preface: Cyrus Townsend Brady, *A Little Traitor to the South: A War-Time Comedy with a Tragic Interlude* (New York: Macmillan, 1904), 9–10.

107 an Army Corps of Engineers report: E. Milby Burton, *The Siege of Charleston, 1861–1865* (Columbia: University of South Carolina Press, 1971), 239.

108 Lake quizzed Hasker: Simon Lake, letter to Horatio L. Wait, February 6, 1899, Augustine Smythe Papers, South Carolina Historical Society, Charleston.

110 "It is this author's humble . . .": (Lt.) Harry von Kolnitz, "The Confederate Submarine," United States Naval Institute Proceedings, October 1937, 1457.

110 submarines even practiced anchor-dropping: Interview with Vice Adm. (Ret.) Al Baciocco.

110 Simons, a native Charlestonian: "World War II Hero, Adm. Simons, Dies," *Charleston News and Courier,* July 20, 1971.

111 Simons had methodically studied: "Adm. Dietrich Hauls Down His Flag of Command Here," *Charleston News and Courier,* June 16, 1957.

111 By late spring they actually thought: "Salvage of Sub *Hunley* Has 50-50 Chance for Success," *Charleston News and Courier,* June 18, 1957.

111 "at some future, indefinite date": "Navy Still Plans Hunt for *Hunley,*" *Charleston News and Courier,* August 28, 1957.

112 Built by students: Russell Maxey, "The *H. L. Hunley,*" *Sandlapper* magazine, January 1969, 52.

CHAPTER 6: "THIS COULD BE IT"
The primary sources of material for this chapter were the authors' interviews with Edward Lee Spence, Clive Cussler, Mark Newell, Ralph Wilbanks, Harry Pecorelli III, and Wes Hall.

121 He would later: Spence mentions the sea whip in the *Orangeburg (S.C.) Times and Democrat* article and the rivets in an article he wrote in the *Argosy Treasure Hunting '77 Annual* titled "Civil War Shipwrecks," 34.

121 "The *Hunley!* . . .": This quote and some other details of Spence's account come from his book *Treasures of the Confederate Coast: The "Real Rhett Butler" and Other Revelations* (Miami: Narwhal Press, 1995).

124 He even appeared: Gary Kinder, *Ship of Gold in the Deep Blue Sea* (New York: Vintage, 1999), 299–300.

126 Cussler's first venture: Some information not gathered in interviews with Clive Cussler comes from his book, coauthored with Craig Dirgo, *The Sea Hunters* (New York: Simon and Schuster, 1996), 197–200.

127 "We don't know where . . .": "Search Ends for Confederate Sub *Hunley*," *Charleston News and Courier,* June 27, 1981.

128 "If it floated out to sea": Ibid.

130–137 It would be a disaster: In addition to the interviews with major participants, this account of the 1994 search for the *Hunley* was aided by the newspaper article "Bad Blood, Thin Egos May Torpedo Salvage," by Tony Bartelme and Schuyler Kropf in *The Charleston Post and Courier,* August 27, 1995, which detailed the feud between NUMA and SCIAA.

130 He had followed Cussler's exploits: Mark Newell, "Raise the *Hunley!*" *Sport Diver* magazine, March–April 1981, 81.

134 He believed the crew: Mark Newell, *Preliminary Proposal for the Recovery and Management of the CSS "H. L. Hunley"* (North Augusta, S.C.: CSS *H. L. Hunley* Project Group/Sons of Confederate Veterans, 1995), 5.

135 "Carl Naylor in panic. . . .": Notation from Mark Newell's expedition diary, on file with the South Carolina Institute of Archaeology and Anthropology.

135 "Time up to last day . . .": Ibid.

136 "Too old to be dredge pipe . . .": Ibid.

136 He was identifying the iron hulk: "Divers May Have Located *Hunley*," *Charleston Post and Courier,* January 28, 1995.

CHAPTER 7: *VENI, VIDI, VICI,* DUDE

The account of the day the *Hunley* was discovered was crafted from interviews with Ralph Wilbanks, Harry Pecorelli III, Wes Hall, and Clive Cussler.

140 Cussler described Wilbanks: Clive Cussler and Craig Dirgo, *The Sea Hunters* (New York: Simon and Schuster, 1996), 213.

150 "Clive, we're going to send you . . .": Harry Pecorelli III, "The Find of a Lifetime," *Charleston Magazine,* January–February 1996, 41.

CHAPTER 8: THE WAR BETWEEN THE STATES
The material in this chapter came primarily from interviews with Glenn McConnell, Chris Amer, Clive Cussler, Ralph Wilbanks, Wes Hall, Harry Pecorelli III, Mark Newell, and Robert Neyland.

154 "The worst possible thing . . .": Amer interview.

156 "This is without a doubt . . .": "*Hunley* Will Be Slow to Rise," *Charleston Post and Courier,* May 12, 1995.

156 "I think they paddled like hell . . .": Ibid.

156 "If Lee could have . . .": Ibid.

157 "I didn't spend fifteen years . . .": "Cussler, USC Split on Sub," *Charleston Post and Courier,* June 3, 1995.

159 The local congressman, "Sonny" Callahan: "Alabama, S.C. Wrangle over *Hunley,*" *Charleston Post and Courier,* July 28, 1995.

159 One man from Mobile: "Share Custody of Sub," John E. Ellis, letter to the editor, *Charleston Post and Courier,* August 14, 1995.

161 Archaeologists at SCIAA: "USC Continues Hunt for *Hunley,*" *Charleston Post and Courier,* June 22, 1995.

161 "competent research was pre-empted . . .": "Bad Blood, Thin Egos May Torpedo Salvage," *Charleston Post and Courier,* August 27, 1995.

161 In one report SCIAA said: Ibid.

161 "If I'm proven wrong": Ibid.

162 "I've been accused of ransoming . . .": "Author Says Money, Glory Not *Hunley* Searchers' Aim," Clive Cussler, letter to the editor, *Charleston Post and Courier,* September 13, 1995.

162 Spence figured: Interview with Lee Spence. Other information about Spence's aborted expedition to relocate the *Hunley* comes from "Diver Asked to Lead Team to *Hunley* Site," *Charleston Post and Courier,* October 11, 1995.

162 It was November 9, 1995: "Author Releases Sub Site," *Charleston Post and Courier,* November 10, 1995.

163 One year after discovering: Except where otherwise noted, the

account of the 1996 dive on the *Hunley* comes from *"H. L. Hunley" Site Assessment* (Santa Fe: National Park Service, 1998). This report— put together by the National Park Service, the Naval Historical Center, and the South Carolina Institute of Archaeology and Anthropology— was the first detailed study of the submarine. It includes a technical narrative of what the divers did—and what they saw—on the first official survey of the *Hunley*'s wreck site.

164 Among the divers: Interview with Bob Neyland.

166 "Now we can quit . . .": "It's Official! Experts Verify Sunken Wreck as Confederate Sub *Hunley*," *Charleston Post and Courier,* May 18, 1996.

168 The politicians and reenactors: Minutes of the *Hunley* Commission meeting for September 12, 1996.

168 By January of 2001: Ibid.

CHAPTER 9: THE BONEYARD

This chapter is based on interviews with Randy Burbage, Warren Lasch, Glenn McConnell, Adm. (Ret.) William L. Schachte, Jr., Edwin C. Bearss, Steve Wright, and Leonard Whitlock.

172 the Charleston City Council decided: A. J. Tamsberg, clerk of the Charleston City Council, letter to Col. D. S. McAlister, chairman of the Municipal Stadium Commission at the Citadel, October 20, 1947.

175 Jonathan Leader, an SCIAA archaeologist: "Remains Linked to *Hunley*," *Charleston Post and Courier,* June 27, 1999.

177 It had caught a pickle-shaped: "Sub Care on War Week List," *Charleston Post and Courier,* April 7, 1996.

178 So it could be hauled into port: Ibid.

179 The *Cairo* was: The story of the *Cairo* was compiled from an interview with Edwin C. Bearss and from his book *Hardluck Ironclad* (Baton Rouge: Louisiana State University Press, 1980).

181 "He's the person": Schachte interview.

181 "What's the *Hunley*?": Lasch interview.

182 "Warren," McConnell persuaded: McConnell interview.

CHAPTER 10: RAISE THE *HUNLEY*!

This chapter is based on the authors' daily reporting through the summer of 2000, including interviews with Bob Neyland, Harry Pecorelli III, Glenn McConnell, Warren Lasch, Paul Mardikian, Randy Burbage, Maria Jacobsen, Jenkins Montgomery, Steve Wright, and Leonard Whitlock.

191 The engineers who built: The movie technicians who built the models for the TNT movie *The Hunley* believed there was no way a wooden, top-mounted spar would have been used by the men who built the submarine. The movie model featured an iron pole mounted at the bottom of the submarine. Aside from the mounting brackets, the movie version of the spar was remarkably accurate.

CHAPTER 11: GOLDFINGER

This chapter is based on the authors' daily coverage of the excavation of the *H. L. Hunley* through 2000–2001, including interviews with Bob Neyland, Glenn McConnell, Warren Lasch, Maria Jacobsen, Paul Mardikian, Harry Pecorelli III, and Shea McLean.

235 The plan was: Maria Jacobsen's discovery of Lt. George E. Dixon's gold coin was recorded by South Carolina Educational TV cameras, which were documenting the excavation for the *Hunley* Commission files. Chairman Glenn McConnell and Friends of the *Hunley* chairman Warren Lasch were kind enough to let the authors review that tape.

CHAPTER 12: WANT OF AIR

This chapter is based on findings of the 2001 excavation of the *Hunley* along with historical accounts, all of which was merged with interviews with Glenn McConnell, Warren Lasch, Bob Neyland, Maria Jacobsen, Paul Mardikian, and Shea McLean.

250 an ideal location for preservation: Bruce Smith, "Scientist Says Where *Hunley* Rested Helped in Preservation of Sub," Associated Press, July 6, 2001.

Epilogue

The information for these endnotes, except where otherwise cited, comes from the authors' reporting.

251 James McClintock: Rich Wills, "The *H. L. Hunley* in Historical Context," Naval Historical Center, www.history.navy.mil, 4.

251 Robert Ruffin Barrow: Ruth H. Duncan, *The Captain and Submarine CSS "H. L. Hunley"* (Memphis: S. C. Toof & Company, 1965), 50–51.

252 William Alexander: "Builder of First Submarine Dead," *Mobile Register,* May 14, 1914.

252 Queenie Bennett: Biographical information and account of the photo's discovery are from Sally Necessary, the great-granddaughter of Queenie Bennett.

252 B. A. "Gus" Whitney: Duncan, *Captain and Submarine,* 70.

254 *Pioneer:* William H. Shock, letter to Gustavus Fox, assistant secretary of the navy, January 24, 1864, original in the National Archives, copy in the Institute of Museum and Library Services's June 2001 newsletter.

256 USS *Housatonic*: "*Housatonic* Got Direct Hit," *Charleston Post and Courier,* July 10, 1999.

257 Horace Lawson Hunley: "Submarine Tender *Hunley* Has Played a Mighty Role in Vital Defense Mission," *Charleston News and Courier,* July 5, 1971.

BIBLIOGRAPHY

Alexander, William. "The Heroes of the *Hunley*." *Munsey's Magazine,* August 1903, 746–49.

———. Letter to J. G. Holmes, September 7, 1898. Augustine Smythe Papers, South Carolina Historical Society, Charleston.

———. Speech to the Iberville Historic Society, December 15, 1903. Transcript in the Eustace Williams Collection, Mobile Public Library.

———. "The True Story of the Confederate Submarine Boats." *New Orleans Picayune,* June 29, 1902.

Barrow, Robert. Letter to Horace Hunley, September 1863. Tulane Special Collections, Barrow Family Papers, Tulane University.

Beauregard, Gen. [P.]G.T. "Torpedo Service in the Harbor and Water Defences of Charleston." Southern Historical Society Papers, vol. 5, no. 4, April 1878, 145–61.

Bowman, Dr. Berry. "The *Hunley*: Ill-Fated Confederate Submarine." *Civil War History,* September 1959, 315–19.

Brady, Cyrus Townsend. *A Little Traitor to the South: A War-Time Comedy with a Tragic Interlude.* New York: Macmillan, 1904.

Burton, E. Milby. *The Siege of Charleston, 1861–1865.* Columbia: University of South Carolina Press, 1971.

Cardozo, J. N. *Reminiscences of Charleston.* Charleston: Joseph Walker Stationer and Printer, 1866.

Churchill, Lt. W. L., U.S.N. "Report to Rear Admiral J. A. Dahlgren on Condition of USS *Housatonic*," November 27, 1864. Copy in the Eustace Williams Collection, Mobile Public Library.

Civil War Naval Chronology, 1861–1865. Washington, D.C.: Government Printing Office, 1971.

Craighead, Erwin. *From Mobile's Past: Sketches of Memorable People and Events.* Mobile: Powers Printing Company, 1925.

Crosby, John K. Letter to Irene Crosby, February 18, 1864. Copy of letter in private collection. Donor wishes to remain anonymous.

Cussler, Clive and Craig Dirgo. *The Sea Hunters.* New York: Simon and Schuster, 1996.

Davis, William C. *Jefferson Davis: The Man and His Hour.* New York: HarperCollins, 1991.

Dixon, George E. Letter to Capt. John F. Cothran, captain commanding Cedar Point, Company A, Twenty-first Alabama Regiment, February 5, 1864. Copy in the Eustace Williams Collection, Mobile Public Library.

Duncan, Ruth H. *The Captain and Submarine CSS "H. L. Hunley."* Memphis: S. C. Toof & Company, 1965.

"Fate of Confederate Submarine Is Still the Subject of Mystery." Associated Press, *State and Columbia Record,* November 19, 1961.

Faust, John W. "Archeologist Claims *Hunley* Remains Found." *Orangeburg (S.C.) Times and Democrat,* June 13, 1975.

Fennell, Edward C. "Search Ends for Confederate Sub *Hunley.*" *Charleston News and Courier,* June 27, 1981.

Folmar, John Kent, ed. *From That Terrible Field: Civil War Letters of James M. Williams, Twenty-first Alabama Infantry Volunteers.* Tuscaloosa: University of Alabama Press, 1981.

Fort, W. B. "First Submarine in the Confederate Navy." *Confederate Veteran,* vol. 26, no. 10 (October 1918), 459.

Hansen, Mark. "USGS Assists in Recovery of the Civil War Submarine *H. L. Hunley.*" *Sound Waves,* Coastal Science and Research News from across the Bureau (of the U.S. Geological Survey), September 2000.

Harris, Neil. *Humbug: The Art of P. T. Barnum.* Boston: Little, Brown, 1973.

Holmes, (Gen.) James Gadsden. Letter to Joseph Daniels, secretary of the navy, April 27, 1915. Copy in the *Hunley* Commission files.

Hunley, Horace Lawson. Letter to Gen. [P.]G.T. Beauregard, September 19, 1863. Copy in the Eustace Williams Collection, Mobile Public Library.

———. Letter to James R. McClintock, August 15, 1863. Copy in the Eustace Williams Collection, Mobile Public Library.

———. Memorandum Book, record group 140, folder 12. Louisiana Historical Society.

Kinder, Gary. *Ship of Gold in the Deep Blue Sea.* New York: Vintage Books, 1999.

Kloeppel, James E. *Danger beneath the Waves.* Orangeburg, S.C.: Sandlapper Publishing, 1992.

Lake, Simon. Letter to Horatio L. Wait, February 6, 1899. Augustine Smythe Papers, South Carolina Historical Society, Charleston.

Lee, Francis D. Letter to Gen. [P.]G.T. Beauregard, May 15, 1876. Copy in the Eustace Williams Collection, Mobile Public Library.

Leovy, Henry J. Letter to Gen. [P.]G.T. Beauregard, March 5, 1864. Copy in the Eustace Williams Collection, Mobile Public Library.

Maury, Maj. Gen. Dabney Herndon. Southern Historical Society Papers, vol. 4, 1894.

Maxey, Russell. "The *H. L. Hunley.*" *Sandlapper* magazine, January 1969, 50–52.

McClintock, James R. Letter to Matthew F. Maury, 1868. Copy in the Eustace Williams Collection, Mobile Public Library.

McLaurin, D. W. "South Carolina Confederate Twins." *Confederate Veteran,* vol. 33 (1925), p. 328.

Murphy, Larry E., ed. *"H. L. Hunley" Site Assessment.* Santa Fe: National Park Service, 1998.

Musicant, Ivan. *Divided Waters: The Naval History of the Civil War.* New York: HarperCollins, 1995.

Newell, Mark. "The CSS *Hunley.*" *Sport Diver* magazine, March–April 1981, 79–80, 82.

———. "Preliminary Proposal for the Recovery and Management of the CSS *H. L. Hunley.*" North Augusta, S.C.: The CSS *H. L. Hunley* Project Group/Sons of Confederate Veterans, 1995.

———. "Raise the *Hunley!*" *Sport Diver* magazine, March–April 1981, 81.

Official Records of the Union and Confederate Navies in the War of Rebellion. Washington, D.C.: Government Printing Office, 1921.

Olmstead, Col. Charles H. "Reminiscences of Service in Charleston Harbor in 1863." Southern Historical Society Papers, vol. 11, 1883, 118–25, 158–71.

Pacha, H. "The Torpedo Scare." *Blackwood's Magazine,* June 1885, 745–46.

Palmer, Mrs. Edwin J. "Horace Lawson Hunley." *United Daughters of the Confederacy Magazine,* May 1962, 14–15, 44–46.

Pillans, Harry. Letter to the editor, *Montgomery Advertiser,* November 8, 1924.

Proceedings of the Naval Court of Inquiry, February 26, 1864. Transcript in the Eustace Williams Collection, Mobile Public Library.

Ragan, Mark K. *The "Hunley": Submarines, Sacrifice, and Success in the Civil War.* Charleston: Narwhal Press, 1995.

Ripley, Gen. R. Letter to Gen. P.G.T. Beauregard, February 19, 1864. Copy in the Eustace Williams Collection, Mobile Public Library.

Roman, Alfred. *The Military Operations of General Beauregard.* Vols. 1 and 2. New York: Harper and Brothers, 1884.

Smith, Gardner. Letter to Volumnia Hunley, November 29, 1863. Tulane Special Collections, Barrow Family Papers, Tulane University.

Spence, E. Lee. *Treasures of the Confederate Coast: The "Real Rhett Butler" and Other Revelations.* Miami: Narwhal Press, 1995.

———. "Civil War Shipwrecks." *Argosy Treasure Hunting '77 Annual,* 1977, 34–38, 90.

Stanton, C. L. "Submarines and Torpedo Boats." *Confederate Veteran,* vol. 22 (1914), 398–99.

Tomb, J. H. Journal. Copy in the Hunley Papers file, Tulane University Library, New Orleans.

von Kolnitz, (Lt.) Harry. "The Confederate Submarine." United States Naval Institute's *Proceedings,* October 1937, 1453–57.

The War of the Rebellion: A Compilation of the Official Records of the Union and Confederate Armies. Washington, D.C.: Government Printing Office, 1901.

Wills, Rich. "The *H. L. Hunley* in Historical Context." Naval Historical Center, www.history.navy.mil.

INDEX

Page numbers in *italics* indicate illustrations.

ABOUT THE AUTHORS

BRIAN HICKS is a senior writer with *The Post and Courier* in Charleston, South Carolina, and the coauthor of *Into the Wind*. The recipient of a number of journalism awards, including the South Carolina Press Association's award for Journalist of the Year, Hicks has covered the *Hunley* since 1999.

SCHUYLER KROPF is a senior political reporter with *The Post and Courier* and the recipient of numerous reporting awards. He has followed the *Hunley* story since 1995, longer than any journalist in America.

Both authors live in Charleston.